Faith, Culture and Conflict

By the same author –
What On Earth?: The Church in the World and the Call of Christ (1993)
Watching for the Morning: Global Chaos and Cosmic Hope (1999)
God's Credentials: Belief and Unbelief in a Troubled World (2007)

Faith, Culture and Conflict

A Middle Eastern Odyssey

Philip Blair

with sketches by Joanna Blair

Mansion Field

Mansion Field
An imprint of Zeticula Ltd
Unit 13,
196 Rose Street,
Edinburgh,
EH2 4AT,
Scotland

http://www.mansionfield.co.uk

First published in 2014. Reprinted 2015

Text © Philip Blair 2014
Sketches © Joanna Blair 2014

Every effort has been made to trace copyright holders. The editor will be pleased to hear about any omissions, and correction will be made in future editions.

All rights reserved. No part of this publication may be reproduced, stored in a retrieval system, or transmitted in any form or by any means, electronic, mechanical, photocopying, recording or otherwise, without the prior permission of the publishers.

ISBN 978-1-905021-15-4

For Alexander, William, Beatrix and Catrin

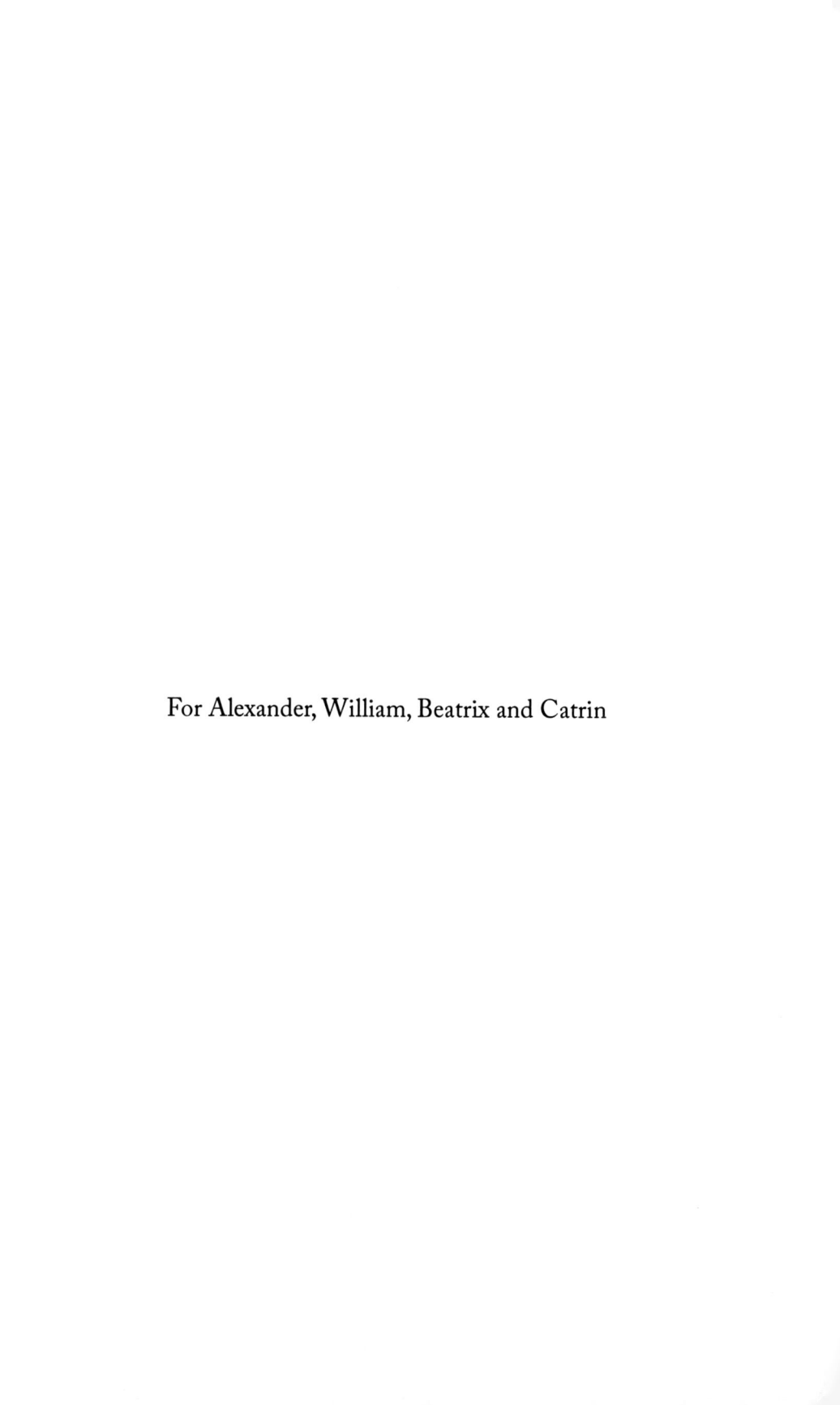

Contents

Illustrations		ix
Preface		xi
I	Island of Love	1
II	Joanna – and the Way Back	33
III	Omdurman	53
IV	Limbo	85
V	Pastures Old	94
VI	Watersheds, Private and Public	123
VII	'Kings of Arabia and Saba'	150
VIII	A Family Business	172
IX	Quite a Liberal Society	195
X	Another Return	213
XI	Second Time Round	224
XII	A Drive Home – and 'Dilmun'	246
XIII	A Surprise or Two	259
XIV	Holy Hill of Balamand	280
XV	State of Disunion	299
XVI	Signing Off	322

Illustrations

The island of Cyprus on a contemporary postcard	2
Philip's batch of police trainees at RAF Netheravon	4
Philip with Mustafa Darwish (right) and his family (centre)	8
Philip in 'khaki drill' outside camp guardroom	12
Colonel Grivas with young EOKA 'martyrs'	14
Philip on Varosha (Famagusta) beach with friends	16
Philip outside his tent with Brian	28
Ridley Hall rugby team	35
Joanna	37
Philip and Joanna's marriage	40
Philip and Joanna cut the cake	40
Philip's sister, with toddlers, in USA at the time	40
Visa to Sudan, with passport photos	52
The River House gate, featuring 'spears'	54
Omdurman, with site of a 'holy dream' in the foreground	57
Khartoum North in silhouette, from across the Nile	60
Philip with the Bishop of Sudan and Khartoum clergy	68
Souq	80
The pyramids at Meroë	82
Typical Beit al-Māl houses	102
Joanna and friends Tricia and Christine	106
A Sudanese Christmas	109
Desert trip with Philip (The General), Rosie, Abdul and Tricia	111
Poster for Philip Gordon's company SEATS	115
Philip with graduating students, 1984	117
Pantomime poster, by Joanna	120
St Martin's	122
A Beit al-Māl style laundry, sketched from our balcony	124
Philip's certificate from the British Embassy	128
Harold Blair aged 82	132

Crowds celebrating the fall of Nimeiri	136
Philip and Joanna at Azraq in Jordan	141
The Brisley family	141
Gate of ruined Suakin, on Red Sea	148
Sana'a street seller, chewing *qat*	151
Philip and Joanna with friends on trip to Shehara	161
Map to advertise central Family Bookshop	178
Philip at FB Bookfair with Omani minister	178
Tackling General Sir Peter de la Billière	186
Philip talking with Wilfred Thesiger before his TV interview	191
Edmund when AFP correspondent in Kuwait, with Annabel	197
Dramarama, a pleasant leisure activity	200
The Gordon family celebrate a birthday	204
Trip with friends up the Karpaz	229
Practicing Turkish with a local shopkeeper	229
Edmund Joseph Norris, RN (Joanna's father)	232
Philip's uncle and godfather, John	236
Marriage of Manga and Mirindra in Kyrenia	238
Philip's mother and father at time of marriage, early 1930s	242
Marriage of Edmund and Rania	263
Nigel in Sherborne, with mother, Uncle Jim, father; early 1980s	282
Lebanon's famous cedars, national emblem	288
View one evening from our Balamand apartment	304

Preface

'Thank you for this, Philip. I will read and enjoy it. But what we really want, you know, is something on what you have been doing in life, not just what you think. How about it?'

The speaker, one Michael Keat, put aside the book I had just given him and looked up at me. I muttered something to the effect that I might one day get round to the task.

This narrative, the fruit of my subsequent autobiographical labours, sets down what to me stand out as the most significant episodes in my adult life – mainly spent in the Middle East and shared for all but a brief initial period by my wife Joanna, cousin to Michael. The book could well be dedicated to the latter; in a way it is because of what I write now. Sadly, he passed away in April of this year – a sorrow to Joanna in particular as he was like a brother to her. The official dedication, anyway, goes to four young souls who appeared on the scene well after the above conversational exchange. I refer to our four grandchildren, who in due course may derive some amusement – if not instruction – from what I have written. I should mention here that our fourth grandchild, Catrin Grace Blair Williams, does not feature in the 'odyssey' that follows as she only arrived in this world on the eighth of the month in which I now write.

My account depends almost entirely on memory, apart from the historical digressions, since I have never kept a diary for anything other than future engagements and the noting down of the occasional important but not necessarily personal event. People with whom I shared certain experiences and who are thus included in these pages may perhaps remember things a little differently from me, in which case I ask their pardon. I should point out, in particular, that the dialogues included are not verbatim transcriptions of conversations that occurred but reconstructions reflecting their remembered general content.

Whom do I thank for assistance in an undertaking that has occupied the twilight years of my professional career? Joanna, 'my better half', is beyond thanks or praise, having given unflinching support to me throughout our married life and having thus become an integral part of the story. Annabel and Edmund, our two adult children, as well as my wider family, I thank simply for being their loving selves. Friends, too numerous to mention, I also thank for being themselves and offering succour and encouragement in times of need. Others … well, some others, I thank for making my life on occasions a tad more interesting than I might have wished!

Philip Blair
July 2014

I

Island of Love

'Look thy last on all things lovely.'

I was waiting in Nicosia airport to board the DC 6 military transport plane due to touch down in RAF Lyneham in Wiltshire, UK, some eight hours later. My kitbag stowed, there were just a few personal items with me, including an edition of Father Trevor Huddleston's bestseller *Naught for your Comfort* recently sent me by a friend. I had just completed my period of military service and was flying home to be demobilised. It was 17 September 1959, a few months after Sir Hugh Foot had engineered a settlement due to be signed the following year giving independence to the strife-torn Mediterranean island of Cyprus.

'Look thy last on all things lovely.'

The words from Walter de la Mare's poem stared up at me from the first page of Huddleston's book. For the author, recalled from South Africa to Britain by his religious Order, those words summed up what he felt – a mixture of love and anguish – as he left 'his' land and people to the mercies of a racist government. For me they reflected feelings less intense, no doubt, yet not dissimilar; I had learnt and experienced so much on the island. I had discovered how to think for myself, untrammelled by the bonds of family. Like the priest whose story lay open before me, I had come to know and feel affection for a foreign land of unusual beauty, with two distinct communities, and to hope for a resolution to its problems and conflicts. I had, finally, made acquaintance of a third people of the region, formative for me in the extreme. There was much to ponder as I was leaving this sad yet suddenly hopeful 'island of love'.

The island of Cyprus on a contemporary postcard

***

I had arrived in Cyprus off a troopship.

On my nineteenth birthday, at the end of February 1958, HMS Devonshire set sail from Liverpool bound for Limassol. The band on the quayside played the Royal Air Force signature tune as I and other airmen, kitbags on our shoulders, walked up the gangplank and boarded the ship. The moment was, for me at least, strangely moving. I was of course aware that when we finally disembarked we would be on active service. Perhaps that had something to do with it.

We put into Gibraltar and Malta on the way out. We were allowed four hours to look round the Crown Colony on the rock – and encounter the apes. In Malta we were given six hours. As we steamed into Valetta harbour with most of us standing on deck, a line of soldiers was standing along the edge of the quayside watching us. I remember someone behind me bellowing, 'One step forward, march!'

Apart from being seasick in the Bay of Biscay and the two welcome breaks on shore, my main memory of the voyage is of eating huge quantities of fruitcake from the NAAFI canteen. I had never much liked cake and realised later that this newfound appetite stemmed from the vague tension I began to feel early on in the voyage and which grew more insistent with every nautical mile covered. (During basic training I couldn't stop eating bread and jam and consequently put on a stone in weight; tension, induced by drill-sergeants breathing down your neck, was no doubt the cause in this case too.)

Two weeks after leaving Liverpool we were docked off Limassol and an hour or two later were being herded into vehicles for transportation to one or other of the military bases. It was now mid-March. It had been sunny and warm during our progress through the Mediterranean and the island of Aphrodite dispensed the same favours. There must have been a fair amount of greenery around after the winter rains, yet my memory is of prevailing whiteness and a stony aridity as the bus wound its way inland from the coast.

Philip's batch of police trainees at RAF Netheravon

I reminded myself that I was now in the Middle East – as the posting was designated. It was something of a thrill.

We saw little of the island's capital, Nicosia, before being disgorged onto the large base a mile or two away, originally the civilian airport. Together with some others I was taken to a low-slung but quite capacious tent, my first home on the island. It was only transit accommodation, however, for we were shortly to be dispersed to outlying stations. The duties of our chosen 'trade' would then begin.

I had opted for the police, for which I had subsequently undergone training at RAF Netheravon, quite near my home in Wiltshire. In retrospect, I can only be thankful that I made this choice because it led to my being posted overseas. Our intake of trainees was, to a man, ordered to Cyprus in response to a fresh wave of EOKA violence.

It was thus with slight apprehension that, a week or two after my arrival on the island, I travelled to a signals station just outside Famagusta for my permanent posting. This was some fifty miles east of Nicosia, near the coast. I was not an obvious candidate for the police, it has to be said. The force had a reputation for toughness second only to that of the RAF Regiment. I had just left public school, was slight of build and had hardly begun to shave. At Cardington, the reception camp for new recruits, the NCO responsible for my billet had thought the idea of my becoming a military policeman ridiculous.

'What you, a snowdrop?' he exploded in amazement when I told him. 'Tell you what, if you ever are, I'll hand you my stripes!' A kindly fellow, I remember Corporal Nesbitt well. Strange that I remember him at all, you might say, after only a week in his charge.

For the next eighteen months my permanent home was also a tent. There were brick-built billets on the station to which I had been assigned but police were supposed to live apart from others; we accordingly had 'tented lines' alongside the Regiment. I shared my four-berth shelter with another station policeman and two police dog-handlers. The latter would on occasions return from nocturnal patrols with kitbags full of oranges, which they handed round.

'Are you really allowed to pick these?' I inquired rather primly soon after my arrival.

'Of course we are', retorted one of them, a muscular-looking type. 'The farmer invited us, didn't he? We're doing him a favour, guarding his trees.'

After a while my tent companions became 'the provost', who patrolled off-camp in Land Rovers. I envied them their life-style but as a national serviceman could not join their ranks.

Station police were mostly assigned to camp security duties. I was given shifts around the clock to man the main guardroom or watch over signals installations, the main storehouse, or the MT (motor transport) section. The night shift, from eleven to seven, was superficially tedious yet in a deeper sense very satisfying: the starry brilliance of the Mediterranean night never palled; I enjoyed scouring the surrounding land with a searchlight; and coming off shift to a cookhouse breakfast and the bliss of morning sleep was almost enough in itself to make the long hours of duty worthwhile.

Yet I had scarcely become accustomed to this way of life before I found myself in Jerusalem.

***

I came straight off night duty, hitched a lift with one of the armed convoys to Nicosia, and boarded my plane. The flight to Jordan was via Beirut and Damascus. As we were waiting at the Syrian airport, I could just make out Soviet Mig fighters parked some way off. We were in an old Dakota or DC 3, the 'air workhorse' of the Second World War. Rather than flying at thousands of feet, it flew at hundreds, at which altitude you can get a lot of turbulence. By the time we reached Jerusalem I was feeling distinctly unwell and romantic thoughts of stepping down from the plane and – metaphorically at least – kissing sacred soil had long since evaporated. I was simply glad to have left behind the noise and discomfort.

I was booked to stay at the Claridge Hotel, a favourite resort of tourists. It was situated on the hillside overlooking the Kidron valley, more or less opposite the massive stonework that supports the eastern side of what Jews call the 'temple area'. The site is occupied today by the exquisitely decorated Mosque of Omar, or 'Dome of the Rock', as well as the al-Aqsa Mosque, both important Muslim shrines. Viewed from across the valley to the east, the two monuments set against the backcloth of East Jerusalem, the 'Old City', form a magnificent vista.

My choice of the Claridge had been dictated by the fact that my former school chaplain and friend, the Reverend Cuthbert Shaw, would be there. He was leading a party of pilgrims to the Holy Land over the Easter period, something he did each year for a tourist agency. Knowing of his plans, I had put in for a short period of leave and could hardly believe being granted it only a month after arriving on the station.

I nodded off during the meeting organised by our leader my first evening at the hotel. I was sitting next to him in front of everyone and at the end of the proceedings he nudged me gently.

'Sorry to wake you, Philip, but I've finished at last.' He gave me an understanding smile. 'You know how we clergy tend to go on!'

The earnest American with whom I found myself sharing a room (he described himself as an evangelist) was rather different. I had to sit through an account of his spiritual adventures around the world before finally resuming my slumber.

The week I spent in and around Jerusalem was memorable – less because of the sites visited than because a young Jordanian befriended me. Towards the end of the week I absented myself from party trips to spend time with him. He took me to see his family and they invited me to share an evening meal.

Mustafa Darwish and his family lived in the village of Silwan, situated a little further down the Kidron valley. Their home, built of stone and perched precariously on the rocky hillside, was very simple. The meal was tasty enough and certainly wholesome (the sheep's testicles especially so, I imagine) but as most of it was steeped in olive oil the consequences for my digestive tract were dramatic; I was grateful that night to have the Claridge bathroom at my disposal. More significantly, my chance encounter with the Darwish family constituted my first lesson in the 'Palestinian predicament'.

Philip with Mustafa Darwish (right) and his family (centre)

I don't want to belittle the impact upon me of the 'holy sites'. Especially moving was an Easter morning service at the Garden Tomb. This sepulchre, hewn from rock and considered by some archaeologists to date from Herodian times, is situated in what must once have been a vineyard or garden, for excavations have uncovered an ancient winepress nearby. Its dimensions and internal arrangement fit well the description given in the gospels of the place where the body of Jesus was laid.

The tomb is near the north gate of the Old City of Jerusalem, commonly called Herod's Gate, and close by a rocky outcrop bearing some resemblance to a human skull. This was noticed in 1883 by General Gordon, taking a vacation in the region before his final, fateful assignment in Sudan, and he became convinced he had stumbled on the location of Jesus' crucifixion – Golgotha, the 'place of the skull', or Calvary. Circumstantial evidence for this exists since the area immediately in front of the skull-shape (a bus station when I saw it) is thought once to have been a place of execution – by stoning.

Whatever one makes of this identification, Gordon's Calvary (as the place subsequently became known) was for me a holy and haunted area, with the Garden a stone's throw away more numinous still. The best guide to both is Gordon himself. Following his death in Khartoum at the hands of the Mahdi's hordes, an essay he wrote was published under the title *Reflections in Palestine*. I have a copy; it is a prized possession.

Sudan and Palestine – unlikely collocation. For Charles George Gordon the common factor was most truly Calvary. As for me, still in my teens as I contemplated rocky skull and sepulchre that long-gone Eastertide, had I then been told how significant the two nations and their peoples would one day be for me, I would no doubt have been surprised.

Of course, most people favour the traditional site for the death, burial and – according to Christians – resurrection of the teacher from Galilee. This was 'discovered' in the fourth century by Helena, mother of the Emperor Constantine; it lies within the present Old City, the Church of the Holy Sepulchre being built over it. What

I suppose all the holy places impressed upon me, leaving aside the question of their authenticity, was the fact that Christianity is rooted in history. Not all religions can make this claim.

The question of Christian origins was important for me, to be sure, but it was the recent history and contemporary situation of the Holy Land that captured my imagination most vividly on this holiday. Jerusalem was the world's most famous divided city in 1958: just outside the Old City one could walk beside the 'green line', a tangle of sandbags and barbed wire pushed together in January 1949 when the truce was agreed by opposing Arab and Jewish forces. One could approach the Mandlebaum gate, the only one through to the State of Israel – if you had a pass. As others who have visited such places will testify, as any boy will know who has shinned up a tree to look into a neighbour's garden, there is a thrill, a kind of romance (as well as a challenge) about looking across a barrier into inaccessible territory. For me at the time not only the clumsily erected frontier but the whole area – every tree, stone, street, stranger – oozed both romance and history. Names, phrases, half-formed ideas vaguely recalled but not fully understood crowded into my mind: *Zion, Arab nation, kibbutzim, Lawrence, Balfour, Palestine, King David (Hotel), Elijah, Olivet, 'I will come again'.*

The last found a double echo: as uttered by the original speaker the words both fascinated and eluded me, but I knew that I myself would have to 'come again', I knew I must revisit this city, this land, this people. My friend Mustafa prepared the way.

'Why is this goodbye, Sayyed Philip?' he murmured as we were saying our final farewells. 'Are you not coming back to see us?'

I reassured him. 'But of course, I'd love to, and hope to. But I don't at this moment know when or how that can be.'

'You can come and stay with us in Silwan. I have asked my parents and they would like it very much.'

'Really?' The offer took me by surprise and needed pondering – but not for long. 'That's a nice idea, Mustafa, and extremely generous. I will keep it in mind, definitely, and let you know when it seems possible.'

We exchanged addresses and, the farewells over, parted company. One of the first things I did on arriving back in Cyprus was to procure a copy of *Teach Yourself Arabic*.

***

I began to feel quite comfortable in my role as station policeman, or 'SP'. The work was generally routine: checking identities, signing people and vehicles in and out of camp, patrolling security areas, doing traffic duty (not my forte). You of course had to look smart, especially when wearing 'khaki drill' in the summer. Boots had to shine, white webbing and putties gleam, brass accessories glisten. I quickly learnt the secret of getting knife-like creases in my shirts and shorts: you mix starch into some water, take a big mouthful and spray out the liquid onto your item of clothing – then and only then applying the iron.

Once in a while a situation would arise that required some actual initiative.

There was the cookhouse riot. I can't recall how it started but it involved members of the RAF Regiment who had some sort of complaint – the food, or the queuing, or fury at some gratuitous insult. (The 'rock apes' were very conscious of their status as fighting troops and could easily be offended.) Anyway, I was on guardroom duty and a call came through from one of the cooks for help since the 'apes' were getting out of hand. I could hear a lot of noise and shouting down the phone so there was nothing for it but to see for myself what was happening. Leaving a colleague in the guardroom, I walked down to the brick-built refectory for non-commissioned ranks wondering what I'd find and, more to the point, what I could do.

The place was in uproar, the Regiment generally throwing their weight around. I told them (in best public school English) to stop. The largest and most muscular ape stepped forward, caught me by the lapels and lifted me off the ground. He was roaring something I did not understand but I looked him in the eye – no choice about that, we were eyeball to eyeball – as he riveted me to the cookhouse wall.

'Put me down!' I ordered him. After a moment's thought I added, 'If you don't, I'll place you on a charge.'

Philip in 'khaki drill' outside camp guardroom

The effect was electric: the spirit seemed to depart from the fellow, he carefully lowered me and everyone calmed down. I left the scene with the chef's effusive thanks ringing in my ears.

Life was also good because of the people I was meeting.

There were my police colleagues, a friendly and likeable group, not the toughies I had been led to expect. Most of them were by nature non-conformist; I suppose it takes something of a loner to be a cop at all. Johnny was in some ways typical. A fresh-complexioned Cockney in the provost, he had the knack of spotting irregularities in those of higher rank. He would then quietly investigate and if appropriate place embarrassing revelations, like being drunk on duty, before the guilty party. The latter tended not to re-offend – at least, not blatantly. Johnny's unorthodox interpretation of his role strongly influenced my own attitude; he also became a good friend.

Cypriot auxiliary police served with us on the camp and I naturally became acquainted with some of them. They were all Turkish Cypriots – apart from a Greek married to a Turk. Greeks were normally barred from serving because of violence being perpetrated against the British, and sometimes others, by the Greek Cypriot EOKA movement. The aims of EOKA at this time are summed up in a single Greek word: *enosis*.

Greek Cypriots wanted the British out; so, in principle, did many Turkish Cypriots. But the Greek community were not just looking for independence but for *enosis*, or 'union', with their 'mother country' mainland Greece. This aspiration was part of the wider desire of Greeks in general to restore past glories of empire, destroyed by the Ottoman Turks centuries earlier. Their design after the First World War to regain Constantinople and part at least of Asia Minor had been thwarted; to gain sovereignty over the island of Cyprus would be a step in the right direction. Prime architect of this policy was the island's Orthodox Archbishop, Makarios III. He, however, worked in tandem with and to some extent under political leaders and others on mainland Greece. The autonomous Church of Cyprus of which he was leader formed a useful infrastructure for the nourishment and dissemination of these views. Once EOKA had begun its operations in 1955, it also provided material assistance to

Colonel Grivas with young EOKA 'martyrs', on contemporary postcard.

the insurgents. The active leader of the EOKA guerrilla organisation was one Colonel Grivas – a Cypriot by birth who had, however, served as a soldier in the Greek army.

The aims of Makarios and EOKA were not, needless to say, those of Turkish Cypriots, who became effectively pro-British – hence the Turkish Cypriot police auxiliaries on stations throughout the island, and hence my friendship with Kemal. The latter's duties included manning the barrier at the main gate when I was in the guardroom checking and signing. He was the antithesis of the 'ferocious Turk' stereotype, gentle and diffident, and as he knew some English we were able to converse. We talked about ourselves, our families, our religions, and – inevitably – exchanged ideas on politics, which usually meant the latest turn of events in his unhappy country.

'Things will have to change', I put it to him. 'I mean, this island has had such an unsettled history, ruled for centuries by foreign powers. What about the discussions now going on between the politicians? Do you see something new, something good coming out of them, especially for you Turks?'

His response was cautious, non-committal. 'It's possible, but then we're fewer than the Greeks, and they are very determined. A just solution will not be easy.' We continued in similar vein, as so often.

Those conversations with Kemal, as well as a book I was reading, Lawrence Durrell's *Bitter Lemons*, were two of the ways in which I began to understand, fairly quickly, the complexities of the island situation.

I should mention a third group from which I drew friends, those servicemen who attended Christian meetings on the camp – either in church (a large tent) or in a green hut called 'The MMG'. Those initials stood for Mission to Mediterranean Garrisons and inside this meagre wooden erection Scottish ladies served refreshments and, when asked, offered words of advice to troops missing their families and starved of home comforts. In addition, the ladies organised a Sunday 'Tea-Fellowship' for the more serious-minded. The Regiment armourer, a quiet, thoughtful person, and a flamboyant, Bible-quoting corporal from Jamaica were particularly

Philip on Varosha (Famagusta) beach with friends, including two MMG ladies

good friends of mine from this group. To take services in the church tent there was a resident chaplain or 'padre' for Anglicans while for Other Denominations ('OD') a second chaplain paid regular visits.

There was also Dr Shelley, an Australian.

From the same family as (though not an admirer of) the famous poet, Dr Shelley was an eye-specialist who lived in an old-style, balconied bungalow looking directly onto the walls of Famagusta Old City, inhabited entirely by Turkish Cypriots. Behind the house stretched the more modern Greek urban district of Varosha. This was situated alongside a fine stretch of beach which I and my friends enjoyed once the violence on the island came to an end. The doctor had some years previously moved to Famagusta from Jerusalem, and as in Palestine, so in Cyprus, people with ophthalmic problems came to his house for treatment – at a nominal fee.

The 'Doc', as we called him, was a designated Soldiers' and Airmen's Scripture Reader, and in that capacity would visit the camp and discuss biblical and other themes with those interested. Sometimes he asked servicemen home to tea, where we could meet and chat with his ninety-year-old mother. The house was dark inside, the shutters normally kept across the windows to ward off the sun. Heavy, ornate furniture gave the place a Victorian flavour – as in many Turkish homes. It was nostalgic and soothing for airmen missing home, especially when tucking into sandwiches and cakes, and downing mugs of English-style tea. I owe much to this eccentric wandering Australian but of that I have written elsewhere. Fifty years later I was pleased to see his bungalow still standing, albeit transformed into some sort of municipal office.

The wider world did not encroach much on those whose duties lay on camp. Occasionally station policemen were given outside duties – welcome as far as I was concerned. I was once required to accompany the provost when raiding an unsavoury establishment in town and another time provided escort for an airman sentenced to detention, necessitating a long and enjoyable drive to another base. (Our own guardroom had just one overnight cell.) Off-duty airmen were sometimes allowed – in groups, and armed – into Famagusta but security tightened following bad EOKA incidents and we were then confined to barracks. Once the emergency ended in the spring of 1959 we could travel freely.

In July 1958 we were unexpectedly made aware of a wider emergency. Shortly after the revolution in Iraq in which Hashemite King Faisal lost his life, lines of tents appeared overnight between our camp and the army signals station opposite. Red berets were prominent: it was a brigade of the Parachute Regiment, on its way to assist another Hashemite, King Hussein of Jordan. The 'red devils' stayed a day or two, then, like the Arabs, folded their tents and silently slipped away.

The Middle East did not ignite at this time, as the British government had feared. Yet the fragility of the region's politics and the ease with which war can erupt were truths that were in no way lost on us.

***

Our own emergency was, of course, a kind of war.

I was abruptly reminded of the fact a little later when I found myself clambering onto the back of a lorry – part of a convoy – carrying a Sten gun.

'Keep it at the ready, especially going through Paralimni,' the driver advised me. 'It's an EOKA breeding ground. Can't be too careful!'

I asked myself, as we set out, if I was genuinely prepared to fire the weapon at Greek Cypriots, militant or not.

I cannot be sure of my exact views on the ethics of warfare at the time; moral questions certainly mattered to me so I presume they included a belief that the use of violence to achieve a political end against an established regime – even a colonial one – constituted rebellion. The whole question of violent resistance, freedom fighting, terrorism – whatever the term preferred – has exercised me much since that hot summer day. Anyway, during my time in the forces I presumably assumed that armed opposition to an existing state authority had to be put down.

I was being sent 'on detachment' to a sub-unit of the station I was on. The only way there was along a winding road through several Greek villages, one called Paralimni, the EOKA centre already mentioned where there had been at least one ambush. Our line of vehicles set off and very soon we were entering the village, with its narrow streets, imposing white church and low, close-packed houses. I wasn't too nervous – the chance of an incident was statistically low – but the next few minutes were certainly tense. I gripped my weapon and peered through the dust to locate spots favoured by snipers: corners of buildings, windows, trees.

We came through without mishap and I felt relieved – prematurely, in a way, for mines could be laid on more lonely stretches of road. An hour or so later, having followed the rough track up, down and round low hills, or meandered along dry, sparsely-vegetated valleys, we negotiated 'Table Mountain', the flattering name given by British troops to a slight elevation. A minute or two later we were driving through the camp gate. We drew to a halt inside and, as the water-bowser went off to replenish the tank on top of a rocky mound, I jumped down from the lorry – plastered in dust and still holding my gun.

I could only see tents, the nearest serving as the guardroom destined to be my place of work. After handing in my weapon I was shown my accommodation – another tent, of course, one of a number set in rows. A few larger tents with trailing guy-ropes were set in more isolated spots, one of them (the church, I later discovered) halfway up the mound. Upright posts and a corrugated iron roof in the midst of the tented lines turned out to be the camp dining room. There were no trees or shrubs, scarcely a plant. All was dust and rock.

It suddenly became apparent that my new unit – totalling perhaps fifteen or twenty acres – was almost an island. We had driven along a narrow corridor of land for the last half-mile or so and were now on a cape, widening out from the corridor and slightly higher. As a walk quickly established, sea rather than barbed wire constituted most of the perimeter. Very soon I was rejoicing in what was, in fact, a swimmer's paradise.

There was not, to be honest, much to do in off-duty hours except swim. For one who had learnt the art in open-air municipality baths and occasionally practised it in (generally freezing) waters off the British coast, diving off rocks into the warm, clear waters of the Mediterranean and drifting lazily across the bay was heaven. I became, like almost everyone else, an addict. Apart from swimming, I read quite a bit, talked a lot, and – there being no chaplain – helped organise church services with one or two friends.

Strong friendships, I should emphasise, are a feature of life in the forces overseas. Away from one's family, relatives and friends at home, and with little or no chance of a relationship with the opposite sex, one is thrown upon one's mates for companionship. This can be particularly rewarding in days of general conscription because one comes across people from all sections of society. From time to time, too, these may include someone with a claim to fame – like John, who slept in a neighbouring tent. We got into conversation on one occasion.

'So why did you choose the police?' he asked, when I had introduced myself. 'You're not the obvious type.'

'I don't know, something to do with being challenged. I couldn't see myself as a telex operator – your line, I think. That and the fact that a boyhood friend became a snowdrop. He's in the provost, mind you, having signed on.'

John gave a short laugh. 'Now that I cannot understand. My one goal is getting back into civvy street.'

'Like most of us – national servicemen, I mean. So, what'll you do when you're out?'

He thought for a moment. 'Follow my sister in showbiz, maybe. Half-sister, I should say. But that's probably asking too much.'

'Sister? Would I know her?'

He smiled. 'It'd be odd if you didn't. She was recently on Broadway, opposite Rex Harrison in *My Fair Lady*. That's just for starters. She's Julie Andrews.'

***

There were only three or four SPs on the station and we were relegated to guardroom duties. Other aspects of security – few enough on a camp with minimal land access – were mostly carried out by members of the RAF Regiment.

The Squadron Leader in command of the sub-station rang the guardroom one day to say he'd seen a strange-looking foreigner prowling around. Had I checked the identity of all coming through the main gate? I explained that one or two Turkish Cypriots, cleaners and suchlike, had entered but none whom I did not know.

'Did you check their passes?' he asked.

'Not if I recognized them.'

He exploded. 'What the hell do you mean? Don't you always check passes? This is a vital security matter.'

I assured him again that no unauthorised person had entered the camp precincts via the gate. His fury was not assuaged and he ordered the camp to be scoured for the 'foreigner'. This was a simple matter and the latter was discovered to be a regular civilian helper, a Turkish Cypriot, with a valid pass.

I might have been forgiven this slight irregularity but I blotted my copybook again.

A message came in to the guardroom of smoke being seen on camp. I suppose I was preoccupied with something at the time because I failed to pass this on to the fire section, manned on a rota basis by airmen of various trades. They, however, heard about the smoke from someone else or saw it for themselves; whichever way it was, they discovered a smouldering waste-bin which posed no threat. Nothing further had to be done. Unfortunately my role in the incident reached the ears of the Squadron Leader, who once again interrogated me.

'Yes, I forgot to pass on the message,' I confessed.

'You *forgot*, LAC Blair? Can't you do better than that?'

Soon after this I found myself travelling back to the main signals station, where the officer in charge of Station Police immediately called me to his office. The Squadron Leader, he informed me, had requested my removal from the sub-station on the grounds that I was not cut out to be a policeman. My boss then muttered something uncomplimentary about the sub-station CO, said his opinion could safely be discounted, and dismissed me.

The period of my detachment had lasted about three months. I had enjoyed every minute of it.

***

One of the bonuses of service life is the fact that most if not all your needs are supplied; little effort is required for daily living, which is simple and ordered. The corollary is that you can concentrate on your personal interests with little distraction. In particular, you have plenty of time to think.

I did a lot of thinking that October as the weather cooled. My thoughts revolved in particular around the subject I would be studying at university. In my final year at school I had taken a college entrance exam covering both history and theology and in due course had received a letter from the Principal: he could find a place for me so long as I read theology.

Reading theology meant knowing ancient Greek and Latin. The latter had been a subject of study at school for ten years, but ancient Greek I had only begun. I therefore abandoned my *Teach Yourself Arabic* in favour of a grammar of New Testament Greek. Yet this was not the only aspect of theology that concerned me: my attitude to the discipline was changing. My visit to Jerusalem, the influence of Dr Shelley, a book or two on theology and a brief correspondence with one of the authors, had all contributed to a revolution in my thinking. I had always considered myself a Christian; now I was discovering that grounds for belief were stronger than I had imagined.

Police duties continued smoothly enough until I found myself caught up in a court-martial case. I was not directly involved, being assigned as guard to the accused in court, an Irishman whose duties had something to do with the Regiment. I heard what the case was about, the nature of the charge and much of the evidence submitted. What I also heard one evening, however, or rather overheard, was fabrication of evidence by the two provost police who at the time were sharing my tent. Now, I was far from sure that the accused was innocent; indeed, I was hardly in a position to know. Nor was I unsympathetic to difficulties so often encountered by police generally in bringing the guilty to justice. But I seemed in some sense to have become a party to perjury – unless of course my colleagues thought better of it. It looked to me as if the man, if convicted, would face a stiff sentence and the thought of a miscarriage of justice bothered me. One way and another I became convinced I had to intervene. Yet here I faced a dilemma: what could I do that would not simply be brushed under the carpet?

Someone had told me, 'If you have a real problem, go to the top'. Perhaps it was Johnny; it was certainly his style. Anyway, I opted to apply the principle. I knew a sentence passed on an airman in a serious case had to be ratified at a high level; I would go to that level – by post.

I wrote the letter carefully, saying what I knew and expressing the hope that the information I was presenting would be taken into account. I also made it clear I was not acting out of any ill-will towards the two police corporals, whose names I naturally did not divulge. I addressed the letter to the Air Officer Commanding, RAF Middle East, Episkopi, stuck a stamp on the envelope and dropped it into the camp mailbox.

I had almost forgotten about it when some weeks later I was summoned by the commanding officer, an Air Commodore. I was marched into his presence and he looked coldly up at me.

'What on earth do you think you were doing, Corporal Blair?' he demanded. (Station police had recently been elevated to Acting Corporal Unpaid.) 'It is utterly out of order to bypass proper channels. Never do such a thing again.'

He said a bit more and I murmured something – enough to prompt a parting shot which I have never forgotten.

'You're either an idiot, Corporal Blair, or a bloody hypocrite.'

There was a postscript. Not long after this a Regiment officer abruptly stopped me in the camp road.

'I'd like to congratulate you on what you did, Corporal Blair,' he remarked quietly, his eyes smiling.

He said nothing more but I have always assumed he was giving me the nod that my letter to the AOC had had a satisfactory outcome. As for my two police colleagues, nothing seemed to happen to them.

***

1958 gave way to 1959 and I had around two weeks' leave to enjoy before being demobbed in September. I had not forgotten Mustafa's invitation to return to Jordan and stay with his family. I put in for a week's leave over the Easter period again and in late March was once again walking the streets of Old Jerusalem with my young Arab and Muslim friends.

But it was not only the Holy City and its environs that I visited this time. Mustafa was determined I should see as much of his country as possible so he took me to various centres of life in what we now know as the occupied West Bank, most notably Nablus.

'If you look over there,' Mustafa suddenly said, pointing across me as we bumped along on a bus on one of our trips, 'you can see a camp for refugees from the war with Israel ten years ago.'

I strained round in my seat to have a look. I was naïvely expecting to see tents, I recall, but what I could just make out through some shrubs some way off was a lot of flat-roofed dwellings built of breeze-blocks.

'Some of my family had to leave their homes in 1948,' Mustafa went on, 'but they managed to find a place like ours in Silwan.'

We fell to discussing the whole Palestine problem, and in particular the concern of young people about future employment. Mustafa was one of these and he asked me whether there were opportunities for further education in UK. I subsequently made efforts to inquire, through my parents and others, whether grants might be available for those in his position. I was young, idealistic and ignorant about such things and gave a few people, not least my busy father, a hard time of it as I pushed the Palestinian cause. Nothing came of these efforts and I was in no position as a national serviceman to pursue the matter further. Once I got back to UK there were too many other things to think about and I let the matter drop. Yet I did not forget my Arab friends and their problems.

Mustafa also took me to Amman, across the Jordan. There we stayed with the family of his elder brother, a stone-mason. I remember him as very good-looking and, like the rest of his family, extremely generous. I was of course experiencing for the first time what strikes every visitor to the Middle East, the depth and range of Arab hospitality. We in the West have come near to losing this human quality altogether.

Amman struck me as shapeless and sprawling. Indeed, Mustafa told me it was an agglomeration of seven villages. In those days there was little in the way of commerce and industrialization, roads were mostly narrow and poorly paved, and the magnificent villas and palaces that now overlook the older part of the city from the surrounding hills were to be built two or three decades later. There were one or two ancient structures to visit, however, like the Roman amphitheatre.

***

My flights to and from Jerusalem had all been via Beirut but on my return to Cyprus on this occasion I had twenty-four hours to spend in the Lebanese capital. These were halcyon days for the city, nicknamed 'the Paris of the Middle East'. I certainly recall its aura of wealth and style. Tall, smart office or apartment blocks intermingled with traditional red-tiled residences. Shops displayed the latest fashions. Streets were replete with gleaming cars, many of them American, and controlled by crisply-uniformed gendarmes.

As in Jerusalem I found myself befriended by someone of my own generation, in this case a student – or maybe a young teacher, I forget – at the American University of Beirut (AUB). I chanced upon the well-known institution as, late in the day, I was wandering round the al-Hamra district and I slipped through the gates to have a closer look. The young man – not a local, in fact, but himself an American – approached me, we got talking and he showed me something of the campus. I remember being rather impressed. He then made a suggestion.

'How about staying the evening at AUB. Some of us are having a bit of a party. You know, some eats and so on. Should be good and you'll meet some interesting guys.'

'Really? I've nothing else to do, so thanks, I will.'

I accordingly joined the festivities. I have no idea now what was being celebrated, though it was still the Easter season. I remember being offered – strangely – 'gingerbread man' biscuits, as well as some lusty singing, which included (I seem to recall) communal rendering of a song *about* gingerbread men. I have long wanted to know, but never managed to discover, what precisely those biscuits denoted.

Beirut in 1959 was the hub of the Middle East politically as well as culturally and commercially. All countries of the region and many lesser groups and factions were represented there, while larger nations from East and West had embassies. The city therefore spawned much gossip and intrigue. Its reputation for the latter had not quite reached the level of a few years later, however, when a major film set in the city could be entitled, 'Where the spies are'. (The film, starring David Niven, still turns up on TV channels.)

The idea that Beirut was crawling with spies and the Middle East Centre for Arab Studies (MECAS), opened in 1947 by the British in nearby Shemlan, was a 'School for Spies', took root after the Russian agent George Blake was unmasked and arrested while studying at MECAS in 1961. The notion was assiduously promoted by the Syrians and strengthened further by the Kim Philby affair. Philby was working as a journalist in Beirut when, in January 1963, he suddenly vanished to reappear in Moscow; he too, it transpired, had been working for the Soviets. It then got about, falsely though perhaps understandably, that he also had been a student at the 'Spy School'. MECAS was of course nothing to do with training spies; it was a school for the teaching of Arabic, drawing students from a variety of backgrounds, but especially the British diplomatic service. It was finally forced to close in 1978 because of the Lebanese civil war.

I would have much appreciated a course at MECAS, for sadly I learnt no Arabic on my second visit to the Arab world. I no doubt tried a few phrases but this was my first encounter with a fact of life native speakers of English have to accept: the difficulty of learning any foreign language, but particularly Arabic, from native speakers of that language – unless you travel to the back of beyond. This is because almost everywhere you go in the world today (it was much the same fifty years ago), people either speak English or wish to speak it better or are keen to learn it. This means it is a constant battle to keep any foreigner you happen to be with, speaking his or her own language. English people generally display great patience with halting – even good – speakers of their language, modifying the form of their diction, their use of vocabulary, structures, idioms to suit the listener's level. Finding such patience in speakers of a language you, as an English speaker, are trying to learn is rare indeed. The notion, sometimes pedalled, that the English are by nature poor language-learners has to be dismissed.

***

An assortment of other memories and thoughts stand out about the time I spent as a serviceman in Cyprus.

I recall a quick trip up 'the panhandle' – the long, finger-like peninsular on the north-east of the island. There was a tiny signals unit almost at the end, next to an Orthodox monastery, where a friend was stationed. I had two days off so it was a pleasure trip but I had to travel in a regular convoy, comprising Bedford trucks carrying supplies and water, with armed Land Rovers front and rear. One convoy on this route had been ambushed with some loss of life but at the time of my trip there was little EOKA activity, so no one expected trouble. We passed through a number of Greek villages where narrow, winding streets slowed us up, but in the open country we breezed along merrily – until tarmac gave way to a rougher surface. The road skirted the coast for a lot of the time, swinging from south to north, then back to the south. There were spectacular vistas, particularly over the last stretch where we drove through rich pastureland flanked by low, flat-topped hills. Not a building could be seen but for the observant there were fauna aplenty, not least the wild donkeys. A final hill was breasted – a magnificent white beach suddenly opening out behind us – and we passed through the camp gate.

I never visited the monastery – dedicated to Saint Andrew, who nineteen hundred years before had (it is claimed) clambered from a boat onto the rocks now overshadowed by the monastery, making it a popular place of pilgrimage – and as for the magnificent beach, it was out of bounds. But it was nice to see my medic friend and sample a life-style even simpler than my own. Many years later I enjoyed both monastery and beach on an almost regular basis, an

Philip outside his tent with Brian, with whom he toured the island

unusual feature of the former being a free-ranging sow, sometimes suckling a cluster of piglets.

Sir Hugh Foot was appointed governor-general of Cyprus during my period of national service, with a brief to bring the armed struggle to an end. Some six months before I was due to be demobbed, a cease-fire was agreed between the British colonial administration and the Greek Cypriot EOKA movement. This meant that servicemen could at last travel freely.

I had one more week of leave to take and wondered about visiting mainland Greece for my final holiday. However, a friend asked if I would join him on a trip round the island to show a film to the troops; it told a true story with a message and he felt it could do some good. This seemed an interesting idea so I agreed to accompany him. We hired a car and made our tour, visiting perhaps half-a-dozen camps, where the halls or cinemas we utilized were well filled. We met and talked with a lot of friendly folk and saw much of Cyprus for the first time – pretty villages, green valleys, wide arid plains, soaring mountains. Whether or not the film did any 'good', we ourselves benefited from the whole experience.

Perhaps my most cherished moment on the island was a brief reunion with a much-loved uncle.

James was one of three brothers: Harold, my father and the eldest; John, two years younger and my godfather; James (Jim to us), the youngest. All three were born in India, where my grandfather, Arthur, and my grandmother, Agnes (née Edmonds; an early woman doctor), were missionaries in the United Provinces. The three boys were educated in England, my father, born in 1902, being sent home for this purpose at the age of six. Apparently my grandparents thought life in India was doing him no good as he had begun to behave rather haughtily towards the servants. He lived with maternal grandparents or aunts until joined by his brothers – brought home by their mother – some time later. When Agnes rejoined her husband overseas the boys remained in England with relatives or at boarding school, seeing their parents when on furlough. The outbreak of war in 1914, however, made such home visits difficult. On leaving school all three brothers went up to Oxford, after which my father spent eleven years in the colonial service in the Gold Coast (Ghana) before returning home and being ordained. John followed the same path in Nigeria until, in 1949, he resigned and soon after emigrated with his family to Western Australia. James, having joined the Oxford Mission to Calcutta, returned to India, where in due course he became a national.

At the time of our meeting in Cyprus my uncle was the Anglican Bishop of Dacca (Dhaka), in East Pakistan (Bangladesh). According to the custom of his Order, of which he remained a member, my uncle had home leave every five years and this was now due. He was to spend most of that summer in UK but would be returning to the sub-continent before my own repatriation. To make sure he saw me he arranged that on his outward journey he would stop off in Cyprus. This he did in April, staying in Nicosia at the Ledra Palace Hotel. I was able to arrange a few days off over the weekend and hitched a lift to the RAF station at the airport.

Uncle Jim and I spent our time wandering around the capital, seeing the sights and generally catching up on news. The Anglican padre, meanwhile, hearing there was a bishop in the vicinity got in touch with my uncle and invited him to preach in the garrison church. This was a generous offer on his part because he was a staunch evangelical and might well have queried the doctrinal credentials of an unknown 'colonial' prelate. As it happens, my father and uncles had been brought up in the Anglo-Catholic tradition and though Catholic practices like praying to the Virgin are frowned on by evangelicals, the two traditions are at one on the important fundamentals of the faith. So the following Sunday evening, in front of a sizeable congregation, my uncle was ushered to the pulpit. After a formal prayer he looked up at his audience.

'I am going to speak tonight about *angels*,' he began.

The opening was scarcely arresting and I prepared myself for a run-of-the-mill clerical address. I had badly misjudged my uncle: as he warmed to his theme I became more and more enthralled, the climax moving me as deeply as any preacher's words have moved me since. Those creatures of reflected light he spoke about served simply as his stepping stones to the Light of the World.

***

And so the time closed in and I began to think more and more about what lay ahead. I could perhaps have reflected on what my time as a national serviceman had done for me. I did not do so at the time, consciously at least, though I have often done so since.

Was I a good policeman, a good soldier? (An airman is of course a soldier, of a kind.) I was not good at protocol – police, military, whatever. I sometimes wonder how I would have performed in open conflict. I imagine I could and would have engaged 'the enemy' without too much hesitation – as I was trained. But I'm glad I never had to put this to the test. I'm relieved that I did not, for instance, have to open fire on some indistinct yet threatening target whilst on guard duty at night. The case of a soldier in Northern Ireland on duty at an army store, charged with murder for shooting someone he judged to be posing an imminent threat, appalled me when years later the case was highlighted in the media.

What I can say with certainty is that my experience of service life was a happy one. I may not have been fully aware of this at the time but the proof lies in the fact that for a number of years afterwards I had the recurring dream that I was back in the RAF and in every case I was thrilled to be in uniform again.

Why the happiness?

Perhaps it was because, as I have already said, in the forces one's day to day needs are supplied, making life simple and ordered. Few decisions have to be made, and making decisions – we all know – can be stressful. But I think the reason was deeper. I was once told, to my amazement, that veterans of the First World War sometimes felt home-sick for the trenches. One can only assume they experienced a measure of amnesia about the horrors of that conflict. Yet I would venture a rationale for this phenomenon. My own experience of active service represented a tiny fraction of what those soldiers went through but it was nevertheless the same in kind. And what for me sums up that experience is twofold: ardent pursuit of a common goal and great dependence on friends, with little to detract from these twin passions. It could perhaps be explained more simply: for a soldier, life is a unity – a unity lost the moment the uniform is put off. In an increasingly fragmented world we crave such unity, and any we have known but subsequently lost beckons like a siren.

Service life made me happy, yet what is much more it gave my life permanent direction. Eighteen months with Her Majesty's Forces in the Middle East, plus, I have to add, a particular book I read during that period, made me certain – as that plane lifted off from Nicosia one September morning in 1959 – that sooner or later I would return.

II

Joanna – and the Way Back

Having disembarked from the plane at RAF Lyneham later that September day, those of us whose term of service was coming to an end were granted an immediate pass to spend the weekend with our families. The following week we were to return for the completion of demobilization formalities.

My father was vicar of a parish in Devizes, only some twenty miles from the military airport, so I was with the family soon after touching down. After eighteen months away it was exciting to be back, yet I don't recall extravagant displays of emotion. My sister, Lorna, four years my senior, was probably not at home but my brother, Nigel, seven years younger than me, certainly was; our relationships were excellent but as with most siblings we tended to take each for granted. My sister and brother had some consuming interests, too, music in the main for the former and naval history/tactics for the latter, so they were seldom at a loss for things to do.

My mother and father would undoubtedly have given me the most loving of welcomes in their own way but neither was of a demonstrative disposition. My mother, Honor Blair (née MacAdam), whose first concern was her family, had a wide range of other interests – tending the garden, running the Young Wives, leading a Guide Company, painting in water colour or oils – and having seen that we were all fed, watered and happy was wont to disappear to pursue one or other of these pastimes. As a parish priest my father had plenty to do that weekend. He was ex-officio chaplain to a nearby garrison and it was Battle of Britain Sunday. (I wore my Number 2 and general service medal, saluting a high-ranking RAF officer as I emerged from the parade service.) Making final preparations and giving a polish to a couple of sermons would have kept him fairly occupied.

Within two weeks I was on my way to Oxford, with the invigorating if slightly daunting prospect before me of three years in the university city of dreaming spires studying theology. I well remember the drive up, my father at the wheel of our 1936 Morris 10 (synchromesh between gears two and three), through wonderful English countryside. I couldn't get over how *green* everything was – this following a summer everyone said had been a scorcher. My parents saw me into a room at St Edmund Hall with its pretty quadrangle, particularly satisfying for my father as this had been his own college (as well as his father's). My sister, up at Oxford as well, was arriving independently. Having completed a diploma at the Guildhall School of Music she was now reading for a degree in music.

What can I say about those Oxford years? The theology was interesting and in many ways challenging – though I met a degree of bigotry. I mean among the academic staff, not students.

'This kind of essay really annoys me,' was the reaction I once sparked from a tutor after I had read to him, in the presence of a fellow-undergraduate, one of my weekly offerings.

'You simply cite Dr Pusey for your early date to the Book of Daniel,' he went on. 'What about modern authorities on Daniel and Jewish apocalyptic, Eric Heaton's book, for example? E.B. Pusey may have been a fine nineteenth-century priest, and scholar in his way, but theology at Oxford has moved on since then.'

I did my best to salvage something. 'Surely, sir, there are linguistic features in Daniel that are best explained by positing an exilic, Babylonian provenance.'

'So it may have been argued. But the date of the pseudepigraphical work we know as Daniel is settled by its content, its references to history. These, unless you take the idea of predictive prophecy to unconscionable lengths, make a second-century date imperative.'

It seemed pointless to take the issue further so I listened quietly to some more donnish comments while privately remaining

Ridley Hall rugby team

unconvinced. As already indicated, I had done some background reading in Cyprus and decided that the liberal, somewhat destructive approach to questions of scriptural authorship and dating was flawed. Scholars were too inclined to base their conclusions on dubious ideological premises rather than unbiased research. While I had little opportunity to air these unfashionable views at university, I did so decades later in published form. It was later, too, that I met the above tutor by chance after he had become a bishop; he quite spontaneously brought up the incident of his abrupt dismissal of that essay on apocalyptic, effectively apologising for the way he had reacted.

Disputes with dons notwithstanding, at the end of my three years at Oxford I was awarded a degree in theology – the main thing.

From Oxford I went to Cambridge. This was in 1962, when I entered Ridley Hall to train for the ordained ministry of the Church of England. The course lasted two years and was very satisfying. Cut-throat croquet on the college lawn remains a vivid memory. Sport was, in fact, my main recreational activity at Cambridge as at Oxford. I played tennis in the summer and competed at middle or long distance running the year round, representing both universities in cross-country and athletics. Ridley also gave me the opportunity to renew my acquaintance with rugby, which I had enjoyed to the age of thirteen but dropped on entering a soccer school.

***

Far and away my most significant achievement during this five-year period was meeting, falling in love with and finally marrying Joanna.

I first saw her one Sunday in June 1960, a neatly-costumed figure with a curling mass of light brown hair walking up to take communion in Truro cathedral. It was early in my first summer vacation from Oxford, when I had joined the family in Cornwall, my father having a month or two previously taken up the post of Canon Chancellor. I not only saw Joanna on this day but also spoke to her. As I was leaving the cathedral by the west doors at the end of the service I was called over by a young man.

Joanna

'Hello,' he said as I came up, 'I was wondering if you were thinking of joining the ringers. A peal of ten, you know, very exciting.'

My response was cautious. 'I ought to have a go one day, but I'm afraid …'

'Ah, excuses, excuses!' he interrupted. 'Now, we have a learner right here, who can tell you what it's all about.' He turned to the quiet, oh-so-pretty girl standing beside him. 'It's fun, Joanna, isn't it? I'm sure you'd recommend it.'

'Well,' she said slowly, 'it's certainly a fascinating hobby. People tend to get hooked on it.' Then, with a hint of a frown, she added, 'But as you know, Gat, I had a bit of a tussle with a rope the other day. So … yes, I'd recommend bell-ringing even if I'm not myself a natural.' No frown now, just smiling eyes briefly turned my way.

A three-cornered conversation ensued but I was scarcely concentrating, in thrall to those sea-blue eyes. I thought at the time how lucky this encounter was; Joanna has long since put me right. It was not luck at all but feminine guile, swiftly translated into action. And she was only seventeen.

For some reason, having fallen in love with Joanna at first sight – that, in retrospect, is indisputable – I dragged my feet. It was two and a half years later that I realised it was time to get serious. We occasionally met casually during the intervening period but were not in any sense 'an item'. Joanna has forgiven me though I'm not sure I deserve it. My excuse is the exigencies of undergraduate life – its academic demands as well as sporting attractions. What I can say with utter truthfulness is that my waywardness was not because someone else had stolen my heart.

It took an act of God to bring me to my senses. Just after Christmas 1962 the whole of England – the West Country most spectacularly – entered an ice-age. 'Snow chaos' it was not; this occurs annually when the land is subjected to a paltry sprinkling, enough to whiten the landscape for a day or two. What happened at the end of '62 and lasted nearly three months had not been experienced for decades – even centuries. Snow fell by the bucket load and drifted to unheard of depths. Ponds, lakes, rivers froze hard and deep to enable almost any activity – skating, lighting fires, the driving of cars even – to be practised on the ice. The country was paralyzed, with many areas made inaccessible – including a conference centre on Exmoor where I had booked myself in for a week. Being unable to get near the place (helicopter drops were not on offer) I found myself at a loose end in Truro. Not entirely, however. I was invited to a party. This was most agreeable, and made all the more agreeable because the invitation came from Joanna.

How well I remember the evening: the intimate atmosphere in their two front rooms; music by grace of Joanna's father, Joe Norris the Second, who had an early Grundig tape recorder, with numbers like Acker Bilk's *Stranger on the Shore* and Cliff Richard's *Bachelor Boy* (not the Beatles, however, *Love Me Do* entering the charts the previous October but failing to rise to the top while *Please Please Me* only did so that January); plenty to drink, and great food prepared by her mother, Mary Cecil; the quartet of friends from her school days – Joanna herself ('nicely'), Judy ('loosely'), Ann ('nearly'), Patsy ('mostly'); male friends too, of course, like Simmo (still a close friend). We ate, drank, talked, danced or twisted à la mode. Yet I was preoccupied, having eyes for just one – my captivating hostess. The penny had finally dropped, as Judy noticed at the time.

'He never took his eyes off you,' she later divulged to her friend.

The rest, as they say, is history. Our first outing together was – a little inappropriately perhaps – to 'Hell's Mouth', a famous spot on the cliffs just north of Camborne.

I didn't quite declare my intentions on the spot but did so in effect in a letter I posted just before leaving Truro on a train for Cambridge, Joanna leaving a little later for her teacher-training college in London. Idyllic days together in one or other of the cities (walks *on* the River Cam, for example, or *Lawrence of Arabia* at the Odeon Leicester Square – our first film together) put the seal on things and we soon became engaged.

Yet joy is seldom untainted. A great sadness for Joanna during the period of our 'going steady' was the sudden death of her father through a heart attack. This was no more then a couple of months after that all-important Christmas party. The funeral was held at Truro Crematorium, my own father officiating.

Philip and Joanna's marriage. Above, from left, Philip's father, Joanna's mother, Michael Saunders (best man), Joanna's uncle Clifton (behind), Philip and Joanna, Judy (bridesmaid), Joanna's cousin Michael (behind), Philip's mother, Philip's brother.

Philip and Joanna cut the cake.

Philip's sister, with toddlers, in USA at the time.

Edmund Joseph Norris was around seventy at the time, having married Mary Cecil Harris at a mature age, with Joanna (their only child) appearing a decade or so later. Daughter and father were understandably very close and his passing hit her hard. I think my recent arrival in her life eased things a little, and possibly even helped her mother. But I am very sorry I never got to know Joe Norris properly – a wonderful character in every sense of the word.

A comforting fact for us both, in a way, was his declared liking for me. 'That is the kind of young man I would like our daughter to marry', he had apparently said of me to Joanna's mother following the Christmas party, adding tersely, 'And we *don't* interfere!'

In this context, too, I must mention that my own parents, having already in their own way fallen in love with Joanna, were utterly delighted when we announced our engagement.

We were married in Truro cathedral on 25 July 1964. The wedding was not in this setting because I was the Chancellor's son but because the cathedral was also the parish church of St Mary's, Truro, of which Joanna was a member. The Dean of Truro read the opening words; my father took the central part tying the knot (he took a deep breath before commencing, I remember); my Uncle Jim, once again on leave, gave the address; the Bishop of Truro gave the blessing. With bishops in attendance, a cathedral organist accompanying hymns and playing us in and out (Widor's Toccata and Crown Imperial), an anthem 'Love is strong as death' composed for the occasion by my sister and sung by the choir, it wasn't quite a royal occasion but came passably close. My beautiful bride deserved it all, including God's final gift – wonderful weather. Thus happily our married life began; even so has it continued.

Following the wedding reception the guests – as many as were able – went off to the Minack Theatre, on the edge of the cliffs at Porthcurno in the far west, to watch a Shakespeare play. It was, we were told, a wonderful evening as the players performed before the backdrop of a silken, sun-streaked sea. Joanna and I have sometimes wished we had gone with them. Instead we set off for our honeymoon. We had a couple of nights in Glastonbury at a hotel opposite the abbey ruins before going on to Wales. The gorgeous weather – a heat-wave, no less – kept going, the street outside was so noisy we couldn't open the window, hot air rises and we had a top room under scalding tiles. That first night we endured the kind of temperature we later became used to in a very different part of the world.

***

After our holiday we went straight back to Cornwall so I could take up the post of assistant curate in the parish church of St Martin and St Meriadoc, Camborne. This 'dull brown, two-storey town', as John Betjamen once described it, was probably better known overseas than in UK as it stands at the centre of the tin-mining district and has given its name to a famous School of Mines. (It used to be said that wherever in the world there was a hole in the ground you'd find a Cousin Jack – a Cornishman – at the bottom.) Its brass band and rugby team have also, from time to time, brought the town a measure of fame. I had not been ordained before taking up duties in the parish but my help was needed immediately as the rector was unwell. Ordination as deacon followed in a couple of months and as priest after a year; a deacon can in fact perform most clerical duties. This post represented my first full-time employment – discounting the two years spent in the RAF.

I say 'employment', yet I feel this is not the right word for those working for the Church. There is plenty to do, of course, but strictly speaking the ordained minister, if not the lay church worker in quite the same sense, is given an allowance by the faithful to enable him or her to serve their spiritual needs. In other words, ordained members of the Church allocated a stipend are freed from the obligation to 'earn a living' in order to devote themselves to such things as prayer, organising church meetings and services, 'ghostly counsel and advice' (as the Book of Common Prayer has it), and the teaching or preaching of the Word. None of these activities are directly productive in a material sense so can hardly be expected to earn material reward. In a nutshell, church work of any description is ultimately directed towards people's spiritual not physical welfare. Much unnecessary effort would be saved – and a few nervous breakdowns avoided – were this properly understood.

We spent four years in Camborne, Joanna teaching at a nearby primary school while I served the parish. This is not the place to give an account of a very eventful time. The rector of the parish, Canon G. F. Sandfield, not at all well when I arrived, gained little in strength and late in 1965 suffered a stroke and died in hospital. The latter, situated in an isolated spot on the edge of a wood near the sea, had formerly specialised in tuberculosis patients and the wards, all at ground level, were spread across attractive grounds. I and a second curate, John Pridmore, a friend from college days who had joined the parish six weeks earlier, were with him at the end. It was a crisp, clear November night and together we stepped outside and looked up at the stars.

'Look at that, John!' I spoke in awe. 'Countless millions, stabbing, like diamonds.'

'Yes,' he said softly, eyes remaining aloft, 'one almost feels they're singing. Maybe they are, to welcome a saint to glory.'

For the next ten months we ran the parish, assisted by our two churchwardens – both salt of the earth. Basil Brown, a previous curate, became rector in September 1966 and life settled into more of a routine – though not for us at home because six weeks later Joanna gave birth to Annabel, our first child.

John and I immensely appreciated our two spiritual mentors in Camborne. Too often one hears of soured relationships between curates and incumbents. We learnt three things from ours: faith, hope, charity. What else matters?

I would mention just one shared achievement during those Camborne years. John, who had a special gift with children, initiated an annual Christmas play to be performed by members of the Junior Church. He left the parish after only two years and following his departure I continued the tradition, turning the story 'The Other Wise Man' into a play. When it had been performed in Camborne church I took the children down to St Hilary, near Marazion, for a second performance. This was, I believe, the first Christmas play to be performed at St Hilary church since those produced annually by the then rector, Bernard Walke, in the nineteen-twenties and thirties. His productions were broadcast to the nation by the BBC, so became something of a tradition. (Walke's haunting narrative *Twenty Years at St Hilary* tells the full story.) My latter-day effort did not attract the BBC, but John, that Christmas Eve, journeyed to Cornwall especially to witness it. I couldn't have asked for more.

I relinquished my post as curate at St Martin's in the summer of 1968, after having had something of a struggle about where to go next. My intention since national service days had been to serve the Church overseas – more specifically, in the Arab world. I told Joanna this when we first got together and she went along with the idea. But she was the only child of a mother who was a widow. I knew her mother was unhappy about our leaving UK and when the offer came of a second curacy at a church in Oxford, this seemed the answer. Yet soon after I had accepted this proposal – and received a letter of welcome onto his team from the vicar – I began to have doubts.

I found myself in the Chancellery garden with my father one day and, on impulse, decided to share my feelings with him.

'I don't know if you've noticed anything, Dad, but something makes me unhappy about the Oxford post. It's not the job that worries me. On the contrary, it's most attractive. Could hardly be better at this stage, working among students in a popular church under such a man. It's just … just not what I had envisaged. I mean, it's not what I felt when I was in Cyprus.' We walked on slowly together, navigating one of my mother's rose beds. 'I decided then that I should work overseas, as I think I mentioned.' I turned towards him. 'So what do you think?'

My father fell silent and we stopped walking. He didn't spend long in thought, however. 'If you really feel like this,' he said quietly, 'then you'd better withdraw.'

He didn't find it easy to give this advice, I could see; he had liked the idea of Oxford and certainly had no wish to see us disappearing over the horizon. I decided to give myself a deadline, hoping my thoughts would clarify or even that something tangible would occur to make it obvious which path I should take. I told only Joanna about the deadline – midday on a Sunday some weeks later. By that time, having left Camborne, I would be on a final paid holiday.

The day rapidly approached and I was still in two minds. Nothing new had occurred to persuade me it was right to withdraw from the Oxford post and I wanted total conviction; in default of this, I would let my acceptance of the curacy stand. The Sunday came and Joanna and I decided to have a change and attend morning service in a little country church. We arrived at its doors on the stroke of eleven – to find there was no service that Sunday. There was nothing for it but drive back to Truro and the cathedral, where the service started at 11.15. We were a little late so slipped in by a side door.

At about ten to twelve the Archdeacon of Cornwall mounted the steps to the pulpit. I remember nothing of his sermon except the first words: 'This morning I wish to speak on behalf of the Church Missionary Society.' Joanna, sitting beside me, knew as quickly as I did that this was the 'something tangible'.

I wrote two letters over the next few days: the first to the vicar in Oxford explaining – and apologising for – the fact that I felt compelled to go back on my decision to accept his offer; the second to the Church Missionary Society (CMS) saying my wife and I were interested in offering ourselves as candidates for work overseas.

***

Once the ball had been set rolling with the CMS, things went smoothly. We were interviewed in London and accepted as missionaries, conditional upon completing a period of training. We had reason for not wanting to start this immediately so it was arranged that our training should commence the following spring. Meanwhile, temporary clerical duties were found for me in two local parishes.

Our period of instruction at the training college lasted four terms, the first ending in July 1969, immediately after which I attended a course in general linguistics designed to prepare one for learning a foreign language. We had already been told that our destination was likely to be Sudan, where the national language is Arabic, so we would be facing a tough language-learning assignment. I in particular would be up against it as it was intended I should give biblical instruction in Arabic. I enjoyed the summer course, however, and received a good grade.

Sudan had a romantic ring about it, not least because of what I had read since my Cyprus days about 'Gordon of Khartoum'. I had first become acquainted with this intriguing character while at Lancing College. The sixth form history teacher wanted us to review a book and I was assigned Lytton Strachey's *Eminent Victorians*. As the reader may know, Strachey was a cynic who managed to rake up gossip about four notable Victorian 'saints': Cardinal Manning, Florence Nightingale, Thomas Arnold, and England's Christian soldier and hero, General Gordon. Even before the dramatic Khartoum episode, this small, dapper army officer had as 'Chinese Gordon' become a figure of legendary military prowess. Strachey painted him as a brandy-swigging misfit of doubtful propriety. Seeing 'Gordon's Calvary' while visiting Jerusalem brought him to my attention again, and shortly afterwards the Anglican padre on my station lent me a book which, though not directly concerned with Gordon, made me determined to learn more about him. I have already referred to this book as giving – together with my experience in the RAF – direction to my life. It is appropriate at this stage to speak of it more fully.

For those interested in the genre, *Temple Gairdner of Cairo*, by Constance Padwick, is a classic of missionary biography. It tells of a man of great academic and even greater musical accomplishment who might have been a 'prince of the Church' but who chose instead, as a young man towards the end of the Victorian era, to bury himself in the Muslim world. It is also a poignant love story, leaving the reader almost as desolate as the wife he left behind as it lifts the veil on his slow death from consumption at the age of fifty-three. But the book also reveals, touchingly, a lifelong passion of its subject. The gentle, scholarly Gairdner was – aside from his devotion to the Master – inspired by the life and death of one man above all others: our eminent Victorian, Charles George Gordon. To this hero, rescuer of orphaned boys as well as soldier extraordinary, he would turn again and again for encouragement in moments of disappointment, despondency, doubt. If 'he' through prayer and dedication to his cause could keep on keeping on when life seemed black and every effort frustrated, then how could any be downcast, how could any complain, how could any with the same Christian profession think of quitting? Even so, our missionary never faltered; he kept the flame of witness burning, never succumbing to expediency.

This story of a missionary priest's life by Constance Padwick, 'half in love with him herself' (as someone who knew her told me later), did more than move me; it constituted a call. I became convinced I should, in some sense, take the same path.

Having found myself a new hero, I was anxious to discover more about my hero's hero. So I searched libraries and bookshops for works on Gordon – to discover he was one of that band of mavericks who perennially fascinate biographers. As with T. E. Lawrence, who for different reasons also interested me, the famous general was a book-a-year personality. In no time I had collected a shelf-full of titles: *England's Hero and Christian Soldier*, *Gordon: Mandarin and Pasha*, *Gordon at Khartoum*, Gordon this, Gordon that – my prize piece, a gift from my friend John, being a copy of the facsimile edition of his last journal from Khartoum. I was only surprised there hadn't been a film about him. (Hollywood soon put that right.) I finally moved to books on the aftermath of the Gordon story, *With Kitchener to Khartoum* for example, and read how at Omdurman in 1898, when the Royal Army made its last cavalry charge, the national hero was avenged – Winston Churchill, none other, witness to the deed.

Omdurman. How it rolls off the tongue! Simply pronouncing the word – as with some other place-names: Samarkand, Kathmandu, Rangoon – evokes adventure, romance, mystery. And it was specifically to Omdurman, the mission now announced, that we would be sent on completing our training.

The CMS college had in the summer of 1969 moved from Chislehurst to a site in Birmingham and while we were students the new complex was officially opened by Queen Elizabeth the Queen Mother. Our two-storey apartment – one of a number built for married couples – was chosen as the one to be visited by the royal guest.

'Welcome to our home, your Majesty,' I said as the Queen Mother, clad in pink coat and huge navy hat, and having negotiated various plants placed in the covered approach, reached our front door. 'It's small but very comfortable. Suits us perfectly.'

There was a flash of white frills and a flurry of little legs as three-year-old Annabel, who had been waiting with us, scampered off. She had heard that a Very Important Person would be visiting us and the moment itself was too much.

We moved into the sitting room and our august visitor looked towards the sofa, where a baby-chair with occupant had been placed.

'And whom have we here?' she inquired politely. 'A little *boy*?'

'Yes, Ma'am,' responded Joanna. 'Edmund is ... about five months now. Yet to reach the troublesome stage!' Her majesty nodded in agreement and went over and tickled baby's tummy – thus conferring, we fondly hoped, a royal blessing.

Joanna had plenty to do at the college looking after the children, though she was able to attend important college sessions, while I divided my time between such sessions and the study of Arabic.

Sometimes we wondered whether our training for life overseas was fully appropriate. For example, no guidance was given on the way to deal with servants – essential in countries like Sudan, swept by sandstorms and plagued by power cuts. This instructional oversight stemmed, we began to feel, from the fact that at the end of the swinging sixties the whole idea of authority (master over servant, teacher over student, parent over child) was becoming suspect. In many circles, not least that of our fellow trainees, it seemed to be assumed that egalitarianism had won the day and we should be matey with everyone. Paid servants, if you had to have them at all, should be treated as personal friends. When we finally arrived 'on station' and had a servant to clean the house on a daily basis, we found the relationship to be more complex, mutual respect rather than matiness proving best for both parties.

The servant question was not in itself of great significance, but I was becoming worried about the Society at a deeper level: its growing preoccupation with political issues. As implied above, the sixties were par excellence an era of social awareness, resulting in the desire for change. The Paris student riots of 1968 epitomise well the spirit of the times, as do the constant marches over the decade in support of such causes as nuclear disarmament, championed frequently by prominent churchmen.

The CMS, founded in 1799 to evangelise those in foreign lands with no knowledge of Christ, had begun subtly to change its stance. Instead of describing its mission as evangelism it was now saying that its task was mission. The words 'task' and 'mission' are of course virtual synonyms, indicating but not defining work undertaken or responsibilities assumed by a person or group. To talk of a task being mission is therefore a tautology. Such a formula, however, suited the Society because the time-honoured word 'evangelism' was at best too narrow and at worst an embarrassment. While not actually abandoning the idea behind the word – proclaiming the good news of Christ in the hope of bringing people to faith in him – the Society was anxious to broaden its brief to encompass social and political activism.

The issue of the day was racism and the CMS, like many another Christian body, spent much time, effort and money in denouncing the evils of this attitude. The South African regime and its policy of apartheid was an obvious target; the British government was another because of what was perceived as racist legislation on immigration. For me, the question was not about whether such governmental policies were right or wrong; clearly they were often ill-conceived. The question was whether the Church – whether any specifically Christian body – should be in the game of politics at all, whether moral denunciation of governments, or indeed anyone other than church members, was appropriate. Moralising is the norm in politics; I had always understood it to be the Church's role precisely *not* to moralise or condemn beyond its own borders but rather to help the sinner of any and every description to know God's love in Jesus and find the forgiveness he offers. I felt strongly enough about this at the time to write an article expounding my views for a Society publication.

The politicisation of the Church of England generally, and the CMS in particular, was thrown into relief by an incident that occurred towards the end of our missionary training. We were invited to a meeting at the Society's London headquarters to learn more about Sudan – which of course seemed an excellent idea. There was a speaker who spent most of the time talking about politics, which was fair enough as a background for prospective residents in the country. But it quickly became apparent that what we were listening to was a thinly-veiled attack on the essentially Muslim government in Khartoum for its oppressive treatment of the southern and strongly Christian region of the country. As soon as the speaker had finished, copies of a magazine were handed round. Called *Grass Curtain*, this turned out to be propaganda for the southern separatist movement which had mounted and was still pursuing an armed struggle against Khartoum. A member of CMS home staff at this point turned to us with a suggestion.

'You two can be a help to us in all this, you know, as channels of information. You can pass on what you glean about the situation.'

I was appalled, and before the meeting ended summoned up enough courage to stand up and express my feelings.

'Joanna and I are not going as missionaries to Sudan in order to be politically involved,' I announced. 'And to be honest, I feel compromised to be attending a meeting in Society premises that appears to encourage such a stance.' I sat down.

No one responded to my protest, either visibly or audibly. Afterwards, however, in the street outside, one of the senior ex-Sudan missionaries who had attended gave us a vague hand signal. For some reason I have always remembered this – maybe reflecting my disappointment at the fact that he didn't speak to us. Ever since, I have wondered what precisely was in his mind.

Throughout our year of training in Birmingham I was doing my best to study Arabic, using an old-style grammar book. Beyond this, I and a few others were once a week taken through verses of the Qur'ān in Arabic by our lecturer on Islam. I soon realised what a massive challenge the language represented and managed to persuade my seniors to send me on a summer language course in Tunisia before we set out for Sudan. I badly needed to supplement my sporadic study of Arabic in Birmingham and to kick-start its oral use. I felt sick at heart to be leaving Joanna at this juncture; her mother was finding the prospect of our leaving hard to take and the situation had become quite tense.

The course itself, at the Bourguiba Language Institute in Tunis, was officially conducted in Arabic but was in practice taught through the medium of French. I had done my best to brush up my school French, lingering in France for a week before taking the boat from Marseilles, so I was not completely floundering on arrival. However, I soon found the mountain of Arabic words flung at us daily by the professor impossible to assimilate so began absenting myself from class. I was inevitably – shades of my experience in Palestine – befriended by youths, one in particular, and with them took my first faltering steps in conversation. Yet I actually learnt more French than Arabic and when at the end of six weeks I returned to UK my French was fairly fluent; for the first time in my life I was able to speak a foreign language. (I had passed my French oral for the school certificate exam on the strength – as far as I could see – of repeating a list of vegetables.) My unexpected mastery of the language of diplomats and lovers was not directly relevant to my role in Sudan but it certainly boosted my confidence.

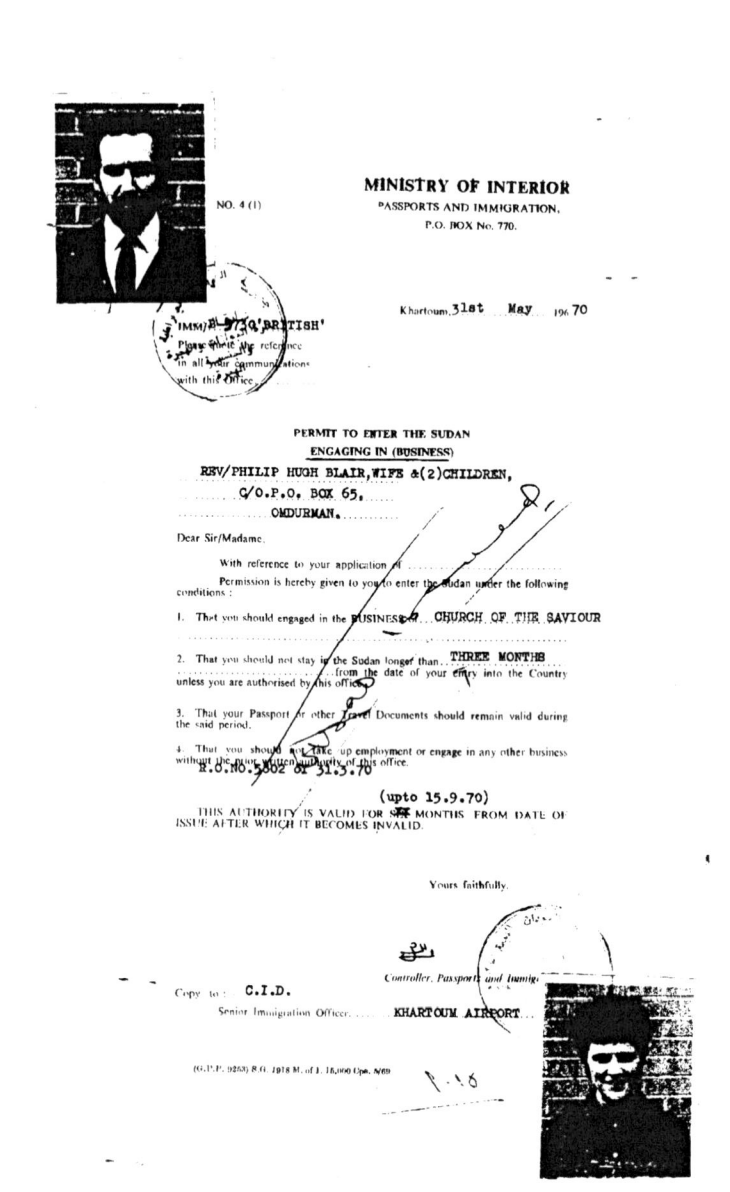

MINISTRY OF INTERIOR
PASSPORTS AND IMMIGRATION,
P.O. BOX No. 770.

NO. 4 (I)

Khartoum, 31st May 19 70

'IMS(I)/M-973/Q'BRITISH'
Please quote the reference
in all your communications
with this office.

PERMIT TO ENTER THE SUDAN
ENGAGING IN (BUSINESS)

REV/PHILIP HUGH BLAIR, WIFE & (2) CHILDREN,
C/O.P.O. BOX 65,
OMDURMAN.

Dear Sir/Madame,

With reference to your application of

Permission is hereby given to you to enter the Sudan under the following conditions :

1. That you should engaged in the BUSINESS OF CHURCH OF THE SAVIOUR

2. That you should not stay in the Sudan longer than THREE MONTHS from the date of your entry into the Country unless you are authorised by this office.

3. That your Passport or other Travel Documents should remain valid during the said period.

4. That you should not take up employment or engage in any other business without the prior written authority of this office.

R.O.NO.562 of 31.5.70

(upto 15.9.70)
THIS AUTHORITY IS VALID FOR SIX MONTHS FROM DATE OF ISSUE AFTER WHICH IT BECOMES INVALID.

Yours faithfully,

Controller, Passports and Immigr

Copy to : C.I.D.
Senior Immigration Officer, KHARTOUM AIRPORT

(G.P.P. 9263) 8.G. 1918 M. of I. 15,000 Ups. 8/69

Visa to Sudan, with passport photos

III

Omdurman

On 29 August 1970 we flew Swissair to Sudan, on a Caravelle to Geneva and a DC8 to Khartoum. As a journey it was less than ideal. It was Joanna's first experience of air travel, she was understandably nervous and she had to cope with a nine-month old baby and a three-year-old – not to speak of a husband. With the transfer to another flight in Geneva (we almost missed it), a stop in Athens and another in Cairo, it took us over ten hours. Had we flown direct on a BOAC VC10 we would have been in the air just six hours. The date of our departure was for some reason written in stone, however, and there was no VC10 flight on that day. Anyway, we finally touched down and after around two hours in the hot, cramped customs hall retrieved our baggage. Waiting for us outside was the Mission Representative, Rachel Hassan, who drove us through the darkness to Omdurman. A seasoned missionary, she was putting us up for several nights before we moved into a bungalow some way down the road.

'But you won't be in the bungalow very long,' she told us. 'You'll be coming back here to live.'

'Here? In your house?' I reacted in surprise.

'Yes, right here, in this very Sudanese style of dwelling. But it won't be my house then because, you see, in a few months' time I'm due to retire. This place, which the mission has owned for years, will then be vacant. I'm sure it'll make an excellent family home.'

The mission property was an older, single-storey villa overlooking the Nile. Known as 'The River House', it dated from Turkish times and was rather attractive. It lay within a compound or *hawsh* which

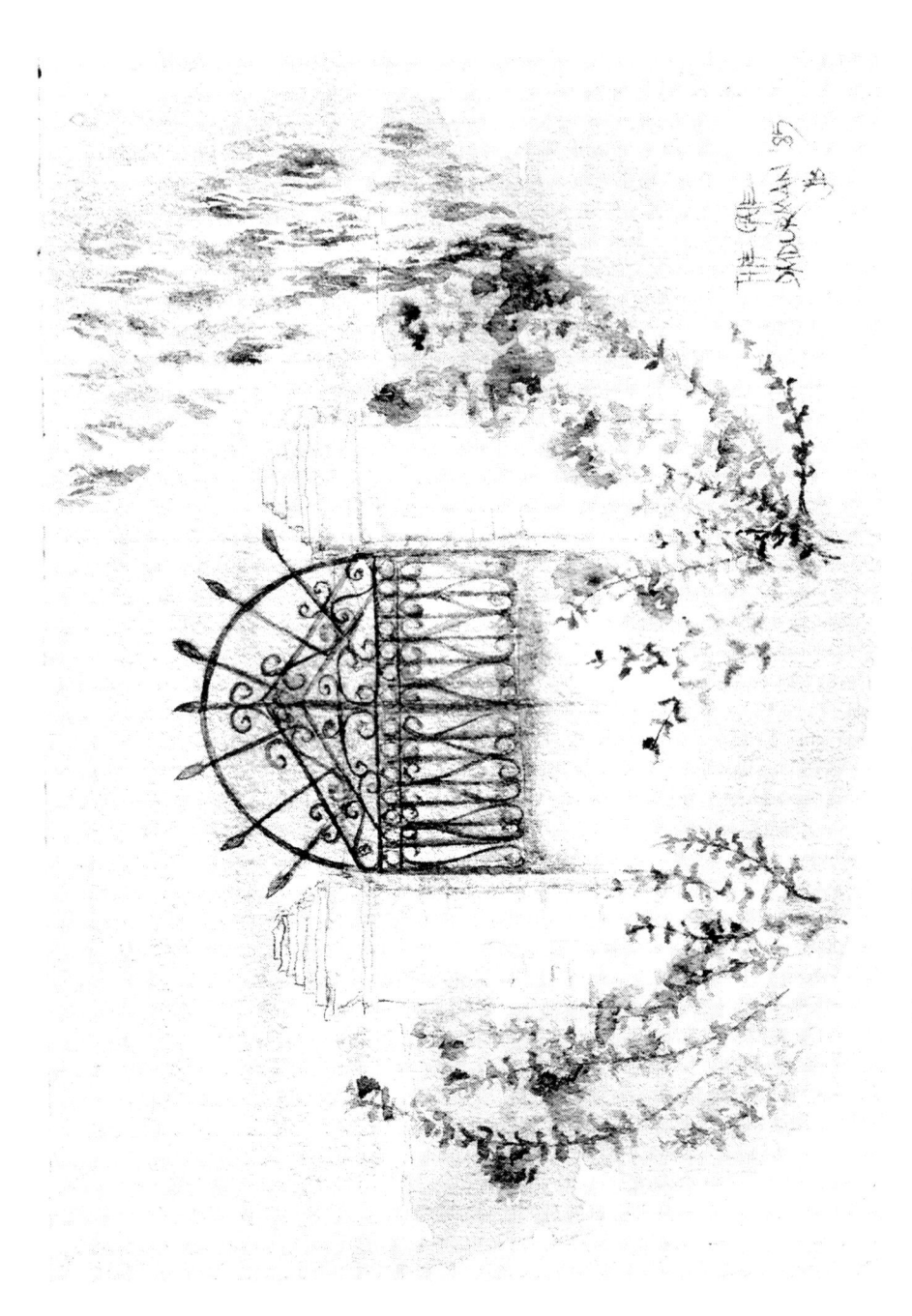

The River House gate, featuring 'spears'

had several outbuildings, including a mud dwelling in a corner of the compound housing a family from the Nuba Mountains. The house itself was built of brick and painted white, having a flat roof of traditional design – mud laid on palm fronds in turn laid over wooden joists (stripped tree trunks or their limbs). The latter had a propensity to leak during summer rains. There was a large high sitting room with similar-sized bedrooms leading off each side, and a third bedroom making the house L-shaped. Double doors led from the sitting room onto a wide veranda at the front. The kitchen and bathroom were separate rooms situated outside the back door.

'As for the toilet', Rachel told us, 'I'm afraid that's further off, in a corner of the compound. It's simply a bucket under the seat, emptied daily by municipality officials who take it away through a trapdoor onto the street.' She gave a crooked smile. 'You may be taken by surprise from time to time when you're enthroned. But don't worry, it's all part of the system!'

The house was set on a slight incline and overlooked its own garden – a lawn flanked by crimson bougainvilleas – and beyond the compound wall (where an iron gate featured what some said were spears from the Battle of Omdurman) lay an open area where boys kicked footballs and where, sometimes, flags were planted to denote a holy spot. Beyond this was the old road from Khartoum, lined with tall neem trees. Beneath and through the trees gleamed the Nile.

We discovered the house had had an interesting history. It had at one time been the property of Deim al-Zubeir Pasha, a slave-trader in southern Sudan whose son Suleimen was executed during Gordon's first period as governor-general. The Pasha had a significant role in the later Gordon story. Gordon's brief for his second assignment in Sudan was to take over once again as governor-general in Khartoum, arrange the evacuation of the Egyptian garrison and some foreign civilians, establish and hand over to a competent authority representing the Khedive in Egypt, and then himself withdraw. What was to be done if the third of these tasks proved impossible was left unclear. In the event, Gordon met Zubeir Pasha in Cairo on his way out to Khartoum and decided that he – and he alone – had sufficient standing among the Sudanese populace to become his successor. He advised Prime Minister Gladstone accordingly. Not surprisingly, Gladstone refused to accept the appointment of someone mixed up with slavery. Not surprisingly, Gordon – finding no viable alternative – refused to withdraw.

Our first night at the River House was memorable. We were in *Africa*: it sent shivers down the spine. The Nile was in flood and probably on that very first occasion the frogs on its banks were into their rhythmic croaking.

'I wish they wouldn't keep playing that music in the eating house down by the river,' Joanna said one evening after we'd moved into the River House permanently. 'It gets so boring!'

'Music?' I responded in astonishment. 'No, Joanna, those are frogs, not Sudanese folk musicians!'

It was of course pretty hot that first night so we slept – as so often later – in the open. We were on the veranda under mosquito nets draped over bamboo uprights tied to local-style wooden bedsteads: Joanna and I together, Annabel in a single bed and Edmund in a cot. Rachel's bed was further off in the garden.

'I always sleep on the lawn,' she explained. 'It's a lot cooler down there. But you'll no doubt feel happier more or less in the house.'

'Absolutely,' I agreed. 'We've much to get used to before we start being adventurous.'

The mosquito nets under which we lay did not provide total protection against bites (which could be malarial) but we had begun taking prophylactics a week or two before flying. We had, as advised by the mission, purchased mosquito nets for ourselves in London; these and other 'essentials' were yet to arrive.

Alisons Tropical Outfitters, where we had bought the nets, was an education. More of a warehouse than a shop, it was rather dark, multi-storeyed, labyrinthine and prehistoric. Shelves were cluttered with tarpaulins, tents, nets, topes, jackets, shorts, leggings, socks, boots, boxes, trunks, hampers, cutlery, crockery, tins, kettles, pocket-knives – in fact everything Boy's Own Annual would tell you was required for the Dark Continent. I remember thinking it must have been just the same when my father sailed for Africa in 1928.

Omdurman, with site of a 'holy dream' in the foreground

Indeed, I was half expecting Dr Livingstone, or perhaps Stanley, to step out from the shadows.

Two of the essentials we had been urged to buy and bring out in huge quantities were toilet-paper and toothpaste (we were warned that Sudan suffered acute shortages of these); we naturally obeyed, though of course it wasn't necessary to purchase them from Alisons. Blankets, sheets, kitchen-ware, clothes, books, toys were some of the things that joined the nets, loo-paper and toothpaste, all of which were packed in barrels, originally used for crude oil. We also decided to bring out a 'dulcitone' given us by elderly relatives; a keyboard instrument playing on tuning forks, the dulcitone is ideal for the tropics as it never goes out of tune. It wouldn't fit into a barrel, however, so we made a special box for it. We then dispatched the whole lot 'deep-sea baggage' – five barrels and the box. These would be off-loaded in Port Sudan and brought by lorry across the desert to Omdurman. The whole process, we were advised, would take up to six months.

We were, as I say, in Africa. Yet also in the Arab world – even in the Middle East according to Hilton International, who some years later built a luxury hotel at the confluence of the Niles and considered it part of their Middle East chain. But to us this was Africa, as quickly became apparent. Joanna still talks of the shock she experienced next morning on finding herself entirely surrounded by brown faces. But she adapted speedily enough – as witnessed by the fact that she also talks of the reverse culture-shock she experienced on seeing only 'white' faces confronting her in the classroom back in England some years later.

We were soon exploring Omdurman – colourful, noisy, dusty. We passed through ancient mud gates, saw the Mahdi's tomb and the Khalifa's house (mud-built yet uniquely two-storeyed, befitting the rank of its original occupant), and then saw our bungalow-to-be in a compound that included the Protestant church, as well as the home of Bishop Butrus, Sudanese Assistant to the Anglican Bishop of Sudan, an Englishman.

'Omdurman is the friendliest town in the world', Bishop Butrus told us at our first meeting. 'You can go anywhere, day or night, in perfect safety.' And so we found – the two exceptions being the occasion when I was punched in the face by a mentally-disturbed man and another when, in the crowded *souq*, a pickpocket tried unsuccessfully to lift money from my shirt pocket.

Exploring further, we crossed the river to the south (the White Nile) and were in Khartoum. Next, we crossed it to the north (the White and Blue Niles combined, after 'the longest kiss in history') and were in Khartoum North. These, 'The Three Towns', comprise today's capital.

Khartoum proper is sandwiched between the two Niles, the spit of land between the converging rivers assuming the shape of an elephant's trunk – *al-khartūm* in Arabic. It used to be said of the town that the British, following the victory at Omdurman, had laid out the central area on the pattern of a Union Jack. This was because one grid of parallel roads intersecting at right angles is diagonally superimposed on another such grid; an intersection can thus have eight roads leading into it. If you look at a map, there is a vague resemblance to the British flag but the idea that this was intentional is almost certainly mistaken; more reasonable is the suggestion that the multi-road intersections were so designed because they made for efficient crowd or riot control. More likely still is that the layout was adopted simply because of its general convenience.

The town boasted a number of fine old buildings, notably the elegant white Presidential Palace – formerly the Governor's Palace, though not the one where Gordon met his end – situated alongside the river at the end of an avenue of spreading banyan trees. The Grand Hotel lay down that avenue to the west, famous for its iced lime drunks, to be savoured on the spacious veranda while relaxing in 'Somerset Maugham chairs'. To the east of the Palace and beside the river lay the Sudan Club (the British Club) and then the leafy campus of Khartoum University, with its faintly Gothic architecture, formerly Gordon College for Boys. Finally, a little beyond the university and also by the river was an open-air cinema which Joanna and I occasionally visited, to see pot-boiler films with passé British or French actors – never released at home, we reckoned.

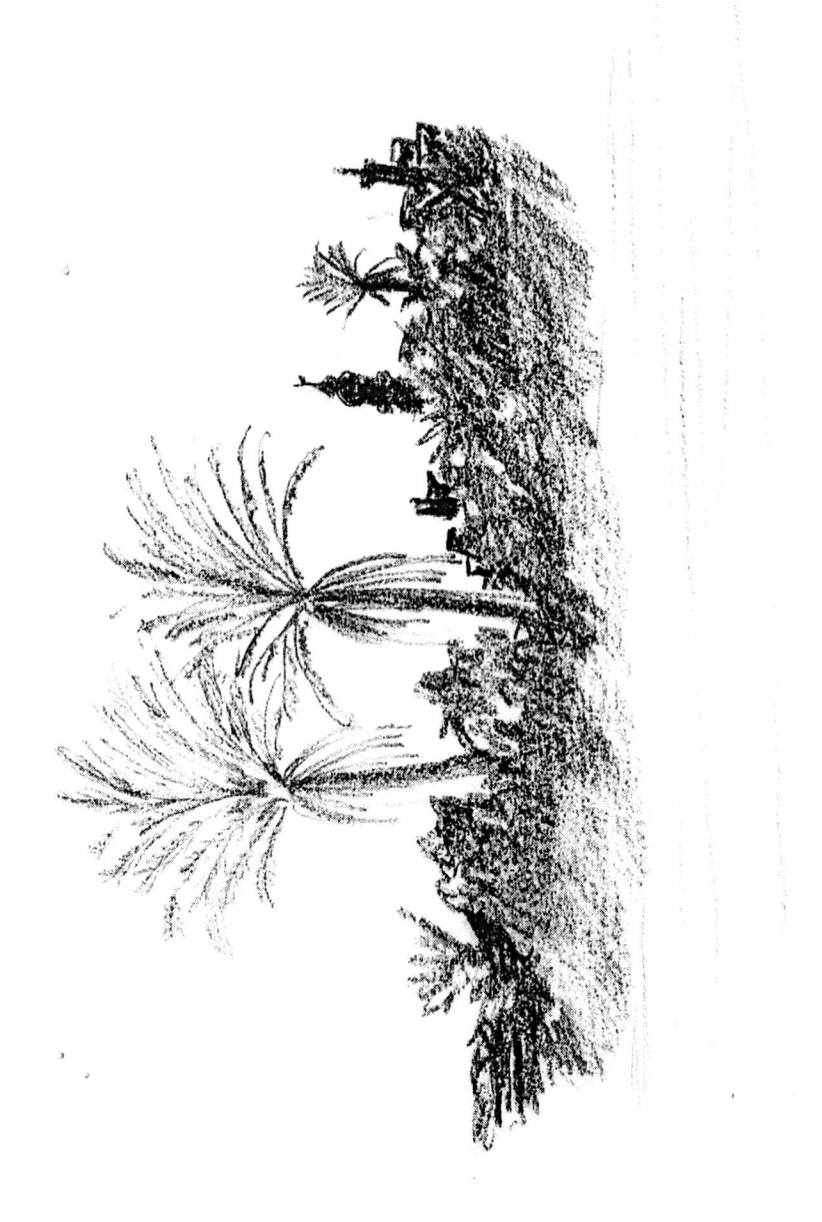

Khartoum North in silhouette, from across the Nile

Away from the river there was an impressive central mosque – together with its quota of beggars, some of them leprosy sufferers. Handsome pitch-roofed and balconied government buildings flanked some streets while others featured modern blocks, quite a few still under construction, incorporating covered pedestrian ways. Yellow taxis, mostly ancient and battered Hillmans or their Russian counterparts, grunted and hiccupped painfully along, their drivers conserving 'benzine' by refusing to move out of top gear. Flowing *toubs* – rather like Indian *saris* – of the Sudanese women and spotless white *jallabiyas* and *'immas* (turbans) of the men gave splashes of colour and style to the streets, but on looking away from bustling humanity the overwhelming impression was one of shabbiness.

'Do you know something?' I said to Joanna one day as we were out shopping. 'It seems to me that wherever you look in Khartoum the buildings are either going up or falling down.'

She laughed. 'You mean the word "maintenance" is not in the Sudanese vocabulary.'

Khartoum North, across the Blue Nile, was for the most part an undistinguished urban sprawl. It included the main Kober prison, however, and not far from this was a lyrically green cricket ground, religiously watered and manicured – 'a little touch of England' as an enthusiast once described it to me. Alongside the river, too, were some fine villas with well-stocked and beautifully-tended gardens. Omdurman, to the west of the Nile, was African in character. It had mostly one- or two-storeyed buildings, the older mud houses overlaid with donkey-dung to create a waterproof surface. The season of overlaying, just before the summer rains, forced its attention upon you for obvious reasons.

In around 1900, Temple Gairdner spoke of Khartoum as a mystical world crossroads. He saw it as the focus of four rays: Arab and Muslim to the north; African and animist to the south; Arab or Berber and mostly Muslim to the west; Afro-Arab and Christian (Ethiopia) to the east. Gairdner's construction was somewhat fanciful but the Sudanese capital was certainly a rich mix of races and religions when we arrived in 1970. The indigenous population was – you might say – Afro-Arab and Muslim, together with a few of Egyptian origin, some of them Copts (Pharonic rather than Arab). More recently, pure Africans had come up in considerable numbers from the south, many of them Christian, while others had come from the Nuba Mountains in the south-west. A large expatriate population – diplomats, aid workers, teachers, business people, construction workers – included a variety of Europeans, both Western and Eastern, with others from Russia, Lebanon, Egypt, India, China, Japan, Korea. There were, finally, many refugees from countries like the Congolese Republic, Chad and Ethiopia.

After the few days with Rachel, we settled into our spacious and (apart from its long-drop, cockroach-infested garden loo) quite well-equipped bungalow. Joanna was tied to the house much of the time with the children – though Annabel soon began attending an infant school – while my own main occupation was the continued study of Arabic.

'I hope you can soon begin your Arabic Bible classes for evangelists,' Bishop Butrus said to me not long after we had arrived. 'They're eager to get started.'

I thought before answering, realising how important it was to sound encouraging while at the same time making it clear that my Arabic, more or less self-taught, was not good enough for lectures and group discussions.

'I need a little more time before I start teaching, Bishop,' I said finally. 'But I don't mind preaching in Arabic. I can take time to prepare and carefully practise my delivery.'

The Bishop needed little persuading about the classes and was pleased that I'd offered to preach. In due course, therefore, I was delivering my first Arabic sermon in Omdurman church. As it turned out, developments within the Church of Sudan resulted in this being both my first *and last* Arabic sermon in the country. For the time being, anyway, I was able to press on with language study, my official pastoral duties being minimal.

We attended services in the church of the Saviour, Omdurman, used by members of the Evangelical as well as Anglican Church, and began to enjoy the rhythmic singing of Sudanese Christians. Most worshippers were from the Nuba Mountains, in Kordofan

Province, as was the Bishop; they had all learnt Arabic, the medium of most hymns and songs, but a few of these were in a tribal vernacular. Often late in the day we would hear them from our bungalow as they practised for Sunday worship.

'I love to hear those African voices singing over in church,' Joanna said to me one evening.

'So do I,' I agreed. 'They sound so happy, and the songs go with such a swing.'

Joanna smiled. 'Ah yes, it don't mean a thing if it ain't got that swing!'

We also attended evening get-togethers of the missionaries to study the Bible, these being held at one or other of our homes, often in the garden to keep cool. There were about twelve of us: ourselves, the Representative, the Bishop, nursing staff and administrators at the hospital, staff at the school for girls, and a young teacher of theology we shall be hearing more about, Philip Gordon. We were happy to attend these gatherings but an atmosphere of slight nervousness seemed to pervade them, as if we were engaged in something unlawful. We were of course living and working in a largely Muslim land and though Islam officially suffers Christians to exist it does not always seem to do so gladly. You have the feeling – especially if your official designation is that of missionary – that Muslim religious leaders are uneasy, suspecting you of the 'sin' of evangelism. Yet it was less a threat from Islam in itself or from individual Muslims that appeared to be worrying our fellow-missionaries; they seemed to fear the government.

'What was that?' a fellow-missionary would suddenly exclaim if we were sitting outside. 'I heard something – or somebody – close by.' We would keep silent, and perhaps the sound would come again.

'The secret police!' someone else would whisper hoarsely.

***

The unease exhibited by some of our colleagues raises the question of how Joanna and I, having arrived in Sudan, felt about our role as 'missionaries'. Or to put it differently, what did we feel our mission was? We were working under the aegis of a legally recognised Christian organization, the Anglican Church in Sudan, and were answerable to its leaders. But we had been sent out to that Church and were supported financially by a missionary society. Did we consider ourselves evangelists? And if so, did this include the evangelising of Muslims?

The word 'evangelism' means something like 'announcing good news', and normal Christians find themselves doing this spontaneously. They have discovered a wonderful way of life – this, at least, is their conviction – and it would be boorish to withhold it from others. Evangelism is thus not something Christians engage in out of a sense of duty, in obedience to some religious injunction. They can't help themselves. Isn't it the same with everyone? What enthusiast for exercise, what keen musician, what lover of art does not almost automatically extol to others the benefits and pleasures of his or her chosen pastime?

It is absurd that 'evangelism' should become, as it has in some circles, a dirty word. Atheists are today's busiest evangelists – patently so, with Richard Dawkins announcing that his best-selling book *The God Delusion* is specifically designed to convert, not just inform. Islam is nothing if not evangelistic, openly seeking, by one means or another, to convert the world to its understanding of God. Yet both atheists and Muslims become worried if not incensed when Christians seek to evangelise, announcing and explaining the 'good news' of who Jesus was and what he accomplished – with, of course, the hope that their hearers will be persuaded and converted. Islam, in fact, virtually criminalises attempts to convert followers of Muhammad, countries in which Islam is predominant usually making the practice illegal.

Which raises a crucial point about the religion of Islam, the fact that unlike Christianity it is inherently political as well as spiritual. In a word, it is theocratic, as can be seen clearly from the manner in which it was established.

During the first period of Muhammad's preaching and gathering of converts, between 610 and 622 AD, when his base for operations was Mecca and he was encountering considerable opposition, he seemed largely unconcerned about developing a political role for himself or his movement. But after the Hijrah (or Emigration) to Medina over the summer of 622, both his situation and aspirations changed. An extant document usually known as the Constitution of Medina shows how he established (or helped to establish) a recognizable 'community'. This community comprised nine clans or groups of people: the Emigrants of Quraysh, who were Muhammad's Meccan followers, eight Arab clans or groups of clans, representing the Medinan population, and a number of Jewish groups attached to various of the Arab clans. The new community, or *ummah* ('nation' or 'people'), constituted a political unit of a new type, a federation of clans or tribes, bound together by solemn agreement. The Constitution suggests that Muhammad was the leading light in the design of this community and that it was his position as 'prophet' that led men to accept his proposals; the federation thus had a religious basis. While he was not at this stage considered overall political ruler, he was ruler or chief of his clan of Emigrants, so was on a par with the chiefs of other clans. The Constitution does, however, assign him one overarching political role, that of arbitrating between rival factions.

It was not long before a political role was Muhammad's in a more substantial form: a stunning military success against a Meccan caravan at Badr in 624, followed by his successful military leadership repulsing the Meccans at the siege of Medina in 627, consolidated his position as supreme political as well as religious leader of the *ummah*. From this moment, tribes around Medina began to throw in their lot with him and others were brought into line by expeditions mounted against them. As for the Jews, some of whom had supported the Meccans during the siege of Medina and were still intriguing against him, these he expelled or otherwise kept in check. The Jewish threat was completely eliminated in 628 when the Jewish oasis of Khaybar surrendered to a Muslim expeditionary force, its people agreeing to become tributaries.

In 630 Muhammad led his followers into Mecca with little opposition and shortly afterwards a final enemy confederacy was defeated at al-Hunayn. There was now a mass movement of Arabs to Islam, Muhammad's wealth dramatically increased, and his army numbered 30,000. Islam was now manifestly a nation, not just a religion; it was a community in which spiritual and political concerns were welded together under the rule of God, represented by an acknowledged prophet. What had been established for the tribes of Israel under Moses in the Sinai peninsula had now been established by Muhammad for the tribes of Ishmael in the Arabian peninsula.

What is the Christian to make of this? Indeed, what to make of the later phenomenon of the expansion of Islam at a quite extraordinary rate? Must some validity be allowed to Muhammad's claim to be the messenger of God, his prophet? Is the Christian, commissioned to 'make disciples of all nations, baptizing them in the name of the Father and of the Son and of the Holy Spirit', released from this charge when it comes to the 'nation of Islam'?

In Christian understanding, the covenant or contract made between God and Israel was superseded by the covenant – this time personal and spiritual, not national and theocratic – made between God and man through the life, death and resurrection of Jesus of Nazareth. This new covenant, it goes without saying, cannot be superseded. To Christians, Jesus was the fulfilment of all that Moses and the later prophets of Israel stood for and taught. He was, if you like, the 'seal of the prophets' (a title Muslims reserve for Muhammad), and there is no room for a further prophet with a message fulfilling, amplifying or replacing his. Muslims may argue that the New Testament does not represent the original gospel or *injīl* of Jesus, which they say harmonises perfectly with the message of Muhammad, but they produce no clear evidence to back this claim so Christians unsurprisingly dismiss it.

The Christian in the Muslim world is thus in the delicate position of wanting to show a proper respect for his or her Muslim friends' faith in God without admitting to a genuine prophetic role for the founder of Islam. If Muslims find such a viewpoint offensive, it is not more offensive than their viewpoint is to Christians, namely, that Jesus of Nazareth did not truly die, did not rise again, and was not – is not – divine. Muslims and Christians need openly to debate these questions and if they cannot agree, they must agree to differ.

Neither side should object to the other seeking to convince and convert. What is the point of debate if it isn't conducted in earnest, each side defending and seeking to establish its position – yet ready to modify or even abandon it should the opposing argument be deemed convincing? There is no place for anger at being challenged or worsted, let alone the resort to threats and violence.

***

The staff of Khartoum Anglican cathedral included a Provost, a clergyman who among other things served as chaplain to expatriate members of the congregation. Not long after our first Christmas in Sudan the existing incumbent, an Englishman, relinquished his post and returned to UK with his family.

'We have an ideal replacement,' the Bishop of Sudan announced to church members. 'A priest who was for many years a missionary in the south and is currently a member of the Church Missionary Society staff in London. He will take over as soon as his visa comes through.'

On hearing his name, I recognised him as the ex-missionary who, after the politicised meeting we had attended at the mission headquarters, had given us that 'vague hand signal'.

The weeks passed and the new Provost did not arrive. 'Not a problem, I'm sure,' the Bishop assured us. 'These things take time.'

A little later, however, he was approaching me personally. 'If you don't mind, Philip, I would like you assist me with the pastoral oversight of the expatriate congregation until the new provost arrives.'

I naturally accepted this new responsibility but realised it would cut into the time available for language study – progressing quite well as I was attending Arabic lessons at the girls' school in Omdurman. (When this arrangement began, my presence hugely amused the girls.)

Time passed and still the new Provost did not arrive. Eventually we found out why: the Sudanese government had decided against issuing a visa to this ex-missionary because of his links with the south. I found the news suggestive: it sounded as if the authorities

Philip with the Bishop of Sudan and Khartoum clergy

were worried about the man's *political* sympathies and affiliations. Some years earlier, missionaries of every complexion had been expelled from the south for a substantial period because one or two (Roman Catholics, I was told) had been discovered aiding and abetting the southern rebels. This alone could have been enough to prompt the government's decision not to issue a visa. Yet I couldn't help wondering: might word have got around about the politicised meeting Joanna and I – *plus the candidate for Provost* – had attended? Was the government concerned that the Missionary Society might be promoting the southern separatist movement? If so, I could not condemn the Sudanese stance; any condemnation was more appropriate for the Society whose agent I was.

Meanwhile, I was left with the responsibility of assisting the bishop with the pastoral oversight of the expatriate community.

By this time Rachel Hassan had left and we had moved into the River House. Our belongings were transported there by donkey-cart – more than we started out with, such as the school desk for Annabel and baby-chair for Edmund made from bits of wood I found lying around in our compound. Also a small dog called Christmas, who had turned up, a tiny puppy, under our gate on Christmas Day, and two kids – that is, young goats – a birthday gift to Annabel from a Sudanese friend called Mahjoub. (The goats had been living behind the bungalow where they would nibble at clothes hanging on the washing line – to Joanna's intense frustration.) Christmas and the goats, 'Blackie' and 'Brownie', joined a very large cat.

'You won't mind looking after Ginger when I'm gone, will you?' Rachel had asked us before leaving. 'He won't be much trouble.'

We had no reason to object so of course took him on. But we discovered he had a tiresome habit: if he wasn't fed on time – and occasionally when he was – he would issue a reminder by sidling up to Joanna and biting her leg. This was not ideal in a rabies-infested country. Anyway, Ginger was now ours so he, Christmas (who could also be tiresome, being prone to incessant barking), plus the goats were the founding members of a mini-menagerie we gradually collected at our riverside home.

The year 1971 wore on and Joanna and I, having just about settled ourselves and our children into the not-so-user-friendly

Sudanese environment, began to wear out. In other words, we needed a holiday.

It was the policy of the mission to give home leave of several months every second year to its members serving overseas. Between these periods, intended for parish deputation work as well as rest and refreshment, a shorter period of local leave could be taken. 'Local' did not necessarily denote your country of residence; it was recognized that tropical regions like Sudan, with few facilities and liable to shortages of essentials, were not the best places in which to recharge the batteries. In accordance with this policy, we arranged a holiday in Ethiopia, where there was a well-established 'missionary rest centre'. An advantage of this location was the fact that the Anglican chaplain in Addis Ababa and his wife were old friends, and they invited us to spend our first week with them.

The week we spent at the chaplaincy with Philip and Janet Cousins was a treat. Hot, dry, flat Sudan was, after a short and exhilarating air flight, supplanted by cool, lush, mountainous Ethiopia. We were given the warmest welcome by our friends and their children and despite Philip's busy life-style were ferried around the capital, shown around institutes and schools, taken to a concert at the palace (replete with armed guards) and, as a highlight, taken on a drive further up the mountains.

'I'm due to visit a couple of my more far-flung church members,' Philip told us. 'Brigadier Sandford and his wife are pretty elderly so I regularly take a service for them in their home. You must come with me. You'll see some fine terrain and at the same time meet a most interesting character.'

I was all ears. 'Sandford, did you say? And a brigadier? He's obviously English.'

'As English as you can get,' Philip confirmed. 'Very much of the old school.'

'Tell us more,' I said. 'There's obviously a story here.'

'There is,' our friend assured us. 'I'll give it to you now, in outline. After serving in the Royal Army during the First World War, Daniel Arthur Sandford – that's his full name – moved to this country where he became advisor to Emperor Haile Selassie. Rejoining the army as colonel in 1940, he first organised and then led a force of Ethiopian partisans known as the "Patriots", which in 1941 combined with the British "Gideon Force", led by Colonel Orde Wingate, to liberate Ethiopia from the Italians. Later on he again became advisor to Selassie, on military and political issues.'

'My goodness,' Joanna remarked. 'The man is walking history. It'll be fascinating to meet him, and his wife.'

The route up the mountains took us through spectacular country – grassy slopes, cascading waterfalls, limpid pools, deep dark gorges, misty blue escarpments – until high up on a plateau we came to the old soldier's retirement home. He was in his late eighties though clearly very much alive. His home was a large, timber-built bungalow – ranch-like in appearance and location. From the front veranda there was a superb view, the land falling away to a deep, hidden valley, layers of receding mountains providing the backdrop.

Our friend held a service of Holy Communion for the household and then we sat talking on the veranda with the brigadier, his wife Chris and an elderly sister. We discovered, among other things, that quite apart from the service that we had just attended the day was particularly special. It was the anniversary of Haile Selassie's triumphant return to Addis Ababa in the company of Sandford, Wingate and their victorious troops.

We left Addis and our friends at the end of that week on a high; when we left the missionary rest centre some five weeks later we were on a distinct low. We had to journey *down* to the centre, known as Bishoftu (near Debra Zeit), situated on the edge of a lake, filling a round depression that looked volcanic in origin; but our 'low' had nothing to do with this location.

For the first half of our stay, for which we were assigned one of the chalets set on the steeply-inclining shore of the lake, all was fine – apart from mild culture-shock at the strong North American flavour of the centre, not least its communal food – bits of fish in your teatime cake, for instance. We soon got over this but in around the third week Edmund, now aged a year and a half, developed a persistent temperature and, in due course, a nagging cough. Then Joanna went down with something – a vague queasiness, headache and general lassitude – though brushing it aside as the result of worry over her son. We sought advice from someone with medical experience but no diagnosis was made beyond the possibility of a gastric disorder. As our holiday drew to a close others at the rest centre displayed similar symptoms but still no light was shed on the cause.

We made it home on our booked flight – Joanna hardly knowing how she'd get onto the plane. She began to wonder if she was having a nervous breakdown.

It was a relief to be back in Omdurman and the River House, where we hoped immediately to find the medical help needed. Edmund's condition was by now alarming – the stubbornly high temperature, the coughing, and the tearfulness denoting pain – on top of which Annabel started to be feverish. Yet expert advice was not so easy to obtain: most members of the mission were on holiday, as also were members of the Swiss mission, including the doctor who ran their clinic in Omdurman. On making inquiries, I found that the resident doctor in Khartoum Clinic, where expatriates usually went for treatment, was also away. The attention of both of us was now entirely focused on Edmund, whose condition seemed critical.

Next day, I gathered the lad into my arms, put him in the back of the car and drove to a quarter of Omdurman where I knew there were doctors. I tried several, yet walked away from their surgeries none the wiser. This was getting me nowhere, I thought. Back went Edmund into the car and I drove over the bridge to Khartoum and straight to the British Embassy offices in the centre. I parked the car, picked the child up and leapt up three flights of stairs to a landing at the top. Pushing open the glass door, I spoke to the first person I saw.

'My son is extremely ill and we don't know what's wrong with him. We can't find a doctor to diagnose his condition and we need your advice. Please tell me where I should go, where I can find someone who will help.'

I remember the silence – stunned, you might say – together with visible discomfiture on the part of the official at being near someone who might be infectious. He or she, I'm not sure which, blinked a little, gathered his or her wits and disappeared into an inner room, to return a moment later carrying a piece of paper.

'As you may know, Dr Williams at the Clinic is away. One of our staff can recommend a doctor, however, Sudanese and very good apparently. Here are her details.'

Muttering my thanks I snatched the paper and hurried back to the car. That evening we were all in the doctor's surgery.

'He has typhoid fever,' she announced, after the briefest look at Edmund.

'But he's got a cough,' said Joanna.

'It's a regular symptom.'

'He had an anti-typhoid injection before we came out,' I ventured.

'That doesn't provide permanent protection.'

Joanna was looking troubled. 'I've got a cough too and have been feeling pretty awful. Had you better look at me?'

The doctor quickly examined her and took her temperature.

'You have it too. And what about your daughter? She doesn't look well.'

Annabel was duly confirmed as having the disease in its early stages.

'I will of course take samples of your blood but you should immediately commence a course of chloramphenicol. I'll write a prescription. You'll find a pharmacy open in Khartoum centre.'

The three affected family members began taking antibiotics that night, Joanna very relieved to know she was not losing her marbles. A day or so later results of the blood tests confirmed the diagnosis for all three – and then I began running a temperature. Perhaps rashly, I started taking the drugs immediately, paying a visit to the doctor the next day for a blood test that again confirmed the presence of the disease. Later on we discovered two interesting things: a typhoid carrier of the disease had been working in the kitchens at the rest centre in Ethiopia; and the fear that you are going mad is a regular feature of typhoid sufferers because the disease attacks the brain.

Suffering as we were from what can be a lethal disease, we went to bed and stayed there – well, as far as possible. Both Edmund and Joanna certainly needed a protracted period of recovery and Annabel also needed rest. This was less important for me but if not

A desert party for Annabel's fifth birthday, 1971

in bed I certainly stayed at home for a while. I could do this – we all could – because a nurse from the Swiss clinic, almost the only missionary left in Omdurman at the time, made it her business to come in every day to see how we were and bring food and supplies. Rosemary was, you might say, our lifeline; we shall never forget her.

We were kept on the drugs for a month, the doctor determined to eradicate every trace of the disease. She was right to take the safe course but chloramphenicol is a powerful antibiotic and we were told later that we had taken twice the normal dose. This may have been why Edmund, though over the fever, began to develop boils. At the Swiss clinic he was prescribed a course of vitamin B injections which quickly dealt with the problem. We should probably all have had this treatment – or at least taken vitamin tablets. We got over the typhoid but it left us tired and weak. After a while I resumed my pastoral duties as well as Arabic studies but as the months passed became aware that I was drawing on dangerously low reserves. Joanna, with primary responsibility for the children, was clearly doing the same. This in mind, we suggested to the mission authorities that our UK leave be brought forward so we could recuperate in a kinder environment. They decided that such a step was unnecessary, however, so we soldiered on.

***

While we were still recovering and more or less tied to our house there was an attempted coup.

'What on earth's that!' Joanna exclaimed, sitting up suddenly as we were taking an afternoon siesta together. We had been disturbed by an enormous thump.

'An explosion of some sort,' I said, rather unnecessarily. 'Quite far off but we'd better investigate.'

We got up from our bed and walked out onto the veranda, with its unobstructed view of open ground and the road beyond it running alongside the river.

'Nobody much around,' I said. 'Nothing serious, I imagine.'

'I'll make tea and bring drinks for the kids,' Joanna suggested. 'We might as well be comfortable as we watch for possible developments.'

We brought the children out with us and sat sipping for a few minutes. An even louder bang suddenly shook the windows.

'Definitely time to retreat,' Joanna announced.

We collected up the tea things and took them inside, continuing with our tiffin in the *saaloon*. We kept away from the windows but before long heard heavy rumbling and shouting. Peering through the glass we saw tanks and armoured cars passing along the Nile road. Soldiers and a few others were sitting or standing on the vehicles, crying out excitedly and waving branches of palms.

'You know what they're making for,' I remarked. 'The radio station – first target of all insurgents.'

Sudan's broadcasting centre was situated less than a mile down the road. Soon we were tuning in to martial music, followed by the announcement that Radio Omdurman was under the control of the forces of the revolution. The President, the speaker added, had been seized and placed under guard.

President Jaafar Muhammad Nimeiri – highly popular in certain circles – was not so easily toppled. Three days later the tanks, cars and soldiers were passing in front of us again. Nimeiri, we learnt, had managed to climb through a window in the building where he was held, made contact with units of the army loyal to him and, with a little help from Libya, overcome the dissident elements. These had been led, it appeared, by officers with communist sympathies. As a young army colonel Nimeiri himself had headed the coup of 1969 which overthrew the then democratically elected government, becoming head of a revolutionary command council. Now the boot was on the other foot, yet he had again come out on top. His Houdini-like escape much strengthened his reputation as leader; indeed, it made him something of a national hero.

There were repercussions from all this for the Anglican church in Sudan – the loss of the cathedral, a fine neo-gothic structure situated next to the Presidential Palace. During the initial fighting, rebel snipers had climbed the tower and used it as a handy vantage point to control Khartoum centre. Not surprisingly, Nimeiri feared this could happen again and the building was declared closed. (In due course the government promised compensation in the form of a new cathedral to be built at public expense on a site away from the centre.) I was affected by this development to the extent that cathedral services I was involved in from time to time, including 'the solemnization of holy matrimony', were diverted to other venues, such as private houses.

At the end of November we celebrated Edmund's second birthday. Our close Sudanese friend knew about it and arrived at the River House with a gift. He walked in through the compound gate leading his gift on a string and clapped his hands (the normal Sudanese way) to attract our attention. I walked down our front steps to the garden to see who it was.

'Mahjoub!' I cried on seeing him standing there with a four-footed companion. 'Don't tell me you've taken to riding that creature!'

'A *dahash*, a donkey foal,' he corrected me. 'I might do so as they make an excellent form of transport. But actually, no.' He looked fondly at the beast fretting a little at his side. 'I thought Edmund might like him. It's his birthday, I think.'

I laughed aloud. 'You're not serious! I don't believe it!'

'Of course I am.'

I looked back towards the house and called out, 'Joanna, Joanna! Come and see Edmund's latest birthday present!'

Joanna arrived and regarded our friend doubtfully. 'I'm not particularly surprised, Mahjoub, because I've never really trusted you. The goats for Annabel and now … now *this* for Edmund!'

'*Him*, please,' Mahjoub murmured, placing his hand on the animal's back. 'Male for a boy.'

'You don't miss a trick, do you?' Joanna's eyes twinkled. 'What I find myself asking is where this will end. Meanwhile, Edmund – and Annabel – will naturally be overjoyed at this addition to our zoo.'

The donkey foal – quite large, in fact – joined Christmas, Ginger, and the two goats, Blackie and Brownie. He joined the goats quite literally in that he was dismissed, like them, to the enclosure or *zariba* we had made at the bottom of the garden. The new family member had to have a name, of course, and we debated the matter.

'He shall be called Heath-and-Hurrit-Small,' Joanna announced finally.

I concurred, adding, 'How did you dream that up, darling?'

'My Dad had a pet with that name,' she explained. 'He told me about it – perhaps a dog – but to be honest I forget. Anyway, it's a good name.'

H-and-H-S provided much entertainment – as indeed did the goats – to both young and old inhabiting or visiting our compound. Especially popular was feeding time, when *birseem*, a kind of clover obtainable from the market, was hoist into their enclosure and the animals would fight over it. Not long after bringing the donkey, Mahjoub turned up with two further candidates for our mini-zoo: a pair of rabbits. Joanna had read the runes correctly.

Mahjoub had been introduced to us by a fellow missionary – the young teacher of theology already mentioned. As well as being a person of great charm, and wonderful with children, our Sudanese friend was unusual in another way: he was a convert from Islam to Christianity. He explained to me one day how this had come about. Wanting to learn more about the Christian faith, he had approached members of an American mission in Khartoum who invited him to study the Bible with them. They began reading the story of Jesus as recorded in one of the gospels.

'It was a revelation,' he told me. 'I had no idea Jesus was so human, such a normal person, mixing and conversing with people quite naturally and delivering his message in everyday language – even if he did extraordinary things as well.'

'You mean, you didn't know what was written about him in the New Testament?'

'His life and teaching is a closed book to the average Muslim, even if Muhammad taught his followers to honour the Nazarene as prophet and Messiah. They rely upon what the Qur'ān says about him, which is limited and very different in tone.'

Back to Heath-and-Hurrit-Small, who fast developed a will of his own as he fed on the daily supplies of *birseem* – indeed, became decidedly frisky. The first step was to let him out of the enclosure from time to time and give him the freedom of the compound. This was fine until he discovered the joys of kicking; on one occasion he came to the back door of the house and directed a hoof at Joanna's mother, staying with us at the time. Something had to be done and Joanna – inventive as ever – had the answer.

'You must ride him to school,' she told me one morning. 'It'll give him exercise.' (I was still attending Arabic lessons at the girls' school.)

'Ride him to school? Don't be ridiculous!' My beloved did not budge and of course within a few days I was doing what she said.

I learnt quite a lot about donkeys from this experience, mostly to do with their brains. I discovered after only a couple of trips to school that there was no need for me to use the reins: the intelligent beast beneath me had memorised the route exactly, though it meandered down and around several small alleys. This animal talent was useful as it enabled me to look at my book for the coming lesson as I went. When I arrived at the school for the first time the girls (and, I suspected, some of the teachers) were scandalized. There was much giggling and whispering as I tied H-and-H-Small to a railing on the edge of the playground. Very soon the oddity was accepted, however, which encouraged me to be more ambitious. I took to riding to the *souq* near our home to buy fruit, vegetables or spices. (Years later someone in Omdurman asked me if I was the *khawājah*, or foreigner, who had regularly ridden around on a donkey; I had obviously made an impression, which touched me deeply.)

Heath-and-Hurrit-Small and I had one rather less routine experience. Happily astride my four-legged computer one day on the way to school, and in something of a reverie, I was disturbed by the sound of trotting behind me – a lot of trotting. My steed was disturbed too and took off like a Ferrari. A moment later I and the donkey-saddle were together on the tarmac, with a receding cloud of dust somewhere ahead. I had not fastened the saddle-strap properly. While I considered my plight, three mounted police came up choking back laughter. Having recovered their composure, they apologised profusely.

'I will immediately go off, catch your donkey and bring it back to you,' one announced.

'That's very kind, but really it isn't necessary,' I said. 'I can easily …'

Souq

He wasn't listening and cantered off. But the inevitable happened further up the road: as soon as he approached his prey, the prey took off again. He returned empty-handed in due course, offering further apologies. With some difficulty I persuaded the three officers that I held them in no way responsible and they finally moved off, spirits revived. I trudged after H-and-H-S, fixed the saddle, jumped into it and proceeded on my way.

***

Ata, our Sudanese houseboy (he was actually over sixty), had served with CMS missionaries for most if not all of his working life. He was very reliable and methodical though not the fastest worker. A gentle, sweet-natured man, he was a Muslim devoted to the Christians he served. While with us he suffered a stroke and was admitted to Khartoum general hospital – not a place entirely favourable to healing, apart from the attention of a doctor, for nursing and the procurement of necessary food and drugs were the responsibility of relatives. I visited him and found the family standing round his bed looking very sombre; he himself was unconscious. I turned to a white-coated official, possibly one of the doctors, standing near us.

'Would anyone mind if I said a prayer?' I asked quietly.

He responded drily, 'If you do, they will know he is going to die.'

I had not intended to pray for the peaceful passing of his soul but for healing and that is how I prayed for our faithful servant, laying a hand on him as I did so. It was all rather emotional so I decided not to stay, mumbling in Arabic to the family as I left, 'He'll be alright.'

A day or two later I chanced to meet one of Ata's daughters in the street, and she told me her father had turned the corner from the moment of my visit. Not long after this he was back in our service. I asked him later what he thought of Jesus and was quite startled when he responded in terms that represented, as far as I could see, a Christian profession of faith.

Ata helped to prepare our Christmas dinner at the end of 1971, to the extent of slaughtering the two geese we had been given by Annabel's playschool teacher with this end in mind. It seemed a bit

The pyramids at Meroë

drastic to reduce our burgeoning animal kingdom in such a manner – though to be honest those wily creatures were not the easiest or quietest of guests. We enjoyed our festive meal but there was a certain poignancy about it, Joanna later on adamant that we should have kept the birds.

My friend from college and Camborne days, John Pridmore, came to stay with us that Christmas. It worked out well as he was able to accompany Joanna's mother, also joining us, on the flight from UK. On the Feast of the Epiphany he and I took a trip some hundred miles north to the pyramids at Meroë. There was no proper road, only a rough track across the desert, so we went by rail. Travel on Sudan Railways was not the most comfortable or speedy but some hours later we were alighting at Kabushia, the station nearest our destination.

Transport to the distant cluster of pyramids was not available so we were faced with a trek across the sands. We set off with our knapsacks and, as the sun was dying in the west, arrived at the mysterious, numinous monuments – the final resting place of kings and queens of ancient Ethiopia. There was enough light to wander round the slightly elevated site and peer at the structures but soon we were setting up camp – little more than choosing a suitable spot. We unrolled our sleeping bags and, after a snack, settled down for a night under the stars.

John's rest, however, was interrupted. Looking extremely pale the next morning, he told me about it.

'I'm afraid, Philip, I had a restless night. I hope this didn't disturb you.'

'Not in the least. So what's been the problem?'

'Er … the inner man. Every so often I had to wander off to … to throw up.'

'My dear fellow, how unpleasant! And there was I, stretched out and blissfully unaware the night long. You're actually a hero.'

He was in no state to cope with further exploration so we packed up and started back for Kabushia. Not surprisingly, my companion soon reached the point at which he could go no further … and lo! across the sand towards us, stately and dignified, approached a nomad on a camel. Immediately interpreting the situation, this wandering Arab offered a 'lift' – as well as an aspirin. So it was that the Reverend John Stuart Pridmore, of Ridley Hall, Cambridge, England, emulating the sages of old, found himself making an Epiphany-tide journey astride that most royal of beasts, a dromedary.

Having reached the railway station on four and two legs respectively, we caught the next and possibly only train back to Khartoum. Not long into our return ride, however, the diesel locomotive developed a fault. After a few fits and starts it failed completely and we chugged to a halt. Everyone jumped down onto the sand – everyone, that is, except my languishing friend. Watching developments, I saw one of the drivers, or maybe the guard, donning a heavy overcoat in the considerable heat and walking off down the line. We would have to wait, we were told, until he reached some installation from which he could call for assistance. Five hours later the help arrived and once something had been done up front we moved off again.

It was very late in the day when, finally, we pulled into Khartoum Central. Our trip into the far past had been short but it represented a never-to-be-forgotten experience – for John especially, I dare say.

In March our tour of missionary duty (eighteen months the minimum) came to an end and on the seventeenth day of the month we flew home on a VC10 to London Heathrow. England was enjoying an early heat wave and as we were driven through the streets to stay the first few nights with friends in Ealing, I remember seeing the police in shirt sleeves.

We were back for four months, our first home leave.

IV

Limbo

It didn't quite work out like that.

Once the adrenalin that had kept us going subsided, Joanna and I discovered that we had all but spent our reserves of energy. We were very thin, both of us, but that was a symptom of a more general weakness. I myself just couldn't get enough sleep. If I exerted myself for any length of time, I felt exhausted.

We returned to Cornwall, making our base in a flat on the top floor of my parents' large house in Truro. We had certain duties to perform for our missionary society – deputation work it was called, which involved the visiting of parishes and speaking about our work overseas. This fell largely to me, Joanna needing to stay at home to look after the children. These responsibilities I managed to perform, and of course we visited friends and one or two churches locally. But as our four-month leave drew near to its end we realised we were in no state to cope with the extra stresses of life overseas so requested an extension of leave. We were granted a further two months and then, when that extension had nearly expired and we felt little stronger, were given a further six months.

During this period the missionary society decided that Joanna should consult a psychiatrist. This was odd because she evinced no worrying psychological symptoms. We went to London together so she could meet this shrink, whom we located, after something of a search, up a flight of stairs in a tower with a green door in Soho. I waited outside the consultation chamber while Joanna was interrogated. After a while she emerged unscathed and told me the doctor could find nothing wrong with her. She rehearsed to me just one of the questions he had asked her, as well as her response.

'How is your sex life, Mrs Blair?'

'I'm quite satisfied. But then, I have nothing to compare it with.' (A brilliant riposte, I thought.)

What I think we were both suffering from to some degree was a form of ME, which among other things, they say, can be caused by over-prescription or prolonged intake of antibiotics. Something along these lines was mentioned to me by a doctor friend who noticed my lassitude in contrast to the energy I had shown formerly as curate of his church. In any case, some time into the six-month extension we heard from our missionary society that Bishop Butrus, Sudanese assistant to the diocesan bishop, no longer wanted us back in Omdurman. (When I met him in Sudan several years later, he denied this.) By now Joanna and I had no wish to be sent anywhere else so we felt it best to be taken off the Society's list of serving members.

An ancillary reason for deciding to resign as missionaries was my continuing unease about the Society's preoccupation with political issues. All overseas missionaries were expected to write an 'annual letter' to the Society in London commenting on how things were going and raising matters of special concern. My first such letter had raised this question of politicisation – of both the Society and the wider church – and was highly critical of it. When, later in 1973, the Society's 'annual sermon', preached by Bishop Stanley Booth-Clibborn and subsequently published and circulated, spelt out the reasoning behind this stance and advocated an extension of the Society's political activism, I felt it was time to make a complete break. Joanna and I were still members of the Church Missionary Society, if not as missionaries; we now cancelled that membership.

Having cut all ties with our sponsors over this 'church in politics' question, I decided to put in writing my own theological position. I therefore began collecting material – and my thoughts – for a full-length study. I sketched a plan, wrote notes and even completed some three chapters but the project was put aside when other concerns became pressing. Two periodicals, however, one from the evangelical and the other from the catholic wing of the church, published articles which summarised my thoughts on the issue.

Twenty years later my book *What on Earth? The Church in the World and the Call of Christ* (Cambridge: Lutterworth, 1993) saw the light of day.

The concerns that became pressing were in the main to do with my appointment by the Bishop of Truro as priest-in-charge of the parish of Probus during an interregnum. At the same time Joanna took up a teaching position in a Truro primary school, while our children had already entered another school as pupils. We thus had plenty to do – though here I should pay tribute to the way my parents, with whom we continued to live, helped both us and our young 'pigeon pair'.

Despite my now having a paid position, which I was advised by the bishop could become permanent, I became increasingly determined to get back to Sudan. I felt we were still meant to be there – and Joanna was with me in this. The idea of gaining financial support from the diocese of Truro came to nothing and it became clear that if we were to return it would have to be under our own steam. There was a route that presented itself immediately: teaching, and more specifically English language teaching. My theology degree gave me a university qualification but I was going to need a certificate qualifying me as an English teacher. I discovered the University of Exeter offered a one-year Advanced Diploma in Education specialising in English language teaching, applied and was accepted.

'I'm intrigued to know why you didn't query my credentials,' I asked Reg Roberts, the lecturer responsible, once the course had begun. 'I'm so grateful you took me on but I noticed in your brochure that applicants normally have to be experienced, full-time teachers. Neither description fits me!'

'Ah,' he replied at once, 'everything hangs on that word "normally". When composing such rubrics I always include it.' He paused, and then added with a smile, 'You see, I believe in opening doors for people, not closing them.'

The wisdom of those last words I have never forgotten. They could, in fact, equally well apply to the then Bishop of Truro, Dr Graham Leonard, who had agreed that I could attend the course while still running a parish and drawing a stipend.

Being a student on the course, which commenced in September 1974, involved weekly commuting from Truro to Exeter, which I usually did by train. I had by then left the parish of Probus, having been asked to cover that of St Enoder, near Newquay. Joanna, meanwhile, remained teaching in the same school although it was housed in new premises, the old schoolhouse of the village of Baldhu.

We had some good times during this period – a sort of limbo, as we conceived it. For instance, we bought a small boat, 12-foot and clinker-built, and an outboard motor. We named her 'Joannabel' and moored her at the top of the Truro River. From there we took her down past Malpas, past the Pandora, where the river becomes the Fal, and on to Falmouth, with its superb natural harbour. Or we would go up a creek, such as the one to Tresillian. We would then beach the boat on a sandy or pebbly spit and get out a picnic. On one occasion, near Tresillian, there came gliding towards us round a corner a gondola, in which an elegant female lay back enjoying the spectacle while a no less elegant gondolier propelled her.

'Who on earth is that woman?' Joanna hissed.

'Good gracious,' I said after a long look, 'it's Helena Sanders! You know, my mother's friend. Famous these days for organising a campaign – highly successful, I gather – to control the cat population of Venice. The man in the Venetian outfit is of course her husband.'

We made new friends, or saw old ones, like the McIntyres – Christopher, Linda and children – who, like us, had recently returned from Africa. They were eking out a living as Chris tried his hand at garden design but were desperate to get back to the continent, where he had been a tea-planter.

Over an excellent dinner one evening in their home, Joanna asked if they weren't slightly doubtful about going back to the area they had been in, Burundi, exhibiting a degree of unrest at the time. Linda's response was both immediate and eloquent: 'Better than starving in Stithians!'

Chris then turned towards us. 'Tell me,' he said, 'what exactly led you to go to Sudan and why are you now so keen to return?'

I spoke for us both in replying, after a moment's thought, 'If you want it in a single phrase, I think it is to be a Christian presence.'

And from that day onwards Chris would always refer to me, in his trademark dead-pan manner, as 'The Christian Presence'.

All this time we remained living in my parents' flat in Truro. My father, however, was due to retire from his post within the year and with this in mind we had (with my parents' help) bought a run-down house in the village of Carharrack, near Redruth. One of our leisure preoccupations at this time was gutting this ex-miner's cottage to make it fully fit for habitation. More or less concurrently with the end of my diploma course in June 1975, my parents left Truro for Sherborne, Dorset, while we moved to the cottage.

The third and smallest bedroom of our new home included a 'flying freehold' over the sitting room of the adjacent property in the terrace. We were convinced that were we to enter our cottage for the Guinness book of records it would win hands down as the smallest three-bedroom dwelling in the land. Small it was but it had its attractions: the kitchen (the ceiling an inch or two above my head) was gloriously warm in winter thanks to an old Wellstood range, and the front room (three steps up) had an open fireplace which we had uncovered, flanked by granite uprights. The main entrance to the house from the street was down three steps to a small yard and then through the 'back' door. We made the 'front' door into a French window leading onto the right of way to the cottage adjoining us. Across this shared pathway was a long, narrow garden in which we erected two granite monoliths, originally a kind of tryst gate in the garden next door. Beyond the wall and an old privy at the bottom of the garden lay a field, and beyond that a wood. This, mostly of fir, was unsafe to enter because of mineshafts, the timber caps of which were rotting and collapsing.

At the end of our road was the local rubbish tip and within the immediate vicinity four vehicle scrap-yards. The soil was stony and unproductive, apart from thriving gorse and ferns, the bushes stunted and windswept. Cornwall is famous as a centre of tourism but no tourists came to Carharrack – unless they were interested in tin mining, of which, with neighbouring St Day, it was the old centre, or intrigued by legends of the 'tinner' Joseph of Arimathea coming to Cornwall with the boy Jesus. Once at the hub of both industrial and religious life (John Wesley used to preach at Gwennap Pit, a stone's throw away), Carharrack was now a backwater. Its population included quite a number of settlers who had hit hard times and were attracted by lower-priced houses. It was a village utterly without pretension – and we loved every minute of the time we spent there.

***

Those years, from 1975 to 1978, can be passed over swiftly.

On receiving my diploma from Exeter in June of 1975, I immediately applied for two teaching posts in Sudan, both at the University of Khartoum. The first was in the English Language Servicing Unit, for which I was turned down as lacking experience. The second was as a 'language laboratory expert' at the Faculty of Education in Omdurman. I had no experience at all of such expertise but made a case for myself, I fondly imagined. I heard nothing back.

At the end of 1975 I resigned as priest-in-charge of St Enoder – the second parish of which I had been given the temporary charge – with no alternative post to go to. The intention was by one means or another to launch myself into the world of English language teaching. After a few ups and downs, including the likelihood of a position in Kuwait which then fell through and six weeks 'on the dole', I joined the staff of a language school in Exeter. While there I saw the Omdurman post advertised again so applied a second time; I also arranged (a strategic move) to run the school language laboratory for the month of August, the usual teacher being away.

For that month Joanna and the children, together with Joanna's mother, came to stay in Exeter, Joanna temping at the language school. We hired a pleasant period house for the duration, the only downside being risqué paintings by the owner all over the walls. It was a good holiday, albeit a working one for the adults; it was also a very hot one. The summer of '76 brought temperatures approaching a hundred Fahrenheit for days on end and the language school, with no air conditioners, became a furnace. Students from Saudi-Arabia were incredulous: they had never experienced conditions like it and virtually refused to attend.

Alas, my second application for the language lab post in Omdurman elicited no response either. However, I had meanwhile been accepted to do an MA in linguistics at the University of Exeter and as a result heard of a vacancy at the Language Centre for the post of Tutor in Applied Linguistics. The main responsibility was teaching English to students from Qatar – part of a push being made by Exeter at the time to forge a relationship with the Arab and Islamic world. I applied and, helped by my Sudan experience, was accepted.

The research for my MA was on a phonetic topic and involved Sudanese colloquial Arabic. There were a number of Sudanese students doing advanced studies at Exeter and two of them became my informants for the language. This fulfilled the dual purpose of furthering my research while at the same time keeping my Arabic up to scratch.

In July 1977 the language lab post in Omdurman was, to my amazement, advertised for the third time. I applied yet again, encouraged by the fact that I could now make a stronger case for myself as an 'expert'. Still nothing came back from Khartoum so in September I was back in Exeter, teaching the Qataris. I began to wonder if my determination to return to Sudan was no more than a pipe-dream.

I was still residing in Exeter for weekdays, returning to Cornwall each weekend – where Joanna, day after day, had been driving the children to school in Truro, going on to her own school in the nearby village, returning to pick up the children and take them home, feeding them, getting them to bed, and finally tying up any odd ends for the next day. It was a tough assignment, but she took it in her stride. By now, however, a new and especially demanding responsibility had arisen.

Joanna's mother had been living with us in our tiny cottage for some time, there having been a problem in her relationship with her sister, with whom she had been living. In around January 1977 she was diagnosed with a return of the cancer for which she had already been treated. As the year wore on her condition worsened: she developed cancer of the lung and it became obvious that –

barring a miracle – the disease was terminal. By the summer a nurse was visiting the house regularly to attend to the by now bedbound patient's medical requirements, while Joanna coped with her everyday needs.

We pray at times for special strength to deal with some difficulty – usually short term. I don't know whether we specifically asked for strength to get through this crisis; I do know that my better half either possessed or was granted remarkable stamina and courage to get through, for get through she did.

Early in October the iron gates yielded: I received a telegram from the Head of English, Faculty of Education, University of Khartoum, offering me the language laboratory position. He hoped I could come immediately.

This was difficult. For one thing, my contract with the University of Exeter ran till the end of the academic year, though a clause allowed for an earlier departure. I consulted the university authorities, who agreed that if I stayed until Christmas I could leave without penalty. I was extremely grateful. They had been most helpful throughout my time, sympathetic in particular to the needs of a family man commuting from some distance. The way back to Sudan was now open.

This didn't answer the question of Joanna's mother, however. Terminal the disease was, it seemed certain, but naturally we were not given an expected date of death. I nevertheless said 'yes' to Khartoum, telling them I would come out, without my family, at the beginning of January. The decision was ultimately mine but I had Joanna's full support. I had support from someone else too, equally important in a way.

When I told Joanna's mother of my decision, she responded: 'I'm very happy for you, Philip. I know how much you have wanted this.'

We held on – and waited.

The last few weeks of Mary Cecil's life were necessarily spent in Plymouth hospital. This made it possible for me to visit her in the evening, coming down by train from Exeter once or twice a week. Joanna, too, had a shortish train journey from Truro; she came when she could. At the end, on the seventeenth of November, I was with her on my own. We scattered her ashes at the crematorium just outside Truro a few days later, my father having officiated at the ceremony.

We didn't have long to settle Mary Cecil's affairs, plan our long-anticipated family return to Sudan and organise my individual departure. It was a slightly surreal period, yet strangely fulfilling. Joanna and I had had little time alone together over the previous couple of years and we made as much as we could of this new opportunity. Meanwhile, our approaching separation, though not what we would have chosen, was not going to be protracted. Khartoum University's long vacation, which of course I would spend in UK, commenced in April. I would be off again at the beginning of July but at the end of the month Joanna and the children, having completed the school year, would be ready to join me. It all seemed eminently reasonable.

V

Pastures Old

I flew back to Sudan on the third of January, 1978, and the first person I saw whom I knew was Israel. Yes, Israel.

I say I saw him but it would be more accurate to say I thought I did. The university had initially put me into the Khartoum Hilton. (I was among the last to be afforded this privilege.) I thought I saw Israel – fleetingly, and at a distance – as he was entering a lift. He glanced my way but showed no sign of recognition and a moment later the doors closed on him. Then I thought, no, perhaps I was wrong.

Israel was a *jibāli* – from the Nuba Mountains in Kordofan province. He had been our houseboy in our first home in Omdurman, the bungalow. At that time he was a pupil at a school run by the Evangelical (*injilī*) Church. He took the job with us to help pay his way through the school. Charming and very reliable, he had made a great impression on us; it was somehow fitting that he of all those I had known in Sudan should be the first to cross my path. For indeed, Israel it truly was entering that lift. I met him in the street a little later and we had a good chat.

'When we saw each other I was at work, I wasn't a hotel guest,' he said, a little defensively. 'I was on duty – as a member of staff, the servicing staff.'

'That's interesting.' I nodded approvingly. 'I of course *was* a guest – briefly, at the university's expense.' I explained why I was back in Sudan. 'I really believed it was you, until you turned away. Then I decided I could be wrong.'

'I was completely surprised, you see,' he apologised. 'Imagine, someone suddenly looks like my former boss – but I know he's in England. And … and you've changed. I mean your hair …'

'Oh that!' I laughed. 'Six years has made a difference, I agree!' I stroked a balding pate ruefully. 'I quite see how it confused you.' I became serious again. 'It's good work, in the Hilton – decent pay?'

'The best I can find.'

'You mean …'

'I mean …,' he anticipated the query, 'I mean I took the job to make a living. I'm not interested in the hotel trade. And no, they don't pay well. It's difficult to make ends meet – with a wife and two children.' He looked at me a trace whimsically.

'You're married? Children too? Great news, Israel!'

'Yes, marriage is great. She's great too, and I'm happy. Very happy. But … but of course I'd like more. I'd like to do something important, useful.'

'Teaching maybe?'

'That'd be good. But the pay? – if you get it at all from the government. Impossible. And as for a private school? Few openings and lots wanting those there are. I've tried but …' He shrugged his shoulders.

'I see.'

And I did. He was worth so much more than a cleaning or stewarding job. His situation suddenly epitomised the African predicament. And as this came home to me the romance of being back in Sudan began to fade. It was back to reality.

I asked him a question that intrigued me.

'This is basically an Arab and Muslim country – in Khartoum, anyway. Afro-Arab if you like, but certainly Muslim. I just wonder about your name, your Christian name. It's from the Bible of course, and nothing wrong with that, the nickname God gave to Jacob, once common enough in England but not now, I have to say. In the Arab or Muslim world … it could be a problem.' I eyed him hesitantly.

He sighed. 'So you understand. Yes, it *is* a problem. There are people around who for some reason imagine because I've got this name, I must be a Zionist. There are sometimes comments …' He paused, looking away. 'Yes, it can be difficult.'

'You mean getting a job?'

'I don't know really. I sometimes wonder about that but there's nothing definite.' He paused again, going on more slowly. 'Some friends suggest I change my name. But I couldn't do that.' His look was almost fierce. 'It's absurd, isn't it? My parents gave me the name Israel and that's who I am. Why should I change it?'

I said for the second time, 'I see.' Once again, back to reality.

The most pressing reality at that moment was my new responsibility as 'language laboratory expert'. On my arrival at Khartoum University's Faculty of Education, to the north of Omdurman, I was ushered into the laboratory by Obeid Kheiri, Head of English.

'Here it is, Mr Philip,' he announced. 'We're so happy you're here to put it right. It's been rather neglected recently, you know, and needs an experienced hand like yourself. I'll leave it to you. Just make yourself at home.'

'I'm so glad to be with you, sir,' I replied respectfully. 'You may know I used to live not far from here so it's not all new. It's very exciting to be back. I'll do my best with this important facility. By the way, please drop the "Mr". Just call me "Philip".'

His eyes sparkled. 'Ah, I will do as you say. And just call me "Obeid".'

I was going to like the man, I decided. But I wasn't sure about the lab. We looked around more closely for a minute or two and the neglect was only too evident. The sixteen booths and their instruments were coated with fine red sand, producing the usual acrid smell, and I noticed some of the air vents above the windows had been left open. Northern Sudan is one of the worst regions in the world for sand-storms – or *habūbs*, as the Arabic splendidly has it. To allow any entrance for sand and dust through the smallest orifice into rooms housing electronic equipment is fatal.

After Obeid had left me I did some dusting – then looked for but didn't find a cleaner, or *farrāsh*, to assist me. I did some tests with the microphone and audio equipment. Only five booths were operational. This, of course, was where my expertise was going to be really useful, restoring a piece of sophisticated technology to its former glory.

Which could never be – I'm ashamed to say. Such expertise as I possessed did not stretch to servicing hardware, the intricacies of which both eluded and bored me. I was quite good at manipulating and exploiting such equipment for language drills and suchlike, but that was all. So with the help of my friendly Head, I looked for a lab technician. Such did exist, but not in Omdurman; his remit was the main campus in Khartoum. I finally tracked him down and he came over and coaxed a few more booths into working order. But though over the next few weeks I supervised several groups of students in the lab it was a losing battle because as soon as one dead recorder or its accoutrement was revived, another died. In the end I gave up the struggle; the system was failing too often. So I allowed the lab to return to the dust from whence it had come. Instead of fulfilling my role as language-lab wizard, ready and equipped for working with and maintaining state-of-the-art electronic aids, I reverted to being a chalk-and-talk classroom instructor.

I was never so relieved. And Obeid didn't seem to mind at all.

During this period I was living in a large octagonal oddity on the banks of the Blue Nile known as the Pink Palace. The luxury of the Khartoum Hilton had naturally, after a few days, given way to sterner things in this strange, gaunt structure. Of course, once I was joined by my family I would need accommodation with appropriate facilities, but as a grass-widower one of the eight cavernous bedsitters reserved for single members of staff became my lot. There was an en suite bathroom (of sorts) but otherwise there was only the huge central area – a kind of atrium – and a shared kitchen. The building had served the exiled Emperor Haile Selassie well enough as headquarters while, between May 1940 and January 1941, he and Colonel Orde Wingate had planned the 'Gideon Force' to liberate Ethiopia. (After fleeing the Italian invaders in May 1936 he had been domiciled, together with his family, in Bath, England, as a private guest – and reportedly an impecunious one.) For us 'bachelors', the Pink Palace provided a roof over our heads but not a lot more.

I did nothing more than sleep in my palace at night, or occasionally for an afternoon siesta. I never used the kitchen –

unlike Piers Crocker, the six-foot-six archaeologist in the room next to me – preferring to eat out. My staple breakfast was boiled beans, or *fūl masri*. Dressed with oil and frequently having a raw onion or hard-boiled egg chopped into it, this truly delicious mixture was obtainable from many corner shops, was very cheap and highly satisfying. Very often you had to squat on the ground to eat it, scooping up the preparation with fragments broken from the long loaf of bread supplied with the bowl of beans. A glass of sweet red tea, sometimes provided free, rounded things off. The 'cuppa' came in other forms as well, mind you. I would sometimes wander out early to have a milky brew in a tall tumbler – though I didn't crumble a packet of biscuits into it to make a kind of porridge as the southerners did.

From my temporary base I was well placed for getting to work. I bought a bicycle – a sit-up-and-beg Raleigh – and would ride quickly over the Blue Nile bridge to Khartoum North, thence more or less alongside the northern stream of the briefly divided Blue Nile to Shambat bridge, where I crossed The Nile (that is, combined Niles) to the northern district of Omdurman. I then had to pedal further north, leaving the town proper until I reached the Faculty of Education at Wad Nabawi. This was not far from the site of the Battle of Omdurman – or Battle of Karari, as it is more properly called. My daily trip back and forth was both enjoyable and invigorating. Once the family joined me and we had a car I continued to cycle to work. The car was then available for Joanna.

Under the neem trees and palms that clustered round the Pink Palace there were some bungalows housing married faculty members. In one of them lived the Babikers – Abdul Qayūm, a professor of mathematics, his English wife Tricia, a teacher at Clergy House Primary School, and their children. Tricia heard that a new lecturer from England had taken up residence in the palace and that his wife, soon to be joining him, was a primary teacher so decided to be proactive. I received a message asking me round to the house. Thus began a lifelong friendship between the families.

If the first 'old friend' I saw on returning to Sudan was strictly speaking Israel, I made contact with 'the other Philip' a day or two after this chance encounter. He had by that time – for his own reasons – resigned from the Church Missionary Society but had stayed on in Sudan as a teacher, living in Khartoum North with our mutual friend Mahjoub. It was a happy reunion and I spent much of my leisure time with both of them, sometimes bedding down under the stars in the Mahjoub home or accompanying them on trips outside the capital in Philip's car. Mahjoub's cousin Muhammad Sīd Ahmed entered my life at this time, too. Muhammad was – like Mahjoub – immensely likeable.

'Philip tells me you used to be communist,' I remarked to him one day. 'I'd be interested to know what led you to such a position – what you see in communist ideology.' (Our conversations, I should point out, were always in Arabic since he spoke very little English.)

'Not so easy to answer that, *abū digin*,' he immediately responded, using my regular nickname 'father of the beard'. After a moment's thought he continued, 'To be honest, becoming a communist was not so much a matter of ideology as a practical step.'

'Practical?'

'Yes. You see, after Nimeiri became president in 1969 Sudan turned very much to the Soviet Union for aid and so it became generally acceptable to be thought of as a communist. Indeed, a local communist party was formed on a legal basis and was for a time quite popular.'

'So you decided that this new party might achieve something useful for the country.'

'Not exactly. As I said, becoming a communist was a practical matter, by which I mean it enabled me to do or be something that would otherwise have been more or less impossible.'

'And what was that "something"?'

Muhammad smiled. 'I could answer that in two ways. Firstly, and very simply, it enabled me to be different, in a sense independent. I no longer had to toe the line.'

I considered his words carefully, finally responding, 'What you are saying interests me enormously, Muhammad, especially about not toeing the line. But you must be more specific. What line? *Whose* line?'

'*Khalās*, now we come to my second way of answering. It enabled me, without endangering myself, to oppose much that was going on in government – sometimes outside it – which I felt unhappy about.'

'You really mean Nimeiri, I suppose.'

'Yes. Certainly I was – and remain – unhappy about some of his policies.'

'What about "outside" the government, as you put it?'

He instinctively lowered his voice. 'I mean, of course, religion.'

'You're not a believer, then?'

He looked hard at me. 'I don't quite know. What I do know is that I don't hold with much that goes on in the name of religion.'

'You mean Islam.'

'I suppose so, yes.'

I had to digest this slowly. 'What about God, Muhammad?' I continued finally. 'Are you, like every party member in the Soviet Union, an atheist?'

'No, it would be wrong to say that – though I'm not quite sure what God means to me. He certainly isn't what I hear from the *'ulamā* – you know, the religious experts round here.'

'A final question, Muhammad, which I know you won't mind. What do you make of Christianity – from what you know of it, that is?'

His reply was swift. 'It interests me, *abū digin*. It interests me a great deal.'

John and Deborah Barff, our replacements as missionaries, lived in our old home, the River House in Omdurman. I naturally went to see them as soon as possible and they quickly became friends. We sat together on the wide veranda, looking across the familiar patch of open ground and through the trees to the Nile.

'I find it extraordinary to be sitting here with these barrels we packed so long ago right beside me,' I remarked to my hosts, glancing at our dust-covered baggage. 'I know the mission insists people pack up their stuff when they go on leave in case they never return. But when we did this I never for a moment thought it would be almost six years till we saw it all again!'

'Maybe it should have been sent to you in UK years ago, which is what is normally done ,' Deborah said, the voice of common sense as so often.

'Oh, I'm very glad it wasn't,' I responded with a smile. 'We'll probably be glad of some of the items this time round. I imagine it wasn't sent because it got around that we intended, by hook or by crook, to come back.' I turned to John. 'You may know more about this than me.'

He shook his head. 'I think we heard something about your plans but what should be done with your things wasn't really up to me.'

Someone else I saw very early on was Bishop Butrus Tia Shukai, now no longer assistant to the Bishop of Sudan (who had retired, not to be replaced) but Anglican Bishop of Omdurman in his own right. The meeting had a tinge of sadness, however, for my friend was in poor health – something to do with his liver. He was having treatment but to little effect. Thereafter I dropped in to see him from time to time but one day found him in bed unconscious, with his daughter, a trained nurse, watching over him. He never regained consciousness and finally slipped away. He and his wife Rhoda – both from the Nuba Mountains – were lovable characters and the Bishop was greatly missed.

***

In mid-April 1978 I was back in UK as expected, happy to be with the family again, only to return alone to Sudan in July for the new academic year. In August, however, Joanna and the children flew out and the picture became complete: we had returned *as a family*. Quite a few people had told me in the intervening years not to go back, not to return to old pastures, not to try putting the clock back. To do so would be courting disaster, they warned. The next eight years would show who was right.

What to select from that crowded period to record here? First, I think, the sun.

It is with you so much in Sudan that there are times when you feel you will scream if it rises, bright and hot, just one more time! Not that August, however, not as we sat together in the shade

Typical Beit al-Māl houses

round the pool in the Sudan Club. To be transported at a stroke from the grey skies and chill winds of Blighty – not always grey and chill, of course, but all too often – to the brilliance and warmth of sub-Saharan Africa was a tonic. And this was what we needed after a period in our lives that had not been easy. Sudan the second time round – if I may be permitted to anticipate those further eight years under her sun – was exactly what the doctor ordered. Africa had smitten; Africa healed.

We needed a home other than the Pink Palace, as I have mentioned. Before the family joined me I had been looking for a place in Omdurman – mostly because it was near my place of work for daily cycling. Joanna, meanwhile, had applied for a post in Clergy House Primary School in Khartoum and was immediately accepted. She would be able to drive there from Omdurman by car, taking the children to school with her. We were importing from UK a bright red Chrysler (ex-Hillman) Hunter estate; it was a second-hand, left-hand drive model, with strengthened springs for bumpy roads. (Some time later a visitor to Sudan saw the car parked outside the Sudan Club, recognised it from some tell-tale sign as indubitably his old car, and left a note on the windscreen telling us he'd had it in Iraq and had driven it back to UK!)

I found an apartment in Beit al-Māl, quite near the Nile a little to the north of the River House. It was not far from a stretch of riverbank where you could watch skilled carpenters building the distinctive Sudanese dhows. The flat, one of two in a small block, was not finished so we had to spend nearly two months in a university guest house in Khartoum's 'new extension', where most expatriates lived. This was a pleasant interlude – apart from the locusts that suddenly descended on the region in their millions, plaguing Khartoum for several months.

Thump, thump! The sound of those heavy creatures hitting the window pane every now and then could be alarming. Then, just as Joanna and I were settling down for a quiet evening …

'Mummy, Daddy, quick!' Annabel's voice would rise to a crescendo. 'There's one in our room!'

I would shout back, 'Okay, okay, I'm coming!'

Having rushed through to their bedroom I would do my best, first, to find the invading pest, which could be lurking under a bed or behind a wardrobe, and, second, to trap it in some receptacle and put it outside. If the latter proved impossible I would try coaxing it through the open window. I usually succeeded, one way or another.

Staying with us in the guest house was a Canadian family, originally from France, and they decided to take the lower flat in Beit al-Māl while we took the upper. Christian Fagueret had been hired to teach French in the Faculty of Education, where I was teaching English. He and his wife Josianne had a daughter, Ludmillia, much the same age as Annabel, and the two became firm friends.

Life began to assume a routine, built up around three things: our teaching, our children's schooling, and the Club. The schools were the American School for Annabel and Clergy House Primary School for Edmund. The latter, now aged eight, was in no danger of being taught by his mother as she was teaching the youngest class.

Situated in the centre of Khartoum, the Sudan Club with its handsome white buildings and green lawns was a haven of rest and refreshment for us on an almost daily basis. Our hours of teaching ended at two (apart from an occasional evening lecture for me) so we could lunch at home, followed by a siesta if we felt the need, before going on to the Club; alternatively, we could go straight to the Club and eat in the dining room, then relax by the pool with friends, have a dip, and play squash, badminton or billiards. From time to time amateur dramatics was on the menu, which meant rehearsing or working on the set. The children, meanwhile, met up with their friends and found plenty to do – not least the swimming, at which they became highly adept, enjoying especially the summer swimming gala.

Every now and then we would have a family trip to the beach with friends. The 'beach' meant the sandy shore of the Blue Nile, which offered excellent swimming in its clear waters, or exploring a stretch of river in our inflatable craft equipped with outboard motor.

Our two kids enjoyed family outings by the Nile or in other favoured spots but as time went on they appreciated more obviously youthful pursuits. They made friends from amongst the sons and daughters of other expatriates and used to party and generally hang out with them. At this early stage of their lives they were interested in things British and Western rather than Arab and exotic. This was well illustrated when we stopped off in Cairo on the way back to UK for one of our first summer vacations. We did all the right things – the museum with its ancient sarcophagi and mummies, the pyramids (where we went round on horseback), and a 48-hour trip by train to Luxor to see the Valley of the Kings. What really roused Annabel and Edmund, however, was something very different.

'Hey, Dad, look over there!' Annabel suddenly exclaimed, pointing excitedly across the street as we were out walking one evening in Cairo.

'Yes, I'm looking,' I replied. 'Nothing remarkable as far as I can see.'

'It's a Wimpy Bar!'

'Yeah, a Wimpy Bar!' echoed Edmund.

'What's so special about a Wimpy Bar?' their mother asked, keeping a straight face.

'Come off it, Mum,' Annabel retorted. 'You know very well there's nothing like it in Khartoum. We've been starved of civilised life. Give us a break!'

So off we trooped into the chromium-bright fast-food vendor and ordered a quartet of chips-with-everything-style dishes, plus fizzy drinks.

On a rather different note, back in Khartoum, Joanna and I used to attend Sunday worship with the 'cathedral congregation'. This was served by the Anglican chaplain, Charles Bonsall, whom I had known in UK and whose presence in Sudan I had been partially instrumental in bringing about. The cathedral remaining closed, services were held in his large bungalow in the city centre.

Having got into the swing of it all, we found our new life-style pleasant and surprisingly stress-free.

There were a few irksome features, of course, like the non-availability of certain foodstuffs and occasional shortages of quite staple items – even bread, sometimes, when I would leave the house

Joanna and friends Tricia and Christine

at dawn and queue at the local bakery for up to an hour. From the very first summer of our return, too, it became necessary to queue several hours a week for petrol. This responsibility fell to me but I could arrange it without much difficulty around my lecturing duties. The casual chats I had with neighbours in the queue represented a useful opportunity to get to know people. Moreover, as most such conversations were in Arabic, my fluency in the language increased by leaps and bounds.

On completion of our first year together back in Sudan, Abdul Qayūm and Tricia Babiker returned from Germany, where Abdul (as we called him) had been on study leave. Tricia joined Joanna in the reception class of Clergy House School, where they and a teaching assistant worked as a team. Abdul returned to his position at the university.

We and the Babikers began sharing family activities, most memorably picnics in the desert west of Omdurman. There was a rocky mound, or *gawz*, not far from the edge of town, roughly in the form of a circle (it looked like a small crater). We had frequented this during our earlier period in Sudan, having been introduced to it by our friend Mahjoub. He had christened it *gawz abū digin*, 'Mound of the Bearded One', in my honour. Anyway, to this spot we and the Babikers – and sometimes others – would repair for late afternoon tea parties.

It was magic.

When we arrived it would still be hot, even in winter, but as the reddening sun declined the air would slowly cool. The first duty was to scour the area for kindling. At a casual glance the ground looked barren of combustible material but as we all walked off and round in widening circles there would be a call from someone who had found a few dry twigs that had dropped and then blown over from an acacia bush, or the excited shout from someone else who had stumbled on a pile of donkey dung – dried out and looking for all the world like nuggets of charcoal, which it also resembled in burning properties. Having got the fire going (Joanna's speciality) we would lie back on the sand with sandwiches and mugs of tea, or perhaps wander off to a rocky promontory to sit alone and watch the sun. The silence was immense. The great red disc would slowly decline until finally it touched the horizon, seconds later to be swallowed up – it almost seemed – by the very ground beneath.

And then the miracle would occur. As the sky gradually darkened – from the centre of the great dome above, down, down, down till the velvet mantle was enveloping us watchers – the softly-undulating sand and rust-brown rocks would brighten till they shone a fiery rose, throwing back the last rays of the sunless yet still glowing western sky. To this day, I have not seen a spectacle in nature to equal it.

One such picnic in the western desert surpassed all others. We had developed the habit of celebrating Christmas Eve in this way. As always, we would reach our chosen spot at around four and prepare the tea. We might be a little more hurried as we were awaiting something special – something that occurred regularly on the stroke of five – and we wanted to enjoy it to the full. On the top of a rock would be our short-wave radio and as the appointed hour approached we tuned in. On the occasion of which I speak we had penetrated to a more distant venue than usual. (We had named it 'Gordon Heights', I remember.) The sky was darkening and the sand beginning to glow. All was quiet.

I may have been the first to spot them, three heads bobbing above a fold of sand, heads that became men and men that became riders on camels. They were making for a city, those travellers – not to the west but to the east, and not associated with a famous king, yet like the wise men of yore they had come from far, perhaps from distant Darfur. We watched as, swaying and dipping, they passed us by on the last leg of their journey to Omdurman.

Minutes later the story was being told in thrilling song by a chorister – told to our little group three thousand miles away in an African desert, told to countless others in homes and castles, schools and colleges, ships, shops, shanty towns: *Once in royal David's city, Stood a lowly cattle shed …*

The Service of Nine Lessons and Carols, relayed by the BBC from the chapel of King's College, Cambridge, had begun. And the world held its breath in yearning and expectation.

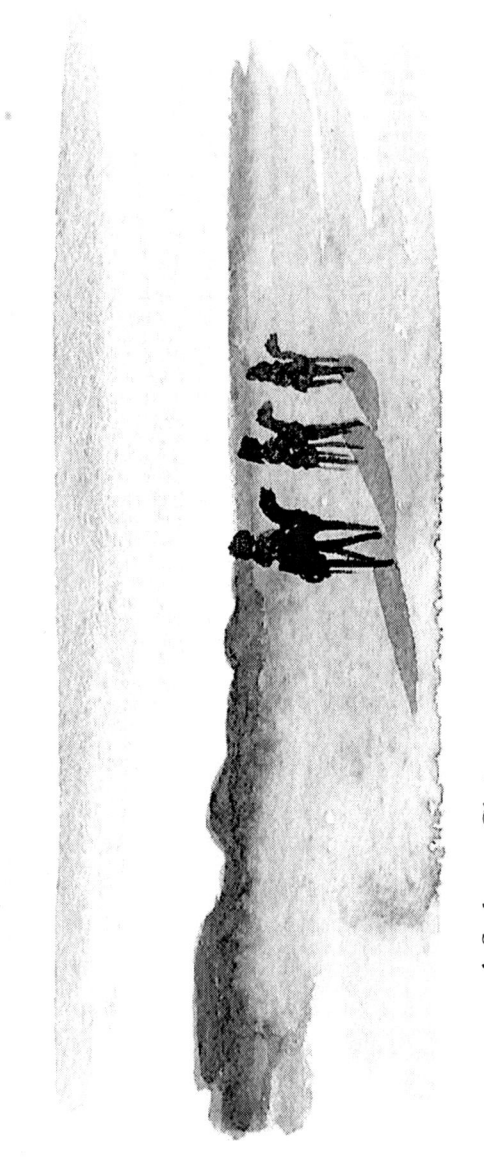

A Sudanese Christmas

***

After a while our friend Philip Gordon came to live with us, Mahjoub and family having moved into a smaller home where they had no spare room. 'The General', as we had taken to calling him after his famous namesake, was granted the third bedroom in our Beit al-Māl apartment. The arrangement worked well, partly perhaps because he lived a roving life and would quite often stay with one or other of his many Sudanese friends. He was an accomplished Arabist – effectively bilingual – and certainly had no problems of communication. By this time he had bought an old Land Rover, which he serviced himself (on one occasion he hoisted the engine out on a pulley attached to a convenient tree), and this enabled him to move around freely on or off road. We sometimes went on desert trips with him – one such featuring a gigantic storm resulting, quite literally, in 'streams in the desert'. Then, in 1980, a friend of ours from UK arrived in Sudan who was to change for ever The General's life.

When we first met Rosie Chard she was hardly out of her teens and singing in the choir of Probus church, where at the time I was priest-in-charge. Then, during our annual vacation in the early summer of 1980, I bumped into her father in Truro.

'You may be interested to hear our Rosie's applied to the Church Missionary Society,' he remarked. 'You were with them in Sudan, weren't you?'

'We were indeed,' I confirmed. 'Now we're back in Sudan – teaching, but no longer with the CMS. We're thoroughly enjoying it, as a matter of fact.'

'A teaching position is what Rosie's looking for.'

'An exciting prospect for her, John,' I said encouragingly.

A shadow crossed his brow. 'It didn't quite work out for you that first time in Sudan, I seem to remember,' he murmured.

'Well, we came back in a rather poor state of health but I wouldn't exactly put that down to the mission. I'm sure Rosie'll be fine.' The concerned parent grunted something and we went our separate ways.

Desert trip with Philip (The General), Rosie, Abdul and Tricia plus kids

A little later our friend passed her CMS selection committee and was assigned a teaching post at Unity High School, in Khartoum. We were delighted to hear this and arranged for her to spend an evening with us at our Cornish cottage. The General was staying in a small cottage he had acquired and was doing up in a nearby village and we asked him over to join us. (The property had a large hole in the roof when he found it and he bought it for one grand borrowed from his father!) Rosie plied both us and him with questions, we gave the required answers and she left in good spirits. A few months later she had increased the 700-odd British expatriate community in Khartoum by one, living in a shared flat in the school grounds. We then had her over to Omdurman to stay the night on a regular basis so she saw a lot of our fast-growing children – and, of course, The General.

***

Over those central years of our second spell in Sudan a number of guests came to stay with us, usually flying from UK and thus with a known time of arrival. Occasionally, however, visitors came overland so we weren't sure when they would turn up.

Our resident houseboy, who had a room downstairs in the yard, was Bolo, a refugee of long-standing from Congo. One morning as we were having breakfast he came up the stairs looking worried.

'*Rajul tihit fi hawsh*,' he announced in his very personal form of the national language. ('Man downstairs in compound.')

'A man?' I repeated. 'Inside the gates? Did you let him in?'

He responded indignantly that he had not and gestured excitedly towards the kitchen window. I looked out. Lying prone below me on a Sudanese *angareib* (rope-strung bed) was presumably a living soul though hardly recognisable as such because wrapped in tinfoil.

'It could be Hugh,' Joanna suggested. 'Wasn't he supposed to be arriving about now?'

I hurried down to the yard and prodded the motionless form a couple of times. It turned over and I found myself looking into the eyes of a young man with sandy, curling hair.

'So it *is* you, Hugh!' I exclaimed, rather unnecessarily. 'What on earth are you sleeping in?'

'Oh this,' he said, patting his bedding. 'Nothing on earth, as a matter of fact. It's my moon-bag. You know, what astronauts use.'

'I don't, actually. But anyway, how did you get in?'

'Climbed the wall, of course. I didn't like to disturb you. It's a bit high but wasn't too difficult. I found myself a bed, crawled inside this lunar thing and slept excellently. You'd be surprised how cosy it is.' It was quite late in the year, when nights can be cold. He climbed out of the bag, followed me upstairs and joined us at the breakfast table. We then plied him with questions about his trip.

We had got to know Hugh when he was studying theology under my father at Sherborne School. (Having retired as Chancellor of Truro Cathedral aged seventy-two, my father signed on as a part-time teacher.) Hugh had not long left the school and was back-packing round the world – highly fashionable at the time. On meeting us in Sherborne he had asked if we could offer him a staging-post, to which we happily agreed.

The trip was designed to get the wanderlust out of his system before going to drama school in preparation for a theatrical career. Pursue that career he successfully has, for Hugh Williams is better known to the public as Hugh Bonneville, of *Downton Abbey* fame.

Similar in some ways to our above friend's arrival though not quite so dramatic was that of a whole company of travellers, driving two new Land Rovers, a Unimog, a Volkswagen minibus and a motorbike. Anglo-German in composition, the party drove up late one afternoon and parked outside our gate. I was living alone in the flat at the time, Joanna having stayed on in England following our summer vacation.

The Land Rovers were the property of our friend Philip – or rather of his newly-formed company SEATS (Sudanese-European Agency for Tourist Services). He had driven overland from UK – give or take a ship or two – with Chris Hutton, an architect friend of ours from Cornwall days. Chris briefly described the experience.

'As you know,' he told me, 'the other Philip beguiled me last summer into being the driver of his second Land Rover on this loony adventure. Maybe I was rash to accept and indeed it was scarcely a holiday, but I actually found it rather relaxing – mentally relaxing, that is.'

'So you actually feel better for it.'

'I do. Life in a London practice is pretty frenetic these days. Simply getting contractors to pay bills can be a nightmare – that, and the fear of litigation if something goes wrong, pushing insurance premiums through the roof. All this I left behind. Indeed, I hardly gave it a thought. The whole trip turned out to be something of a tonic.'

'You also left behind Wendy and the girls,' I ventured.

He laughed. 'I didn't think so much about them either!'

'What of the journey itself?'

'Crossing Europe was fine, as was the ferry to Alexandria. Egypt, however, presented problems – bureaucratic ones. In the end we got the necessary papers and made it to Wady Halfa. Yet once there it seemed we'd get no further – at which point we met the Germans. Somehow the red tape was sorted and from then on we kept together. We would, I suppose, have made it through Sudan's empty quarter without the others, but their expertise was a real help.'

Caked in dust and sand, the weary over-landers were much relieved to be able to use the amenities of our apartment and clean themselves up. They then strolled off to stretch their legs and buy a few things, returning to settle down for the night – and several more, it transpired. Philip and Chris slept in the flat with me while the rest bedded down under canvas or in their vehicles outside. Our building was set back from the road, leaving them a convenient parking space. Chris had to leave after a week but Philip had business to do in Khartoum so stayed on.

I should explain the latter's position. He and our mutual friend Muhammad Sīd Ahmed had started up SEATS with the double purpose of taking European visitors to Sudan on trips into the desert or to Dinda game reserve further south, while at the same time taking Sudanese visitors to UK on trips round London or to other places of interest. Muhammad was to run the show in Sudan, Philip in London – which meant that our friend would no longer be living with us. The venture was carefully planned and theoretically viable, Philip even taking the trouble to obtain a licence to drive coaches and buses. The UK operation never properly got off the ground, however; there simply weren't enough Sudanese visiting the British capital. At our end the company had some success, Muhammad having on occasions

Poster for Philip Gordon's company SEATS

to pull in casual drivers like Abdul or myself. Certain tourists would have been surprised had they been told that the Sudanese guy at the wheel of their vehicle was a professor of mathematics!

I have, in describing the arrival of the overland group, jumped to late 1983. Much had happened in the intervening period.

In the autumn of 1980 Annabel entered boarding school in UK, with Edmund joining her the following year. They came out to Sudan three times a year for the holidays and we were at home for most of their summer term so children and parents were not apart for long periods. The school, however, went through a tricky patch on the staffing and discipline front while our two were there, a new and in some ways rather ineffectual headmaster being appointed the year Annabel entered. There were of course members of staff who were excellent, not least our friend John Pridmore, who had for some time been school chaplain. But both Annabel and Edmund in different ways endured unpleasant spells during their time at the school.

Life in Sudan proceeded smoothly for both Joanna and me until 1982 – apart from the increasingly frequent queuing for bread, sugar, gas cylinders or petrol. In the summer of that year Joanna felt compelled to resign from her position at Khartoum International Primary School (formerly Clergy House School) over the conduct of its new chairman of governors. He was Sudanese and had a reputation for getting things done. The school wanted to implement a number of changes and most parents and teachers were pleased to give him their support. Joanna, however, became worried not so much by what he did as how he did it. His method, consistently applied, was pressure and threats and she wanted none of it.

So that autumn she was out of a job. She found a position as Head of the new Indian Modern School but it was a case of out of the frying pan into the fire. Her hands were tied by the Indian chairperson who, while wanting a British Head, was not prepared to implement British educational standards. Six months later Joanna resigned and was again unemployed.

Meanwhile, all continued well for me as lecturer at the Faculty of Education. My colleagues were the easiest people to work with, while the students were polite, attentive and appreciative. In one or two cases the normal student-teacher relationship was transcended.

Philip with graduating students, 1984

'Why don't you and your wife come and stay with us in Wad Medani for a night or two,' Khalid, an older student, asked me one day. 'I've often talked about you to Jamīla and she'd like to meet you both.'

I was touched by the offer and, as it happened, we had both been wanting to visit his home town, situated in the cotton-growing region known as the Gezira.

'A great idea, Khalid,' I responded, 'which I really appreciate. We'll take you up on it as soon as we find a suitable date.'

'How about the coming *eid* holiday?'

'Sounds perfect.'

The holiday came and the trip was made. Our hosts, who had two young children, gave us a wonderful time, from the carefully chosen destinations for our daytime trips with Khalid to the traditional Sudanese fare of the evening meals prepared by Jamīla. I still recall the glorious shrubs and flowers cultivated in some of the government centres we visited in the fertile region.

Each year Joanna and I held a tea party in our home for graduating students. These occasions involved home-grown music, which could mean me strumming a banjo for old-time songs, or a student called Seif al-Dīn, with lute and voice rendering his own poignant folk-songs. It was no surprise years later to come across a taped recording of his vocal repertoire on sale in the Gulf – by then under the name of Seif al-Jāmia, 'Sword of the University', a judicious modification of the name of his birth, which means 'Sword of Religion'.

Talking of religion, I might point out that every now and then I had to field an interesting question from one of my students, particularly when it was realised I had taken the trouble to learn Arabic. I would be asked, very seriously, 'Why aren't you a Muslim?' Occasionally the query took a more pointed form, 'Are you a Muslim?' In either case I would reply that though the Arabic language and Arab culture fascinated me, this had not led to a change in my convictions. The way was then open for me – indeed, it was no more than a courtesy – to explain why I was a Christian.

***

Sport and amateur dramatics represented enjoyable leisure activities during this period. The former, for me, meant squash in the Sudan Club and running with the 'Hash House Harriers', featuring paper-chases with a beery aftermath. Annabel and Edmund appreciated the latter weekly event when they were on holiday with us. I also competed several times in the annual Three Towns half-marathon and was pleased to discover I was not on the athletic shelf. Later I joined Khartoum Cricket Club, renewing my involvement in the game for the first time since schooldays on that 'lyrically green cricket ground' in Khartoum North.

Amateur dramatics for me meant pantomime and roles like the Wicked Queen, Genie of the Lamp, and Captain Hook. Joanna, meanwhile, worked on the stage sets, both designing and painting. Annabel and Edmund became involved in these annual pantomimes too, even when they were arriving in Khartoum off the 'lollipop special' just a day or two before Christmas.

I was at this time supposed to be working on a doctoral thesis, my MA research having been upgraded, but was inclined to be dilatory.

'Possession of a higher degree is not important to me, darling,' I argued to Joanna.

'Don't be ridiculous,' was her immediate riposte. 'It would be extremely short-sighted to chuck things at this stage. A PhD could prove a crucial asset.'

Her logic was unassailable so I pressed on with my investigation into the segmental sounds of Sudanese colloquial Arabic.

My studies reached a climax in 1983, when students of the university went on strike over 'government interference', armoured vehicles appearing on campus following a mysterious student death. Nimeiri promptly closed the university but staff members were required to remain in place until matters were settled. Nothing was resolved over the next three months and there followed the summer vacation. This resulted in my enjoying six months free from distraction during which to write my thesis up. In September I submitted it and in mid-December flew home for my viva – when I learnt that my two-volume study was acceptable without revision.

Pantomime poster, by Joanna

A final experience from this period deserves to be recorded here: eight days spent in a quite different part of the world.

In July 1982 Joanna and I flew to India to visit my uncle at the Oxford Mission in Behala, Calcutta. We flew Pan Am 'Trans-Continental Clipper' on a Boeing 747 – our first experience of a jumbo. I remember a fascinating conversation between two Indian gentlemen going on near us during the flight. They spoke of their erstwhile colonial rulers almost with affection.

'What do you think about this amazing Falkland Islands campaign the British are conducting against the Argentinians,' one asked the other.

'Oh, we know the British too well, don't we?' the other replied. 'Is it credible they can lose this conflict? I think not.'

'Yes, they are smart. They will never let an upstart like Galtieri have his way. Look at Mrs Thatcher – so tough. She will not flinch, you can be sure.'

We touched down in Delhi, for which, with Agra, we had reserved for ourselves a single day. There we glimpsed imperial splendour dreamed up by Lutyens. In Agra we paid homage to the Taj Mahal and ferreted out an Indian colleague from Khartoum. But it was Calcutta that truly impressed: the Victoria Monument; the bustling thoroughfares (street dwellers scarcely shocked, after Khartoum); Mother Theresa's 'Home for the Dying' next to a garish Hindu temple to Kali; eighty-something-year-old Sister Florence, Oxford Mission, working among lepers (she once declined an invitation to appear on Terry Wogan's TV chat show because of a tea-party engagement, eventually retiring aged around a hundred); the Mission School for Orphans and its orchestra; Father Theodore and a talented young cellist; Father Victor and his work among sailors; the watery, palm-fringed villages of West Bengal with their mildewed yet somehow elegant mansions; finally Uncle Jim, driving us nimbly round a packed city in the inevitable 'Ambassador' (1956 Morris Oxford, as was), showing us the sights, chatting in Bengali to passers-by, introducing us to unforgettable characters from – as it seemed – another world, another age.

Such was our last encounter with my Indian uncle.

St Martin's

VI

Watersheds, Private and Public

In 1983 we sold our home in Carharrack, Cornwall, and bought a new one in Sherborne, Dorset. The reason for choosing the latter market town was twofold: my parents now lived there, and it was a lot closer than Cornwall to our children's school not far from London. It also had a railway station and nearby trunk road, making it very accessible.

St Martin's is a late Georgian house with a good-sized garden, making it an excellent family home. After we had bought it we discovered from my maternal aunt, Lorna Kimber (née MacAdam), that she and her mother – my grandmother – had rented and lived in the house for a while during the war. At the time I was a baby just up the road. My father, having recently returned from Africa, joined the staff of Sherborne Abbey and we were living in the curate's house – until we were bombed out of it in the raid of 1940.

We spent Christmas 1983 at St Martin's, Joanna having stayed on after our summer vacation to take possession of our new home while I extended the visit I had made to UK for my doctoral viva. The festive dinner was notable because my parents, brother, sister and her family all joined us and our two youngsters round the table. We had not had such a gathering for years.

The year 1983 thus proved something of a watershed for us. It was a watershed for two friends as well.

Philip Gordon can be said to have had more than one reason for driving, in company with our friend Chris Hutton, some three thousand miles to Khartoum late in 1983. Certainly he wished to bring out the two Land Rovers for his company, SEATS. Yet he

A Beit al-Māl style laundry, sketched from our balcony

also wanted to see Rosie Chard. Chris having left and the others having decamped from outside our gate, Philip naturally remained with me in Omdurman while seeing to new business developments. Of an evening we would, as so often before, seat ourselves on the balcony overlooking the dusty street and talk things over with a glass of something. (No longer brandy, which we had often enjoyed together; it and other alcoholic beverages were no longer available, as I will shortly explain.) On one of these evenings my companion suddenly became serious.

'Philip,' he said, 'I want to ask you something. It's about Rosie.'

I was instantly attentive. 'No problem. Fire ahead.'

Never a man for preliminaries, he came straight to the point. 'I'm thinking of proposing marriage. What do you think?'

I had no need to ponder the issue as both Joanna and I knew exactly what we thought. 'It's an excellent idea. My other half would say the same, I know.'

'Good,' he responded. 'And thanks. I shall follow your advice.'

That was that. Point settled. Time to talk about something else.

A day or so later Philip wrote a letter declaring his intentions and dropped it in at Rosie's flat in Khartoum – scurrying off immediately. Rosie read it a few hours later. The exact sequence of events from this point I am not fully cognizant of but the upshot was that Rosie accepted this proposal – a rather unusual one for the late twentieth century – and the two became engaged. They were married the following June in Probus church, Cornwall, where, having obtained the bishop's permission, I tied the knot. They were the last couple I was to 'join in Holy Matrimony'.

'I think I must be unique in having driven three thousand miles – and crossed deserts – to propose to my beloved,' Philip announced in his reception speech. He turned to her, smiling slightly. 'I hope, Rosie, you will always remember this.'

***

If 1983 turned out to be a watershed for us and our two friends, it was a watershed on a far larger scale for the Sudanese people.

President Jaafar Nimeiri had been finding things increasingly difficult. Since coming to power as an army colonel in the coup of 1969 (the year Colonel Muammar al-Gaddafi, in Libya, also hoisted himself to national leadership), he had had to fend off a succession of insurrections. One of them, that of 1971, we have already mentioned. He had also found it necessary to suppress two Sufi Orders, the Ansar and the Khatmiyya. By the eighties he was running out of options. Economically the country – though the recipient of considerable foreign aid – was sinking, this becoming very evident as the Sudanese pound rapidly lost value, power cuts multiplied, and queues for petrol, gas cylinders, certain foodstuffs and other essentials lengthened. Petrol was put on rationing but this did not stop the long lines of cars. I once had my car in a queue for three days, sleeping in the back for the second night in order to be ready to move early next morning if the tanker arrived. Nimeiri's popularity plummeted, notwithstanding a presidential election in which he, the single candidate, gained – as his subjects sardonically commented – 110% of the votes. The President needed a miracle, and knew where to find one.

With the backing of his attorney general, the Muslim Brotherhood leader Hassan al-Turābi, the President turned to religion. In September 1983 he poured all the whisky he could find into the Nile (he'd enjoyed his scotch as an army officer, so this must have been difficult), implemented *shari'a* law country-wide and turned to Saudi Arabia. The royals across the water, welcoming such a spectacular conversion (they'd probably stipulated it), shelled out readily enough with the goodies, most importantly black gold – oil, petrol, 'benzine'.

To the disappointment of his people, the queues did not evaporate overnight. Nothing in fact seemed to change – apart from a new and highly distasteful responsibility imposed upon every Sudanese citizen, that of grassing on your neighbour. Instructions were issued by the government that any observed shortfall in religious zeal should be reported to the authorities. Failure to do so would be to risk being taken into custody. Courts of 'summary justice' were set up, victims 'tried' and judicial sentences – lashings, double amputations, imprisonment – were implemented and publicized daily on Radio Omdurman. Married male expatriates were obliged, when out with their wives, to have their marriage certificates with them as on-the-spot evidence to the police that they were not adulterers; similarly, when in 1984 Annabel, having left school in UK, took a year out teaching at our friend Tricia's infant school in Khartoum, I carried her birth certificate if she was with me in the car to prove she was my daughter. The nation had entered an era of the strictest Islamic purity.

The southern Sudanese were incensed by the implementation of *shari'a* law in their region, largely Christian or animist, and soon the civil war that had raged between south and north from 1955 till 1972 (when Nimeiri himself had ended it) flared up again. The American-educated John Garang headed the Sudan People's Liberation Army which led the new offensive against the forces of the Khartoum government.

President Nimeiri was making enemies elsewhere, too.

Colonel Gaddafi's stance was strongly anti-Western and he was very unhappy about Nimeiri's support for the American-brokered Camp David Accords of 1978, which had led to peace between Israel and Egypt. He had already been lending support to groups opposing Nimeiri; now he took the remarkable step of sending a Soviet-built Tupolev TU 22 bomber across the Sudan border to target the capital. This was in March 1984, one Friday morning.

Joanna and I were in our Omdurman flat at the time when a huge explosion, followed by the whine of a jet, stunned us both. Joanna rushed to a back window.

'Philip, here – quickly!' she cried. 'A plane just above us – I can even see its rivets.' She paused for a second or two, and then went on, 'It's climbing away to the north. Extraordinary!'

'Yes, yes,' I shouted back, 'but now *you* come *here*!' I had gone in the opposite direction, to a south-facing window, on hearing the blast. 'Just look at this!' In a moment Joanna had joined me, in time to see a heavy cloud of dust and smoke mushrooming high in the direction of the radio station, perhaps a quarter of a mile away. We watched in silence for a little.

'You know what that might have hit,' I said suddenly. 'The Tuckers' house. I'd better do something.' Colonel Tommy Tucker

```
                                              BRITISH EMBASSY
                                              KHARTOUM

        TO WHOM IT MAY CONCERN

        This is to certify that
        Mr/Mrs/Miss .......P. H. BLAIR................

        holder of Passport No. ...C 620930 C.........

        is a British/.................... citizen.

        As such he/she is entitled to the protection of British
        Embassy Consular Officials, who, under the provisions of
        the Vienna Convention on Consular Relations, have immediate
        right of access to him/her.

        In the event of difficulties, please contact the British
        Embassy, Aboulela Building, Barlaman Avenue, telephone
        numbers 70767, 70768 and 80828. Embassy opening hours are
        from 0800 to 1400 hours Saturday to Thursday inclusive.

        Outside these hours the Consul, Mr. M A Corbett, can be
        contacted at House 41, Street 51, Khartoum II and the Vice
        Consul Mr. Ralph Allen at Plot 31 Street 31E New Extension.
```

السفارة البريطانية
الخرطوم

الى من يهمه الامر

نشهد بان السيد / السيدة / الانسة ...P. H. BLAIR...
حامل / تحمل جواز سفر رقم ......C 620930 C......
الجنسية البريطانية / الايرلندية / .... وبالتالي فهو / تحت حماية ممثلي القسم القنصلي بالسفارة البريطانية . تحت اتفاقية فينا للعلاقات القنصلية . حسب هذه الاتفاقية لممثلي القنصلية الحق في مقابلته / مقابلتها فورا في حالة حدوث صاحب إبراز هذه الشهادة بالسفارة البريطانية .
عمارة ابو العلا الجديدة شارع البرلمان تلفونات ٨٠٨٢٨/٧٠٧١٧
ساعات العمل من الساعة الثامنة صباحا الى الثانية بعد الظهر من السبت الى الخميس . في غير ساعات العمل يمكن الاتصال بالقنصل مستر م . ا . كوربيت منزل رقم ٤١ شارع ٥١ الخرطوم ٢ او نائب القنصل ر . الن منزل ٣١ شارع ٣١ الامتداد الجديد .

Philip's certificate from the British Embassy

was leader of the British Army Training Team (BATT), working with the Sudanese military. He and his family lived a little way south of us on the Nile road.

My responsibilities in Sudan by this time were not restricted to university teaching: the British Embassy had appointed me 'warden' for British personnel living in Omdurman. (I have sometimes wondered if this was the real summit of my career.) I hurried downstairs and got out my bike – or maybe the car – and made for the Tucker home. It was intact, mercifully, but no one was in. There was nothing more to be done so I returned home, where Joanna reminded me that our near-neighbours usually went sailing on Fridays. I couldn't report to my embassy boss as we had no telephone and I had not as yet been issued with a short-wave radio.

Very soon, however, there was a further development: loud knocking on our gate. I went down and opened up. Confronting me was a family of four we knew well. The parents looked distracted, if not distraught; the two children were silent.

'Sue, Evan,' I said at once, 'you look dreadful! What has happened?' Evan carried one child in his arms while Sue gripped a pushchair in which the other, a baby boy, was sitting motionless. Behind them was their car, parked under our tree.

'We've come to take refuge,' Evan explained, his voice not quite steady. 'I'll explain in a minute.'

'Come in, come in, all of you, and we'll make some tea. You need reviving, clearly.'

Evan and Sue France, with their two young children, had come to Sudan under the auspices of the Church Missionary Society as replacements for the Barffs, who had of course replaced us. Naturally, they had inherited our old home, the River House. I closed the gate behind them as they entered and we trooped upstairs. With the family settled in chairs, sipping tea or soft drinks as appropriate, we listened to their story.

'We were at the children's service in Khartoum this morning,' Sue began. 'We usually go, as you know. We stayed for a while but then set out for home. When we got there …' Her voice began to falter and there were tears in her eyes as she looked across at her husband.

He took up the story. 'We'd heard what sounded like explosions of some kind but didn't think too much of it. Then, when we reached the River House, we couldn't believe our eyes. The place was in a shambles, the windows blown in and glass strewn everywhere. But what really got to us was finding bits of the glass in Jonathan's cot, under the window. What the result would have been had he been in it at the time of the explosion doesn't bear thinking.'

Evan stopped abruptly, the enormity of it overwhelming him. Joanna and I kept silent until he was able to continue. What of course had happened, he explained, was that a bomb had fallen well short of the radio station and not so far from their house, resulting in the devastation they had just witnessed.

The Frances went off in due course to some mutual friends, Christine and Abdullah Osman, who opened their home to them. Joanna and I decided to go to the club to relax and we stayed there till evening. On returning to our flat we faced yet another development. Philip Gordon, who continued to use our home as a base, was there with Rosie. She often came over to stay the night and she it was that broke the news.

'You've got visitors,' she announced cheerfully as we walked in quite late. 'The Tuckers. They're asleep in the spare room.'

'Okay,' said Joanna, blinking slightly. 'Anything else?'

'Oh yes,' Rosie replied at once. 'Just listen to this.' She paused for a moment, eyes widening as if scarcely able herself to believe her next item of news. 'Apparently one bomb failed to detonate and lodged itself in the outside loo of the house next to the Tuckers – one of the servants having only just left it!'

We later learnt that though the radio station had escaped damage – it was unquestionably the target – five people had lost their lives in the raid. We also heard about speculation that Nimeiri himself was the culprit, arranging the bombing so that he could blame it on Libya and whip up public sympathy. We have never taken the idea seriously; the attack, coming out of the blue, bore all the hallmarks of the eccentric Libyan colonel.

***

For us personally the year 1984 turned out to be a good one. Edmund's troubles at school were fading into the past and he was doing well, we had Annabel living with us once again from August, and Joanna was offered a job. This was not a teaching post, however, but that of administrative secretary to the director of a design firm. She settled into the position quickly and enthusiastically, especially appreciating the fact that she was encouraged to contribute to certain projects herself. She had always had a flare for art and design and it was exciting to be involved in the sphere commercially. More importantly, the company – wholly Sudanese – was a largely family affair and behaved as such. To this day Joanna looks back on her two years with Afrograph as one of her happiest employment experiences.

The year 1985 began sadly. On 15 January my father died at home in Sherborne. He was aged eighty-two and had for some time been suffering from a progressive heart problem. I had been wondering whether to take a trip home on my own to see him and decided to do so in February, when the visit would coincide with a university break as well as half-term at Edmund's school. My father was on a new drug that was proving effective and there seemed no imminent threat of death. When the news came through that he had passed away, I could have kicked myself for not having gone home sooner. The one positive factor, to some extent assuaging my sense of guilt, was the fact that a few days before he died I had a telephone conversation with him, when we were able to say a lot to each other.

I might mention, incidentally, that at the time making international phone calls was a major operation. Few people in Khartoum and Omdurman had phones that worked at all – ours certainly didn't. To make an international call you had to go to Khartoum central post office, book your call and then wait in a queue for several hours before making it. I phoned my mother in this way on hearing the sudden, so-sad news – which I think came in the form of a telegram. She said she was bearing up and that I should stick to my plan to come home in February, when there would be a memorial service at Sherborne School.

Harold Blair aged 82

My father's death upset me and for a while I only half believed he had gone. (I learnt, incidentally, that he had hastened his own passing by finally declining the new drug he was on; it apparently had some most unpleasant side-effects.) The two of us had been close from my childhood up, sharing much that was personal, intellectual, spiritual. Joanna keenly felt his passing too. Well before we had become 'an item' she had grown to respect him as her divinity teacher at Truro High School, and once we were married she was welcomed with open arms into the Blair family.

But if my emotions were heightened this didn't seem to affect my performance. I have heard the issue discussed on the media, especially in relation to sport. If an athlete decides not to withdraw from an event following a major bereavement, what effect will it have? As it happened, three days after my father's death I played the innings of my life in a cricketing fixture. I remember murmuring (emotionally) to Joanna, on my return to the pavilion, 'That was for Dad!'

My trip home in February for the memorial service represented a form of 'closure' – as the term is these days.

'I've been so touched by the love and respect for your father people have shown,' my mother declared. 'Indeed, the love has overflowed onto me. Relatives, friends, even casual acquaintances have been amazingly supportive.'

'I'm not surprised,' I told her. 'You and Dad have helped so many people. They want you to know.'

'Well, perhaps. But there's something I need to ask you. It's about editing his book, which I've been trying to deal with. It's quite a task – though of course I consider it an honour.' She paused, looking slightly doubtful. 'To come to the point, could you help me, back in Sudan, particularly with the Greek in the text?'

'No problem at all,' I assured her. 'I'll take a copy of the manuscript, work on it and get it back by April. We'll then be home for the vacation – just two months away.'

The Kaleidoscope of Truth had been accepted for publication only weeks before my father's death. It was on Clement of Alexandria, an early Christian thinker awarded the name 'Beloved Teacher' by grateful disciples – a title equally appropriate to my father, I felt. The book, his fourth, finally appeared in early 1986.

The commemoration held in Sherborne School chapel lacked nothing. Harold Arthur Blair had been administrator and man of action (Africa), pastor (England), scholar (anthropology in Africa; theology in England), teacher (England). He was truly a man for all seasons. The service drew those strands together in masterly fashion, thanks to one of his teaching colleagues who both planned the event and gave the address.

My parents had been married for fifty-three years. They experienced a period of slight tension after the war, when my mother was in indifferent health and my father – always super-conscientious – was immersed in parochial responsibilities. But by any measure their marriage was a wonderful one.

***

Death, they sometimes say, comes in clusters; it often comes in pairs – as we found that January, 1985.

Mahmoud Muhammad Taha was the leader of a Muslim sect in Sudan called the Republican Brothers. It could best be described as a Sufi sect since it interpreted the religion of Islam in a more spiritual and liberal way than the norm. For example, Mahmoud taught that adherence to traditional forms and frequency of corporate assembly, public and private prayer, fasting and suchlike, was important but not ultimately essential. All these things, he said, were crutches and supports rather than ends in themselves. They were designed to assist the believer in achieving the spiritual goal: God living within him or her. Especially 'her', for Mahmoud believed that women within Islam should be freed from restrictions with which they had traditionally been bound. Yet while making these points he insisted he was truly Muslim, drawing his inspiration from the Qur'ān.

I had come to know of the Republican Brothers because of students I taught who had become his admirers – one in particular, whom I will call Mansour. The latter impressed me greatly, as a budding academic and as a personality. He had a level of openness and honesty that in my experience was extremely rare. We used to chat together from time to time and on one occasion went quite deeply into his religious beliefs. I found them surprisingly close to my own so, suitably emboldened, put a leading question to him.

'What, Mansour, does the figure of Jesus mean to you?'

'A great deal,' he replied at once. 'I respond particularly to the fact that his message was so spiritual – the idea, for example, that what lies within is what really matters.'

'That's a most interesting point to single out. What about the things he did, and his claims?'

'He clearly did remarkable things, not least his miracles. At its simplest, I would say he was unique.'

I fastened on the reference to miracles. 'What do you make of the supreme miracle, Mansour? I mean his resurrection from the dead.' I thought for a moment. 'I know Muslims normally say he never truly died. But what do you think? Do you believe he rose from the dead?'

He looked me in the eye. 'Yes,' he said, 'I do.'

We discussed the matter no further; I told him his position was essentially Christian and left it at that. Our relationship did not end there, however, or indeed with his departure from the university. Sometime later, after the dramatic events I am about to describe, he went to England for higher studies, where he got in touch with me to ask if I could support his request for political asylum. He was fearful of returning to Sudan because of his known Republican sympathies, fearing imprisonment or worse, and I was only too happy to testify to the gravity of his position. As far as I know his petition was successful.

In the early eighties Mahmoud Taha started to attract a measure of criticism from strict Muslims and then, as the country's problems multiplied throughout 1984 despite the 'moral straitjacket' of *shari'a* law, he was accused of anti-government activities. One day we woke up to find that he and his close supporters (including Mansour) had been arrested, and over the final weeks of the year and into 1985 the media were relentless in reporting the case against Mahmoud and his 'heretical' movement. His views were expounded in detail, and an almost hour-by-hour account was given of the attempts of Muslim clerics and lawyers to persuade the religious leader of the error of his ways and the need to recant. It became evident that he was, first of all, accused of sedition but that failing to make this accusation stick the authorities commuted the charge to that of

Crowds celebrating the fall of Nimeiri, as seen from River House balcony

blasphemy. The story was then put around that his wicked teaching was the principle cause of the country's many woes – including a prolonged drought that had caused the Nile to be at a historic low.

Sedition or blasphemy, it made no difference: the man in the dock would not budge. However, since it was clear his life was on the line he suggested to his closest followers, who seemed likely to share his fate, that they foreswear his views and go free. The trial proceeded inexorably, culminating in recantations by several of Mahmoud's innermost circle – in due course released after strict warning, together with the rest of those apprehended – and the sentence of death by hanging pronounced upon their 76-year-old leader.

Mahmoud was publicly hanged in Kober Prison, Khartoum North, on the morning of Friday, 18 January 1985. I still have an Arabic paper reporting the event the next day. The banner headline read: 'The nation has been purged of his spiritual fornication'.

A few moments before the sentence was carried out someone pushed through the crowd and tossed a single rose onto the raised platform on which the gibbet was erected – a historic gesture symbolizing love and admiration for a Sufi saint. Immediately following the hanging a helicopter flew up and landed in the prison forecourt. Mahmoud's body was dumped on board, the helicopter took off again and flew to an unknown desert spot, where the body was interred. The authorities were worried that if the location were known it would become a religious shrine and place of pilgrimage – perhaps, indeed, the focus of actual sedition.

An uneasy quiet hung over the capital for days, and hushed voices – 'hushed' because of the ubiquitous 'secret police' – discussed the abyss into which the country seemed to be falling. My Sudanese colleagues at the Faculty of Education were scathing in their condemnation.

'This affair will not be forgotten,' one of them commented. 'If you ask me, it will be the last nail in Nimeiri's coffin.'

On 6 April, following a month or more of generally non-violent but insistent demonstrations throughout the capital, General Suwar al-Dhahab, who had a reputation for being 'a gentleman', took over the reins of government. Not a shot had been fired. Nimeiri had lost all credibility, his support collapsing, including that of the army. He was, however, allowed to leave the country and go into exile in Egypt – luckier in this respect than most deposed leaders.

There was universal rejoicing at his departure. Crowds marched round Khartoum laughing and singing, the most popular refrain being *'Yā Nimeiri, yā humār!'* 'O Nimeiri, O you donkey!' (The name 'Nimeiri' actually means 'little leopard'.) Even the weather seemed in sympathy: downpours of rain occurred in many regions, ending the long period of drought. A second ditty quickly became current, *'Nimeiri fāt, al-matara jāt!'*, which could be rendered, 'Nimeiri's done, the rain has come!' The Sudanese people relished the irony.

There was one other immediate and dramatic development: the petrol queues vanished. The reason was soon on everyone's lips: Nimeiri had been funding his 40,000 secret police (this was the figure bandied around) by allowing them to sell huge quantities of the petrol coming from Saudi Arabia on the black market. It was tempting to conclude that a real 'new dawn' had begun for the country. Certainly many felt it had, not least Nimeiri's successor as President, who announced that his term of office would be short-lived as he would hand power over to a democratically elected government within a year.

I personally was left with deep thoughts that April. In particular, I pondered afresh the power of sacrifice, in this case of sacrificial death – for that was how I interpreted the execution of Mahmoud Muhammad Taha. 'Death' was, of course, a theme I had been contemplating: my own father's death three days before that of Mahmoud, as well as the hundredth anniversary of the death of General Gordon in Khartoum eight days after it – a coincidence I noted with interest.

The day after Mahmoud's death I happened to read in the New Testament the following words of Jesus to religious leaders of his day: 'Woe to you, teachers of the law and Pharisees, you hypocrites! … You snakes! You brood of vipers! How will you escape being condemned to hell? Therefore I am sending you prophets and wise men and teachers. Some of them you will kill and crucify; others you will flog in your synagogues and pursue from town to town.

And so upon you will come all the righteous blood that has been shed on earth.'

The parallel was obvious: Jesus was tried by the religious authorities, who wanted to nail him for sedition, but failing in this they got him instead for blasphemy. Mahmoud Muhammad Taha was tried by the religious authorities …

Things don't change much, I thought.

***

In slight mitigation of the solemn events we experienced or witnessed that January, there was a happy development for us as a family early in the year: a return to our old home in the al-Mourada district of Omdurman, the River House.

The France family had returned to UK permanently, following the bombing experience and then, in the summer of 1984, having to survive a full month in Omdurman without electricity. Noticing that the house was remaining empty, we began negotiating with the Church of Sudan in the hope of obtaining the lease. We finally signed the contract on 13 February, hiring a lorry to move our possessions from Beit al-Māl to al-Mourada eight days later. It was almost thirteen years since we had left the house to go on leave at the end of what was meant to be just the first of many missionary tours.

Philip and Rosie Gordon were staying with us at the time and I recall the moment when we were sitting together on the veranda drinking tea, having just made the move.

'This is full circle, isn't it,' I said. 'Here we are, after so many years, back in the River House.' I looked across at Joanna. 'It's like the ultimate seal on our decision to pack up for the second time to live and work in the Arab world. We have, you might say, finally come home.'

After a brief silence, Rosie suddenly shivered. 'Stop it, Philip!' she pleaded. 'You're making me feel quite peculiar.'

Three days after this 'homecoming' I was on a plane to London. I was making the trip to UK already mentioned to attend the memorial service for my father, and was flying 'Skypak'. I must explain what the latter meant.

Joanna and I, like most expats, used to find economical ways to fly to London for short visits home. The Skypak company recruited people on a one-off basis to act as couriers; they paid for your flight on a good carrier to a European destination in exchange for the responsibility of supervising their mail bag. You then had to make your own arrangement for a return flight so naturally looked for the cheapest possible ticket. Bulgarian Airways – or 'Vulgar Bulgar' – was a popular choice, as it significantly undercut other carriers, taking you through Sofia, behind the Iron Curtain, where you had to change planes (Russian Tupolovs). I flew with them a couple of times, my main memory being the in-flight meal, featuring bullet-hard peas and very old, wrinkled apples. A more positive recollection, I should perhaps mention, is being at the airport one December and being directed along an uncovered path beside magnificent, snow-covered Christmas trees.

Joanna flew Bulgarian to be home for the children's half-term on one occasion. She recalls stern, leather-clad females monitoring the airport building, one of whom she found the courage to approach.

'Where should I wait?' she asked.

'Sit there till we tell you!' the woman barked, and pointed to a bench. Joanna dutifully did as she was told. When, finally, she was boarding her plane there was a free-for-all as passengers scrambled for seats. Her patience ran out.

'Give me the ugly face of capitalism any day,' she remarked loudly.

From the back of the plane came a cheery cockney voice, 'Think of the money, darling, think of the money!'

Towards the end of April 1985 Joanna and I were together on a flight to Amman, Jordan, where we were stopping off to visit friends – the Brisley family – before flying on to UK for our summer vacation. We had actually done the same the year before, when our friends had taken us round important sites like the Roman city of Gerash, Mount Nebo, the Dead Sea and, inevitably, 'the rose-red city half as old as time', Petra.

For me, Jordan had nostalgia from the visits I had made over a quarter of a century previously. I think some of this had rubbed

Philip and Joanna at Azraq in Jordan (above), while staying with the Brisley family (below)

off onto Joanna, not least through what was becoming a mutual fascination with the personality of T.E. Lawrence. One of our favourite National Trust sites in England had helped to foster this interest, what must surely represent the Trust's smallest property, Cloud's Hill. This was Lawrence's tiny 'getaway' cottage while he was – long after his Arabian adventures – a private in the army stationed at Bovington, in Dorset. Nearby is the stretch of road where, at the age of forty-seven, after apparently swerving on his Broughton motor-cycle, he crashed and was killed. Joanna and I have visited Cloud's Hill, half-hidden among the trees by the side of the road, many times. It somehow evokes Lawrence's enigmatic character, as well as – to us at least – the Middle East.

In Jordan on this second holiday with Dave and Candy Brisley, our godson Richard and little Victoria (who shares a birthday with me), we took a trip to Azraq, an oasis settlement of Roman provenance but associated also with Lawrence. He and his men sometimes sheltered there during the Arab Revolt of 1916-18. We never made it to Wady Rum, associated even more strongly with Lawrence – a pleasure in store. Standing on the stones of the citadel of Azraq was good enough at the time.

We visited Mount Nebo for the second time, and having looked over the Jordan valley to see if we could make out the domes of Jerusalem on the skyline (we couldn't), wandered down a slope to Moses' Spring, reputedly near the unknown – and, according to the Bible, 'unknowable' – location of Moses' tomb.

After we had had our picnic beside the gushing stream we fell to discussing how Victoria, now around two years old, could follow in her brother's footsteps and be baptized, or, as people generally call it, 'christened'. Joanna and I had already been selected as godparents, plus another friend of the family. The problem, not unusual, was how to get everyone together in one place and at one time.

Joanna suddenly piped up. 'Why can't we baptize Victoria – here, now, in the waters of Moses' spring?'

There was an astonished silence.

'But... er ...', someone stammered, 'we haven't got what we need? I mean, not all three godparents, no prayer books. And this can't be official – we're not in a church!'

My wife swept every objection aside.

'Philip is – or was – a priest. In any case, all Christians can baptize according to the Bible. What we *do* have here is plenty of water, the one thing needful, surely. Philip can remember the service – can't you darling?' She turned imperiously towards me.

'Well, yes, more or less – the basics anyway.'

We were convinced – and preparations began immediately. One of us (I forget who) stood proxy for the missing godparent.

The baptismal candidate was 'sprinkled' with – not dipped into – the waters of the spring, the important words were pronounced, the promises made and the Amens said. Little Victoria had been formally received into the Church of Jesus Christ.

I later wrote to the Anglican chaplain in Amman telling him what we had done and asking if possibly Victoria's name could be included on the official list of those baptized in Jordan. I received a courteous reply, the chaplain turning out to be a member of the Church Missionary Society whom I had met in our missionary days. He was only too pleased to enter Victoria's name into the register and he forwarded a certificate to that effect. We were very pleased – especially Joanna.

On our last full day in Jordan we all took a trip up north, to Gadara. We went, indeed, beyond that ancient town to have our picnic on the slopes overlooking the Jordan valley and Lake of Galilee, to the north-west, with views due north of the Golan Heights. We were, in fact, looking straight at the modern state of Israel, or at territory it had occupied. If our hastily-organised ceremony at Moses' Spring had been the true highlight of our holiday, then this picnic ran it very close.

It was a perfect day, sunny but not too hot. We spread out the rugs and unpacked the picnic hamper and extras in a field of long green grass, laced with wildflowers of every description – scarlet poppies predominating. The tapestry of colour fell away before us into the valley and to the lake. It was breath-taking. Gazing up the smooth waters of Galilee we could just make out the shapes of buildings on its western shore.

'That must be Tiberias,' said Dave.

I commented, 'You mean the lakeside town of Jesus' day – named by the Romans after the emperor.'

He smiled. 'I suppose so. But you know more about that than me!'

I knew a little about landmarks of the Holy Land. But I did not know how important Tiberias had once been to a family who later became linked in marriage to ours. We quickly fell to eating the meal prepared by Candy, washing it down (the adults, anyway) with something stronger than water.

Psychologists and others sometimes talk about measuring people's level of contentment. Even as I write this, the British government is proposing to mount a survey of the nation to discover how happy the populace is, and why. Such information, our leaders imagine, can help towards the design of a more beneficial social programme. I note that commentators are sceptical, pointing to the fact that happiness is a subjective, ephemeral emotion, which cannot be measured. Yet I can say without equivocation that on that April day I was as happy as I can ever remember. Was it the weather, the gorgeous environment, the food and drink, the company of friends?

I fancy there was a deeper reason for the way I felt. Places have memories and those memories – is it too much to believe? – can be tapped.

Late in 1985 we had our second brush with royalty.

Every now and then selected British expatriates would be invited by the British ambassador to Sudan to a meal or party at the embassy residence. Joanna and I were fortunate in being amongst those invited every year to a celebration of the Queen's official birthday. This was because my post at Khartoum University was supported financially by the Overseas Development Administration and we were thus part of the British aid programme to the Sudan. These were pleasant occasions, with drinks and nibbles generously served, and the opportunity for conversations with both colleagues and those you may not previously have met.

It was not, however, a celebration of her mother's birthday that brought Anne, Princess Royal, to Sudan; she had come in her capacity as president of the Save the Children Fund to study British relief efforts in the country. The ambo accordingly organised a drinks party in the residence garden so she could meet a selection of those representing Britain on the aid front in this one-time Anglo-Egyptian condominium. Joanna and I were, with others, ushered into the presence of the royal visitor and graciously received. Pleasantries were exchanged and when there was a lull in the conversation I ventured a question.

'Your Highness, I happened to read in the British Press last summer a report on a previous visit you made to Northern Sudan. It said something that intrigued me, that you saw quite a few crocodiles in the Nile – or perhaps basking on the bank. I say "intrigued me"; it would be truer to say it worried me!'

The Princess Royal raised her eyebrows. 'Why should it have worried you? We were well away from them, quite safe.'

'Indeed, your Highness, but I'm afraid to say it wasn't your safety I was thinking about, but my own. You see, we've been in the habit of swimming in the Nile – the Blue Nile, mind you. It was the White Nile, I think, where you saw the crocodiles.' The Princess nodded.

'The fact is,' I went on, 'we've always been told that there were no crocodiles within two hundred miles of Khartoum. We've seen just one round here – but that's stuffed and fastened over the entrance to Omdurman police station. It's an enormous specimen, apparently shot some twenty years ago. But from that report I read, the accuracy of which you now confirm, there are some very-much-alive crocs uncomfortably close!'

Joanna had a point to make. 'I got the impression from the report, your Highness, that you were some way up the Nile from Khartoum. Is that right?'

'A fair distance, I should say,' she responded. 'But I can't really remember.'

'Twenty, thirty miles up-river, perhaps?' I ruminated. 'You could well have been visiting Jebel Awliya Dam. I'd like the beasties a bit further off, personally.'

Princess Anne smiled. 'Well, I'm sorry if I've ruined your swimming. But there it is, I *did* see the crocodiles.'

***

A year after he had assumed the presidency of Sudan, General Suwar al-Dhahab was as good as his word and handed over the government of the country to a democratically elected government under the leadership of Sādiq al-Mahdi, of the Umma Party. It seemed an appropriate moment for us to be moving on.

Not that there was much choice about it. As already mentioned, my post in Sudan carried a sterling supplement from the British Overseas Development Administration (ODA). When I arrived in my post there had been approximate parity between the Sudanese and sterling pounds, but by 1986 the latter was some six times more valuable than the former. Early in that year the ODA informed me that my supplementation would cease at the end of the academic year in June – though a little later they extended payment for three months at the university's request. Joanna, of course, had a salary from Afrograph but this was very small by British standards and even on our combined Sudanese incomes we could not consider staying. The cost of our children's continuing education was a major factor, for as well as losing my salary supplementation, we would be losing the ODA's educational grants, which included holiday air fares. I began to look for a new post.

My final year or two at the Faculty of Education had been satisfying. This was a lot to do with the fact that our friend Abdul had been appointed Dean of the Faculty of Education some time earlier, his brief being the reform of the administration, in particular the exam system. He did a remarkably good job and efficiency dramatically increased. Meanwhile, I had been appointed Head of Department, the position having become vacant. It was unusual for an expatriate to be given this responsibility because it needed someone proficient in spoken and written Arabic. My knowledge of the language was considered sufficient.

The possibility arose of my obtaining an ODA-supplemented post in the English Language Servicing Unit (ELSU), on the university's main campus. The teaching itself – English for Special Purposes – did not greatly appeal to me but for a time it looked as if I would settle for it. I had, however, also applied for the British Council sponsored post of Director of Programmes in the Language Centre at the University of Sana'a, Yemen.

'It's time for us to move on,' Joanna insisted, as we were discussing our situation one morning. 'We've had a very good innings here in Sudan and I for one am ready for a change – a new challenge.'

'I see the force of what you say, sweetie, but the matter is not wholly in our hands. It boils down to what's on offer and at the moment the only viable one seems to be from ELSU, here in Sudan. But we'll see. There may yet be a twist.'

Twist there was. Days before I was expecting to clinch a deal with ELSU, I received an offer from the British Council for the post in Sana'a. I decided to accept, though first clearing it with the Khartoum people since they had wanted me. Their formal offer had been delayed pending a green light from the university authorities.

I felt sad at the prospect of leaving good friends behind, particularly locals like Mahjoub, Muhammad Sīd Ahmed, Abdul Qayūm and Tricia – the last by now proud parents of *six* offspring. (Philip and Rosie Gordon we would not be leaving as they had by this time moved on to the Sultanate of Oman.) Something occurred, however, to make me feel the road to Yemen was indeed the one to take.

At this time we were worshipping in the new Anglican cathedral, built by the government on the edge of the capital. It had been in use for a year or so. The Sunday following my acceptance of the Yemen post I was having serious second thoughts about my decision. We attended evening service in the cathedral as usual and words from the appointed psalm – usually described as 'messianic' – suddenly caught my eye: 'The kings of Arabia and Saba shall bring gifts.' Saba means the Yemen, I knew, Arabia Felix, ancient Sheba – seat of the famous queen who visited Solomon. The words from the psalm somehow reassured me about serving the modern counterparts of these 'kings'.

One of the last things we did in Sudan was to take a four-day trip to Port Sudan and the ruined town of Suakin, both on the Red Sea. This entailed a five-hundred mile bus drive via Qadārif and

147

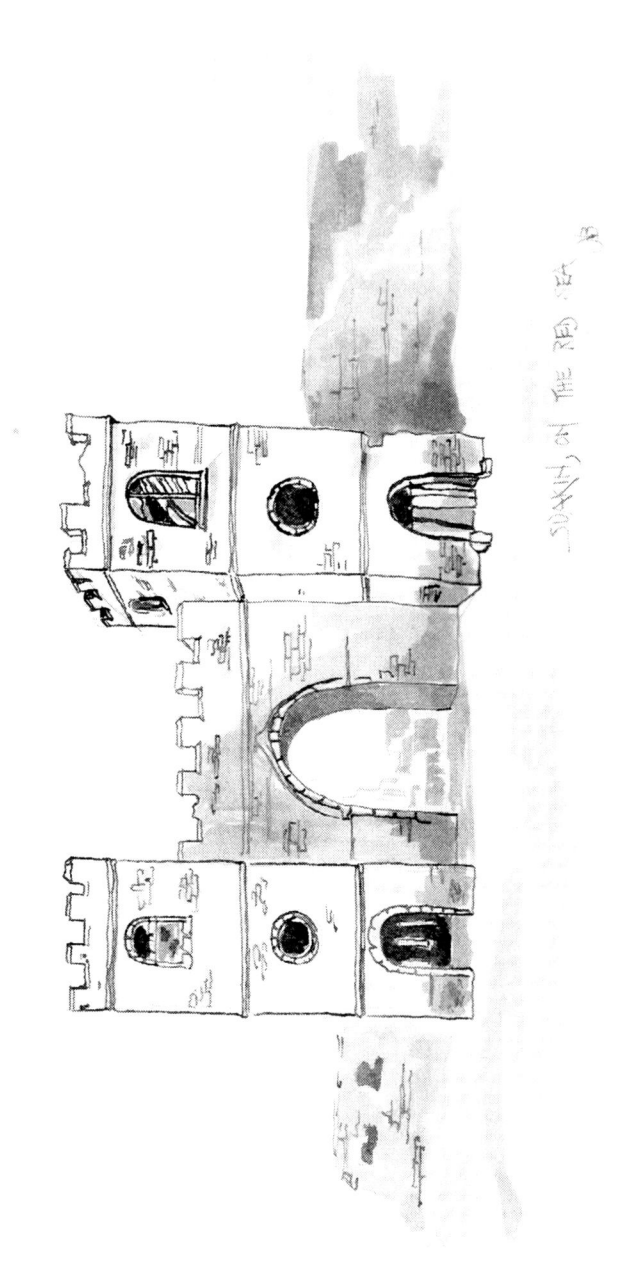

Gate of ruined Suakin, on Red Sea

Kassala, very near the Ethiopian border, and then over the slight elevation of the Red Sea Hills to Sudan's single seaport. On the outward trip we broke our journey in Kassala, staying the night in a primitive though clean hostel. Arrived in Port Sudan we found a comfortable hotel and explored, mostly around Suakin, where we wandered along the quay and stared down at a host of brilliantly-coloured fish darting to and fro in the limpid water. Even more spectacular were the sea-creatures on display as we snorkelled off a nearby coral reef one afternoon. Yet my most vivid recollection of this short holiday is rather different.

Our outward journey, as I have mentioned, was stretched over two days; not so the return journey. We set off from Port Sudan very early and started driving. We drove, and drove, and drove. There were of course brief tea and toilet stops, but nothing that amounted to a genuine rest for our driver – a large, muscular man who reminded me of the former Hollywood star Victor Mature, of 'Samson and Delilah' fame.

This Sudanese Victor drove his vehicle on indifferent roads that day for effectively fifteen hours non-stop. He had a mate – not a co-driver, oh no! – a little fellow who watched the man at the wheel like a hawk every mile of the way. Our chauffeur's eyelids, not surprisingly, began to droop from time to time, at which mate would engage driver in loud conversation. The eyes of the latter would slowly widen in response to the ceaseless flow of remarks and insistent questions. So on we went, without mishap, finally arriving in Khartoum tired but happy. It was a sterling performance. Strength and will-power lay behind the achievement – plus another, more subtle factor.

Just before our hero let in the clutch, both going and coming, he cried three words: *'tawakkulnā 'ala allāh!'* 'Our trust is in God!'

It most certainly was.

VII

'Kings of Arabia and Saba'

Joanna and I flew direct from Khartoum to the Yemen at the beginning of September, 1986. I still had a month of my Khartoum contract to fulfil so this was a short visit, for briefing only, needed by us as well as my new employers. We were met at the airport by a member of the British Council whom we already knew. He had been a government teacher in Sudan and was a good friend. This was a pleasant introduction to the country in which we expected to spend the next four years. A month later we were touching down again for me to take up my new responsibilities, accompanied by a good deal of baggage.

'Enchanting Yemen', the title of an article I read around this time, is how one visitor describes this quintessentially Arab country, and from the moment you arrive you realise why. The architecture, the mountains, the vistas take the breath away. The capital, Sana'a, is a feast in itself. The locals will tell you it is the oldest city in the world, its true name being 'Sam City', that is, the city of Shem, from which we get 'Semite' and 'Semitic'. Shem, the eldest son of Noah according to the Bible, is said to have been the founder. 'That makes good sense,' I thought with a smile on first hearing the tradition. 'If you've survived a flood, you're unlikely to settle on a plain!' Sana'a is in the mountains, more than 7,000 feet above sea level.

We wandered along to Bāb al-Yemen, the main gate to the Old City, from our apartment in a modern suburb on one of our first evenings. It is a hive of commercial activity – like the kiosks where dough is twirled round the head until it is thin, flat and round, ready for baking on a convex circle of iron prior to enclosing a

Sana'a street seller, chewing *qat*

mix of meat and vegetables to make a delicious 'sandwich'. Stalls are there, some piled high with fruit or greens, others selling ice-cream, others trinkets of all kinds. Once inside the Old City you wander round the maze of streets and alleyways, endangering your life from speeding mopeds as you crane your head to look up at the quaint, towering buildings each side of you. These all boast the trademark rounded arches, filled with coloured glass, above all doors and windows. Shops will entice you with wares produced by local artisans, or spices sculpted into pyramids, or (in season) handcarts sporting huge piles of succulent grapes. Suddenly you are confronted by huge, dark walls enclosing the Great Mosque of Sana'a, which incorporates design features and some material from an earlier Byzantine cathedral.

Once you venture outside the capital, into the mountains, the wonders come thick and fast, and astonishment builds. You see a precipitous escarpment, an amazingly-illuminated face of strata, a village atop a cliff-edge or a fortress clinging impossibly to a pinnacle – and you feel you have seen it all. A few days later you realise you haven't.

Enough of this by way of introduction to the social and scenic marvels of late twentieth-century Arabia Felix. What of the new position I was taking up in this remarkable region?

My job title, according to the British Council, was 'Director of Programmes', denoting my leadership of a significant British aid project, under the Key English Language Teaching (KELT) scheme. It was a major professional step for me within the overseas English teaching community. I had been a little surprised to be offered the post, not least because I had only been an English teacher for ten years. True, I had been a Head of Department in the Arab world but it had been a minor role, serving a faculty rather than a university. I had felt, too, that the fact of my having had a previous career within the church might count against me. My appointment proved this wrong, but on arrival in the Yemen I remained sensitive about my 'priestly' and our joint missionary past, not wishing in any way to draw attention to it. It was partly for this reason that Joanna and I didn't initially join any group of Christians meeting regularly for worship, preferring to have a simple service at home. In the event, I need hardly have worried: one of my team of English teachers, an Irishman, turned out to be a Roman Catholic priest who discreetly celebrated the mass for Catholics. It was clear that the authorities were perfectly aware of what was going on.

To return to the question of why I was appointed to this senior position, I learnt in due course that my possession of a doctorate was a factor. That is as may be. My own interpretation of events as they gradually unfolded – quite unforeseen – led me to conclude that a more important factor was the assumption that I would be mostly a figurehead, working hard but not putting my own stamp on things. I would be a 'safe appointment', quiet and amenable. I would not rock the boat.

The position involved leading – under the British Council Representative, of course – a team of experienced language teachers serving the university as 'KELT officers'. There were half a dozen of them. But alongside this was administrative responsibility for some eighteen other English teachers in the university Language Centre, a quasi-faculty with its own Dean, a Yemeni. There were therefore twenty-four teaching personnel serving under me in what was called the English Language Unit, teaching English to students throughout the university. The majority of the eighteen had individual contracts with the university but the Unit included a handful of teachers from the United States Peace Corps. Leading this varied selection of people promised to be interesting.

Soon, however, for no clearly identifiable reason I began to feel under threat. This went further than the joke some of us used to make about our Yemeni employers, that they had the Protestant work ethic: 'You Protestant; you work!' It was the sense that I was not really trusted to do the job for its own sake; I would only work effectively if I were fearful that if I didn't I would pay a price. This atmosphere of threat seemed to emanate from the British Council as much as from my Yemeni boss.

Early on I developed the habit of stopping for a coffee-break at a tiny roadside cafeteria – a sort of cave in a wall – on my way down from my office on the main campus to the Faculty of Education, which had its own campus. I had the responsibility of teaching literary appreciation to aspiring English teachers, a pleasant change from basic language courses. I recall wondering on one occasion, as I was sipping from my cup, whether something sinister was developing, something directed against me personally.

'I wonder how long I'll last', I suddenly found myself thinking. A moment later I told myself not to be silly. But I was right.

Quite early in 1987, just a few months after I had arrived in post, the British Council Representative took me aside and dropped the bombshell.

'How would you like to go to Taiz, Philip?'

'Taiz?'

'Yes, to the branch of the Faculty of Education there.'

I was – despite that premonition of storm clouds gathering – completely taken aback. 'Whatever makes you think I'd want to move to Taiz?'

The Representative spoke slowly. 'We don't think you're really suited to the post up here. An advisory position in education would be much more your line.'

These were weasel words disguising something disturbing, I immediately decided.

I asked him, 'What's this about? There's obviously more to it than you're telling me.'

He chose his words carefully. 'Well yes, there is. The fact is, there have been complaints – about your performance. That you are slow.'

'Slow? Slow?' I repeated. 'What is that meant to mean? And who's been saying it?'

'I'd prefer not to go into details. But think about it. The move to Taiz, I mean. I'm sure it would be best for all concerned. Think about it and come back to me in a day or two.'

I agreed, though having no real doubt about how I would respond. I delivered that response a couple of days later.

'I will not go to Taiz,' I said flatly. 'You've chosen the right person for the job here and I'm staying.'

My boss did not force the issue, though he seemed surprised at my reaction. The matter didn't quite end there, however.

A few weeks later the British Council played host to an academic from UK who was to advise them on some matter of policy. He was known to Joanna and me from visits he had made to Sudan in relation to work being done at Khartoum University by our friend Abdul Qayūm Babiker. We had no idea he was visiting the Yemen but of course he heard that we were around and came to see us. He was amazed when we mentioned the 'loss of confidence' in me and told us he had spoken highly of us to the Council Representative. Following his visit the atmosphere changed dramatically; I found myself being appreciated rather than harried.

In due course I came to hear – I forget how – who it was that had complained. It turned out to be a senior member of the aid project I was leading. She had been in the country for some time and the Council Representative held her in high esteem.

***

A period of welcome calm now ensued, with work going well. Among other things, I was able to oversee a complete revamping of the in-house teaching materials used by the project team. Joanna, meanwhile, had found employment teaching English part-time in the British Council Language School.

One of Joanna's colleagues at the School, a full-time teacher, was a young man who to this day resides in the Yemeni capital. As well as being an accomplished pianist, whose recitals in the embassy residence we used to enjoy, in 1997 he published the highly-acclaimed *Yemen: Travels in Dictionary Land*. This was followed by other, equally well-received works. Tim Mackintosh-Smith should be bracketed with that small and select band of Englishmen who over the years have fallen in love with and then, one way or another, embraced the Arab world. The London *Daily Telegraph* once described him as 'the sage of Sana'a'.

Aside from our work, Joanna and I enjoyed regular trips outside the capital – especially after the arrival in early April of the new, tax-free Land Rover we had purchased in UK.

The most memorable place visited – several times, for we always took our guests there – was Ma'rib, on the edge of the Empty

Quarter. We would drive out of Sana'a, pass through the police check point (for which we had to obtain an official pass each time) and soon begin the long drop to the desert. At first there would be high mountains – more like cliffs – flanking the route. We would crane our necks looking up at these, and occasionally at a building sitting on top, like 'Job's Tomb', a domed structure on the very edge of the escarpment. Down, down we would go, following the road as it twisted and turned. Every so often it would pass through a village, where a local, replete with personal Kalashnikov, might be standing waiting for a lift. This happened mostly on the return journey, but going or coming we would stop, take him on board and carry on. We became used to having a gunman sitting behind us and – surprisingly, perhaps – felt perfectly comfortable. To the Yemeni male a light machine gun was and is an essential badge of adulthood. True, he might occasionally use it – mostly for celebratory purposes or target practice – but there seemed no reason to fear that the weapon would be turned on us.

After about three hours we would emerge from low-lying mountains and begin to breathe the warm desert air. We would first turn to the surviving stones of an ancient dam, first constructed by people of the ancient kingdom of Saba, biblical Sheba. Some speculated that the Queen of Sheba herself (known locally as Belqīs) might have been involved. Joanna and I were no strangers to such ancient monoliths, our home in England being within easy reach of Stonehenge, yet picking our way along the top of the rust-red masonry of this remarkable feat of early engineering was a unique experience.

We would then move desert-ward to an intriguing mound with collapsing mud-buildings over the top; this is what remains of Old Ma'rib, ancient capital of Saba. Like the *tels* of ancient Mesopotamia, the date of the first settlement on this site is unknown; the mound or *tel* is composed of layer upon layer of crumbled dwellings, each version of the city having falling down or been flattened to make way for the next. Wandering around these ruins made the flesh tingle.

The silence was huge – though to be honest it wasn't total. The faint throbbing of diesel pumps, extracting water from deep bore wells to irrigate patches of green (areas where locals grew vegetables), provided reassurance that one wasn't alone. In a strange way this almost subliminal sound served to accentuate the otherwise massive quiet.

You travel east from Sana'a to get to Ma'rib; if you head south, up and over a mountain pass, and then follow the continuous and sometimes tortuous descent, you end up in Taiz. This was once the seat of the country's ruling Imams, where you can still visit the famous lions – or their descendants – of Imam Ahmad, who held the throne from 1948 to 1962. He occupied the royal palace of al-Urdhi, a fortified stronghold which he shared with his harem, the royal treasure, an arsenal of modern weapons and a hundred and fifty palace guards.

Being behind the wheel of our new 110 'safari' Land Rover on the drive to Taiz was an exhilarating experience – especially by night. By day one enjoyed the startlingly green vistas that unfolded before one; by night it became a test of driving skill and endurance, aided by regular applications of strong local coffee.

Taiz in those days was the second city of the Arab Republic of the Yemen – which, it should be remembered, was separated from the southern region of the Arab peninsular. The latter – starting with Aden in the nineteenth century and, from 1937, including the Aden hinterland and the Hadramaut – was under British control until 1967. The city of Taiz is very different from Sana'a, both in appearance and atmosphere. It is at a lower altitude and is consequently warmer; it felt and looked, indeed, mildly tropical. The central area is situated on a gentle slope, but part of it climbs what at first glance seems a vertical cliff. It was some way up this precipitous mountainside that we visited an English language inspector and his wife.

'What a superb view!' I said to them after we had made the climb, parked our vehicle and were sitting with them on their balcony. 'You look right over the city. One has to admit, there are advantages in working overseas.'

'Very true,' Roger, utterly English, politely agreed. 'There are downsides, of course, but we expats seldom come out the losers.'

There was a slight commotion inside and a young child appeared, immediately attaching herself to her mother, Yukari. From that haven of security she shyly regarded Joanna and me.

'Let me do some introducing,' Yukari began, gesturing towards the little girl beside her. 'This is Naomi – or "Mimi" as we usually call her.' Joanna and I made appropriate salutations. 'Jon, her brother and just a few months old, is inside. You must make his acquaintance too.' We walked into an inner room and inspected him in his cot, sound asleep.

It was not long before Joanna was entertaining Naomi, the shyness quite gone, with quick line drawings and paper cutouts, from which developed an impromptu lesson in art. So, in this unlikely setting, began a family friendship between the Blairs and Barnards that was later consolidated in the country of our next posting. Later still it was cemented by the two youngsters asking us to be their godparents, which request was welcomed and granted. The children of a 'mixed marriage', Yukari being (charmingly) Japanese, they have since done very well both socially and academically.

We had a particularly enjoyable trip west to the *sāhil*, the flat strip of coastland along the Red Sea. This has a fully tropical climate, hot and dusty, with sand and palm trees fringing the water. Annabel and Edmund were on holiday with us on this occasion, which we shared with another family. Once again the drive took us down a steeply descending route, winding back and forth alongside the spectacular terracing, such a feature of the country and devoted nowadays entirely to the cultivation of the *qat* tree, with its chewable, mildly narcotic leaf. Long gone are the days when those same terraces were utilized for growing the famous Mokha coffee.

Once the descent was complete and we were on a level we stopped to look at the town of Mokha, some of it in ruins, before ensconcing ourselves on the beach. It was a glorious, lazy day, between hot beach and warm – yet somehow cooling – sea. Even Joanna, hardly a swimmer, enjoyed lounging in the shallows. It was one of those holiday experiences, with good friends – the other family included teenagers, to join up with our own – which remains hazily in the memory as a golden moment, a respite from an otherwise fairly demanding life-style.

Besides major trips we visited noted sites of interest in the immediate vicinity. Wadi Dahar was one such, with its palace perched high on a vertical outcrop of rock; once, further up that *wadi*, we were hailed excitedly.

'Mr Philip, Mr Philip!' The cry came from a figure clambering over some boulders a bit above us and I soon recognised him.

'Ismail, what are you doing here?' I called out. 'You should be in Sudan!' He was a former student and, slightly breathless, he came and sat down on a rock beside us.

'You're right. And I would be if the Khartoum government paid me a good salary – and did so regularly. As they don't do either I'm teaching English in a village over there.' He pointed up the valley. 'Quite a few of your students from Omdurman have come to the Yemen – Khalid, for example, who you'll certainly remember.'

'Well, we've done the same. So tell us, how are you finding the place?' We settled down to a conversation, catching up on our respective news.

Another favourite destination of ours, not too far from Sana'a, was a stream – so clear you wanted to stoop down and drink. In gorgeous little falls and pools it tumbled down a narrow chine, wooded and flowery, in the mountains beyond Haddah.

Joanna and I would often go alone on these shorter outings; when not alone we would be taking an expatriate friend or two. Socializing with Yemenis was a rarity, we discovered, close fraternizing with foreigners being frowned on by many locals. On one occasion, however, we attended an afternoon *qat*-chewing session at the kind invitation of a Yemeni driver employed by the British Council. I was suffering from a cold at the time and it prompted an interesting remark from our host.

'This plant has healing properties, *yā ustāz*. Your cold will now disappear.'

I was sceptical. 'I find that difficult to believe, Abdullah.'

'I swear it, *wallāhi!*'

'I certainly hope you're right. As you see, I'm chewing these leaves as hard as I can.'

My cold obstinately refused to disappear, and I certainly didn't feel like a 'master of the universe' as another enthusiast of chewing had said I would. A vague high, as if I'd had several cups of coffee, was about the sum of it. I suppose I hadn't done enough 'storing', packing my cheek with leaves to make it bulge like a tennis ball in the manner of the locals.

Perhaps the most eventful recreational outing was made to Shehara, a town spread across the top of a mountain, like so many other Yemeni settlements. This was a longer trip and we invited some friends to share our vehicle. After leaving the tarmac of the Sana'a-Ma'rib road we had to drive along a rough track for a good few miles to get to the mountain. The track wound through undulating rocky terrain and then crossed a stony valley, where for a while we followed a dry river bed with large boulders. The Land Rover, I was happy to discover, lived superbly up to the challenge. The light was failing as we set up camp at the foot of the mountain, intending to climb it the next morning. Having unpacked what was necessary for a meal we lit a fire and sat round it together.

'Ugh! Just look over there,' Joanna suddenly cried, pointing into the darkness beyond the fire. Our heads turned as one and we strained to make out what it was she had seen.

'Eyes!' one of our friends exclaimed. 'Shining, pinpoint eyes. Extraordinary! What are they?' He got up and moved a step towards them. A few eyes moved.

'Oh, oh my!' he cried. 'Spiders – big, bulbous ones. In fact some are quite enormous and have more than eight legs.'

The rest of us got up to look closer, though Joanna held her ground.

'An amazing sight,' I commented, peering at them. 'We're more or less surrounded, by the looks of it. As for the ones with *sixteen* legs, it seems to me, they're couples, one on top of the other. Perhaps they're copulating.'

'Horrible, horrible!' was all Joanna could say.

We went on muttering our disgust, only slowly coming to realise that they had been drawn by the fire. Someone threw on more wood and the flames flared up. The unwelcome visitors retreated a little.

We had our meal together but then came the question of sleep. Our friends started unpacking a one-piece tent, prompting me to turn to Joanna.

Philip and Joanna with friends on trip to Shehara, in the mountains

'I feel the idea about sleeping under the stars has been overtaken by events,' I murmured to Joanna, nodding towards the phalanx of eyes. 'I don't fancy sharing my bed with those creatures.'

She almost choked at the thought. 'My golly, no!'

'So what shall we do?'

'Sleep in the back of the Land Rover. There's nowhere else.'

She was of course right. Unlike our friends we had not brought a tent, being used to bedding down in sleeping-bags in the open desert of Sudan. But a desert is one thing; you can sprinkle a circle of special powder on the sand round your chosen territory to ward off marauding invertebrates. This was rough ground, with the odd sprig of vegetation providing ample cover for potential invaders. In any case, we had no such chemical to give us protection.

So into the Land Rover we climbed. Being a long wheel-base model we could almost stretch out lengthwise in the back – but not quite – and the space being narrow every movement we each made disturbed the other. We closed the windows except for a tiny slit – we were taking no risks – but then felt too hot. We had dropped several thousand feet on the drive down and the air was much warmer than that of Sana'a. We eventually fell into a fitful slumber.

We woke the next day feeling surprisingly fresh. Having breakfasted – without any eight-legged onlookers – we set out for the town. The drive began unremarkably but the higher we climbed the steeper became the ascent. The road was paved with large flat slabs and there were moments when I felt as if we might start sliding backwards – or even topple over.

Once in the town we looked around – Joanna finding herself the target of one or two disapproving male locals. She had become used to this in Sana'a, a gob of spit falling at her feet indicating offended feelings. (She always dressed modestly, in fact, exposing little flesh and wearing a head cover when in doubt.) We walked down to a spectacular arched footbridge, spanning the vertiginous chasm that split the mountain on which Shehara stands. Joanna, however, could only walk across while clinging to my hand; heights are not her strong point.

Unlike our outward journey, the return journey was to be made in a single drive. It began with the precipitous slopes to the valley below – a driving experience more alarming than climbing the slopes because it was raining, making the surface slippery. We reached the bottom in one piece, however, crossed the valley as the day was waning (mindful of advice not to do so after dark for fear of bandits) and began wending our way through rocky hillocks on the other side. Now the fun began.

We did not meet bandits but very soon, on turning a corner, we saw heads popping up above the rocks on each side of us, soon becoming armed figures staring down. They issued no challenge so we motored on, only to find our way barred a little later by a makeshift barrier manned by men carrying Kalashnikovs. They gave us a cursory glance, looked into the back of the Land Rover and waved us on. We set off once more along the roughly-graded track until we had almost reached the Sana'a-Ma'rib road. At this point we found ourselves approaching a large concourse of armed men, their four-wheel drives parked nearby. They waved us down and then scrutinised both us and our vehicle.

'*Bita'milū eish hinā?*' A fierce looking guy, presumably their leader, poked his head in through the driver's window to ask the question: 'What are you doing here?'

I reassured him as politely as possible. '*Shāifīn al-manāzir bass, yā sheikh.*' ('Just seeing the sights, your lordship.') As an afterthought I added, 'May I ask what it is you're looking for?'

'A couple who have eloped, each from a different tribe,' was the unexpected reply.

'We can't help you on that, I'm afraid. We've seen no one on the road except some foreigners.' We had stopped to help these folk, their four-wheel drive stalling and refusing to restart; Joanna knew a trick with the air intake which I tried – with complete success.

The men allowed us to pass and a little further on, much relieved, we turned onto the main road. We then began the slow, twisting ascent to Sana'a. It was dark by now and after a few hundred yards we could make out in our headlights *some more* monster arachnids scurrying across the tarmac. I carefully avoided them, mindful of the saying Joanna's mother had so often repeated: 'If you want to live and thrive, let the spider run alive.' A couple of hours later we were back home.

Not long after this trip we heard that tribesmen of the Shehara district had caught up with an unmarried couple and, in a particularly barbaric manner, summarily executed them.

Northern Yemen in those days was essentially a tribal society, not quite like ancient Israel in the time of the judges, when everyone 'did what was right in his own eyes', but not so very different. There was indeed a central government, headed by the relatively young president, Ali Abdullah Saleh, who did his best to control the provinces. A semblance of democracy developed while we were there with the formation of an elected body of representatives. Our Dean, I seem to recall, at one stage showed interest in obtaining a seat in this assembly.

The country had had a chequered history over the previous twenty-five years. In 1962 Imam al-Badr succeeded to the throne of the Mutawakkilite Kingdom of Yemen on the death of his father, Imam Ahmad, only to lose it following a coup d'ètat led by the leader of a republican movement. The Imam managed to avoid capture and rallied popular support. There followed an eight-year civil war, during which republicans received support from Egypt and the Soviet Union, while royalists were helped by Saudi Arabia. Egypt, under the leadership of Gamal Abdul Nasser, sent as many as 70,000 troops to aid the republicans, but the gesture put considerable strain on Egypt's resources and, after the disastrous Six Day War of 1967 with Israel, Nasser began pulling his forces out. In 1970 the civil war ended in a truce, King Faisal of Saudi Arabia formally recognizing the Yemen Arab Republic.

The new Republic's southern neighbour was now the People's Democratic Republic of Yemen, comprising Aden, its hinterland and the Hadhramaut, since 1967 independent of Britain. Relations between the two republics became extremely strained, sinking to open hostilities in 1972. Finally, in 1978, a 'peace envoy' from the south visited the northern Republic. He had a bomb in his briefcase, however, and with it assassinated the then president, Ahmad al-Ghashmi. Ali Abdullah Saleh was al-Ghashmi's successor.

***

Christmas 1987 in Yemen was good.

We hosted a big party in our spacious apartment, with no shortage of food and drink. Being under the British Council we enjoyed the 'diplomatic privilege' of a drink allowance (alcoholic), which we used to the full. We were encouraged to claim the full amount, offloading the excess to those without this privilege. Drink had in fact flowed freely at other parties we had given, in honour of personal or official visitors, which occasions were always well attended.

We were also involved over the Christmas period in the production of the pantomime Peter Pan, with Joanna designing the stage-set while I co-directed and again played Captain Hook. The venture did a lot for the morale of those involved, several of whom were teaching colleagues, and was hailed a success. We appreciated Christmas worship too. By this time we were attending services on a regular basis, in the form of interdenominational gatherings held on Friday mornings in a community hall.

But the Christmas glow did not last.

Early in 1988 I was summoned to the Language Centre conference room to find a group of people sitting round the table headed by the Dean. I can't remember who they were but they didn't include members of my team because the business was conducted in Arabic. They must have been colleagues from other departments within the Centre, like the Head of Arabic, a Palestinian. There was a brief preliminary discussion but then the Dean turned to me.

'Would you say your teachers were doing a good job, Dr Blair?' he asked.

'They're doing their best, generally speaking,' I replied. 'I hope that answers your question.'

'I was wondering whether you were tough enough with them.'

'Tough? Why be "tough"? If they step out of line, I tell them so, and they adjust. But I believe in encouraging people, appreciating them. That's what gets results, not forever pushing, asking for more.'

'What about the students? Are you and your team meeting their needs?'

'I think so. We all monitor our performance, adapting when necessary.'

So continued the interrogation, thinly-disguised criticism. I gave no quarter and the flow of questions slowly dried up. The meeting then adjourned, the Dean – in uncharacteristically quixotic fashion – complimenting me on my Arabic.

On arriving home later I told Joanna, 'I've just been defending myself in a kangaroo court!'

Nothing seemed to come of this experience. Nor did I pick up anything, within or without the university, to suggest repercussions. But it clearly signalled something. I was back to the situation of my first few months in the country.

A few weeks later the Dean informed me that the government was foisting on the university a huge new intake of students, all of whom would require tutoring in English at a basic level. As I recall, they were due to join the military after graduating. Such directives were fairly standard. There was the 'poets' affair, for instance. Would the Unit 'examine' (that is, 'pass') two Yemeni poets in the English language so they could graduate? I arranged a test and found the candidates woefully inadequate. Unable to underwrite educational perjury, I proposed a formula by which the literary gentlemen could graduate without formally 'satisfying the examiners'.

The Dean asked me to absorb the new intake of students within our current programme despite the fact that this would mean them missing a full semester (half an academic year).

'This is not a good idea,' I told him. 'If we do so, classes will be greatly swollen and there will be a major discrepancy between the level of existing students and those of the new intake.'

'The Rector wants them integrated into the programme immediately. Get your teachers to work something out that will take account of the different student levels.'

'I've sounded them out and they're very unhappy at the idea. They believe, and I have to agree, that the result will be little learning at either level – almost none for the newcomers.'

'I don't agree. You listen too much to your teachers, Dr Blair. Please make arrangements for the new students to be taken into the programme.'

I made a final effort to get round the problem. I worked out and submitted to the Dean a separate timetable of classes for the new intake, which I managed somehow to staff. He was not impressed.

This was a no-win situation, I realised: if I acceded to the Dean's request I would be blamed for lowering teaching standards, which the British Council strongly deplored; if I held out against him I risked the displeasure of the university authorities. I decided to go for broke; the balancing act I had so often been forced to perform in the attempt to please two masters had become tedious and the thought of a showdown correspondingly attractive.

I must tread carefully, I knew, doing nothing without British Council backing. So I went to see the Council Representative, telling him how both I and the team felt and floating a plan of action.

'I want to seek an interview with the Rector – with the Dean's blessing, of course. I'll explain the problems involved in allowing this large intake to join our present classes and stress that there's a viable alternative. Maybe I'll convince him – I'd certainly like to try.'

My Council boss was cautious. 'I see your point, Philip, but you're forgetting that argument doesn't cut much ice with these folk. Secondly, the Rector may not be disposed to listen to a non-Yemeni – and not particularly senior – member of staff.'

'Would *you* see the Rector?' I immediately suggested. 'You have more clout.'

He shook his head. 'No, we won't go down that road.' He fell silent for a moment, and then added, 'I'm not against your strategy, so feel free to try it.'

I approached the Dean about seeing the Rector and his response was non-committal. Somewhat nonplussed, I decided to put the matter aside for at least twenty-four hours and then take stock. But events now took over.

On next entering the Language Centre, I found a professor of English from India sitting at the desk in my office. I had been dismissed from my position as Head of the English Language Unit and he was my replacement. I went to the common room to check my mailbox to find it empty, a few remnants of my post identifiable on the floor.

'What appalling behaviour!' I remarked, and moved into the corridor – to find myself facing the Dean.

'You will not be seeing me in the Centre again,' I said, walking past him and out of the main door.

I went straight to the Land Rover, jumped in and drove home.

When I reported to the Council Representative that I had been dismissed as Head of the English Language Unit, and that I had in effect announced my resignation, he was much taken aback.

'You cannot resign like that on the spot,' he told me. 'You're still Director of Programmes and thus leader, under me, of the aid project. Resignation has to be approved by London.'

'Then I'll have to wait.'

'Wait – for what? I hope, Philip, that you will reconsider your decision – made rather precipitously, it has to be said. Whatever you decide, however, you must carry on your teaching duties for the time being.'

I agreed to the latter – there was little choice – though making it clear I still wanted to resign. My reasoning was clear: the job description of the post I had accepted included leadership of the English Language Unit; without this responsibility the position was largely meaningless.

I walked into the Language Centre the next morning as cheerfully as I could.

'Good morning,' I greeted the Dean. 'I'm afraid I was a bit hasty about offering my resignation. The Council Representative tells me I have to carry on teaching for a while. I will of course do so.'

The Dean, sounding perfectly amiable (as he did most of the time), murmured something about me taking on extra classes.

'Thank you, but I would prefer to continue with my present load,' I responded.

No further reference was made to my new situation, nor to the events of a day or two previously.

The case was taken up by the Council and, in due course, by the Embassy. From what I gathered, they were mostly concerned about defusing a situation they felt could be damaging to British interests. In due course I heard on the grapevine that our long-standing friend in the Council (he who had welcomed us at the airport) had been heard to remark, 'I wouldn't like to be Philip; they're going to make him a scapegoat.'

Joanna and I, meanwhile, continued to believe that resignation was the right course to take. We were encouraged in this conviction on hearing that a Yemeni professor of chemistry had also opposed the mid-year intake of students into his departmental programme, losing his supervisory position as a consequence.

The Council and Embassy discussions about my situation took a long time. Meanwhile, the Council Representative I had been dealing with departed, his position being filled by an older man. I wondered if he would be more sympathetic to my cause, but was disappointed. At a party given by our Council friend he addressed me out of the blue on the issue, remarking in acid tones, 'When you decide on something you really go firm, don't you.'

So that was that; we waited. Would I be allowed to resign? It was the last thing my seniors wanted, clearly.

The news finally came through. Yes, they were prepared to accept my resignation but there would be penalties: I would not receive current or pending financial benefits, namely, educational allowances for our children and payment for freight to UK, which could include a vehicle. There was also the matter of my end-of-contract reference.

The freight penalty came to nothing. 'I'm authorising payment of the cost of your baggage home,' the British Council accountant quietly informed me. As for the educational allowances, once back in England I fought the decision in a series of letters to the Council. I also asked my Member of Parliament to follow the matter up. A year later I received a cheque for the full amount, totalling something approaching £4,000 – not a huge sum but invaluable at the time. I was less successful over my reference: in those letters to London I protested that it gave a false impression and asked for it to be rewritten. My efforts were in vain.

'God's Favourite' was the name of the play for which Joanna, in the last few weeks of our time in the Yemen, designed and helped to build a most dramatic stage set featuring, at one point, the burnt out shell of a house. The play is a study of the biblical character Job in modern guise, cataloguing the personal disasters he sustained. People sympathised with Joanna and me for having to return home prematurely and when, just before performances of the play were due to commence, I managed to drive our Land Rover into the side of the road and do a cartwheel they commiserated with us for having to endure Job-like traumas. Their concern was kind but unnecessary. We were by no means unhappy and had no regrets. Eighteen months in the land of Job (remembering that tomb on the cliff-top) had been both fascinating and instructive.

Actually I didn't drive into the side of the road, the vehicle slid there. We were going on a trip and it began to rain for the first time in weeks as we were turning a corner at normal speed. The tarmac instantly became like ice and we glided gracefully into a deep gutter, did the cartwheel and landed back on four wheels. We were much shaken up but no one was badly hurt. We got a lift home and I reported the accident to the police. I was slightly mystified, however, when they wouldn't let me go once I had made my statement.

After five or ten minutes a young man quietly took me outside and led me behind a vehicle. '*Fulūs,*' he murmured, '*fulūs.*' ('Money, money.') I shook my head – and went on shaking it, or else muttering the Arabic equivalent for 'out of the question', for a good half hour before the attempt to corrupt me was dropped.

We put the Land Rover into a garage where it was repaired relatively cheaply, but I was not able to collect it until our last full day in the country. Having got a certificate of roadworthiness, I had to procure an export licence, which meant signatures from officials in a number of government departments. At first sight this seemed impossible but it was a challenge I had to accept.

Small miracles happen because at the beginning of this quest I encountered a Sudanese expat worker who said he knew the procedure well and would like to help. I grasped his hand and together we hurried round building after building, office after office, until desks began to empty and doors close: the Yemenis were drifting off for their afternoon chewing sessions. With minutes to spare we obtained a final signature and stamp – then embraced.

'*Yā ibn an-nīl,*' I whooped, '*alfi shukr limusāʻadatak. Lau kunta ma maʻī, abadan ma najahta!*' ('O son of the Nile, a thousand thanks for your help. If you hadn't been with me, I'd never have succeeded!')

My gratitude remains immense. We drove that Land Rover in a string of countries for the next thirteen years.

On that same last day, teaching colleagues in the Unit had arranged a presentation to me in the university. I told Joanna it was unlikely that I would make it in time and asked her to be ready to take my place. This duly became necessary as a result of my trawl through government offices, so she went to the Language Centre to stand proxy. The proceedings ended in near farce, to the amusement of those present, with Joanna receiving the farewell gift on behalf of her husband from a colleague presenting it on behalf of the Dean.

I say we had no regrets. I would go further, in saying that I understood and understand the reasoning behind my dismissal by the Dean and the slightly hard line taken by the British Council. It was right for me to resign, I have no doubt, but the motives of those opposing me were related to the necessities of real politik, which is the way of the world. I hold nothing against those concerned; I certainly didn't get everything right in the Yemen.

VIII

A Family Business

We made a virtue of necessity.

Joanna and I flew out of Sana'a airport on the first of May not to UK but to Cyprus – for the first leg of a two-week holiday. We spent a night in Larnaca, then hired a car and drove up Mount Olympus (Cypriot version), booking into a hotel near the top. Externally it was not prepossessing, being a corrugated iron, ranch-like structure. But when we got inside we couldn't believe our luck. The owner/manager turned out to be … not Dr Shelley himself, of my RAF days on the island (that was scarcely possible), but a close friend of his, an Armenian whom I had not met but often heard about. He gave us an excellent evening meal, followed by a brim-full – and gratis – glass of Cyprus brandy each. The room we were given looked across the mountain over the top of almond trees coming into blossom, with swallows and swifts darting hither and thither. We were the only hotel guests, as I recall, and we felt like Adam and Eve new in Eden.

We took walks along the heights and up to the ski-slope, where there was still some snow. (I made a mental note to do some skiing before I died – yet to be fulfilled.) We had two nights on the mountain and then returned to the lowlands and explored Nicosia (Greek half: Lefkosia), some pretty villages, and finally my old RAF haunts – particularly Cape Greco, where I tried to locate the concrete base to my tent on the former signals station. From a little beyond 'Table Mountain' we looked across to the ghost town of Varosha, the one-time Greek quarter of Famagusta, since 1974 deserted and in the hands of the Turkish Cypriots. All this was fascinating for me and I hope not too boring for Joanna.

We flew from Cyprus to Greece, in fulfilment of my long-held wish to visit the cradle of European civilization, as well as the grave of another of my eccentric heroes. We were fortunate in being able to stay with friends from Sudan – the Eastwoods. Basil was a diplomat who had served a spell in the British Embassy in Khartoum, where he had been the official to whom I answered in my role as an embassy warden. From Khartoum he moved to Athens, where he was first secretary. (He later became British ambassador to Syria.) He and his wife Alison guided our sightseeing in the Greek capital for two days before we set off on our own, across the Peloponnese and over the Corinth Canal, for the small coastal town of Missolonghi.

If ever a place oozed atmosphere, this quiet fishing port did. It is situated by a lagoon on the edge of flatlands (part swamplands) skirting the mountains. Joanna immediately wanted to paint it but a couple of pen-sketches had to suffice. Why the atmosphere? The answer is chiefly – for us at least – Lord Byron, who on 19 April 1824, at the age of thirty-six, died in Missolonghi of a fever. The house in which he breathed his last is there to see, with a considerable collection of memorabilia, plus a fine portrait of the poet in Albanian dress.

Whatever attracted me to Byron, my reader may ask? Perhaps the combination of creative thinker or artist – mystic almost – and man of action that I descried also in T.E. Lawrence and Charles George Gordon. To say the poet was, like the latter, a 'soldier-saint' would be going rather far. Few, if any, would allow that he was in any sense a saint. Yet the designation would not be absurdly wide of the mark. It is little known that over the last few weeks of his life Byron welcomed visits from a reverend gentleman named Kennedy and that he kept a Bible at his bedside. Some of his last recorded words, in answer to this Reverend, were, 'Yes, not my will but His be done.'

There was always another side to George Gordon, Lord Byron, very different from the rakish stereotype. It is movingly portrayed in George Wilson Knight's classic study, *Lord Byron: Christian virtues*. And has the reader spotted the coincidence: *George Gordon*, Lord

Byron, and General Charles *George Gordon*? The poet's mother was Catherine Gordon, third wife of Captain John ('Mad Jack') Byron, who deserted her not long after their son's birth. She then moved to Aberdeenshire in Scotland, where she brought her son up. So famous poet and equally famous general were, you might almost say, related.

Having read Wilson Knight's meticulously-documented book while at school, I discovered later that this scholar of English literature was living in England's West Country. This was in the mid-seventies, when I was lodging in Exeter, so I made a point of looking him up. I was startled when, having knocked at his front-door, it opened to reveal a figure clad in theatrical garb – Elizabethan costume, I rather think. I have since learnt that, in university circles, he was a highly-acclaimed actor as well as lecturer. Though approaching eighty when I saw him, he was obviously still wedded to the stage. He ushered me into a room with low lighting and we sat together, munching cake and sipping tea. I began talking about Byron, sharing with him my unorthodox ideas about the poet.

'But this is a most interesting analysis,' my host enthused. 'The poet was of course a many-sided character, but the parallel you see with Gordon of Khartoum is fascinating. And his nobler qualities have been neglected far too long. You should develop your thesis – indeed, work it into an article for publication.'

I was greatly encouraged by his words and said as much, though have never managed to follow his advice. The conversation then turned to Wilson Knight's days at Oxford, where he had been my father's contemporary at St Edmund Hall, as it turned out. The latter confirmed this, recalling his striking looks and exquisite attire.

Joanna and I returned from Missolonghi for two days more with the Eastwoods in Athens and then flew, for the third leg of our post-Yemen holiday, to Tunis. As must now be apparent, this holiday was a conspicuous self-indulgence on my part – coupled with a desire to share with Joanna important past experiences.

Tunisia was an anti-climax after Cyprus and Greece. We did the city *souq* – long, tunnel-like, very colourful covered walkways – impressed in particular by the extensive area devoted to gold (we didn't buy any). We visited Sidi Bou Saïd and enjoyed a coffee among all the white, blue-shuttered houses, but we gave ancient Carthage a miss. As we passed it on the metro Joanna muttered irreverently, 'Just another pile of old stones.'

I enjoyed some mild nostalgia, identifying the building where I had studied Arabic. I also made topographical notes for an attempt at fiction with an Arab world theme I was playing with. But that was it.

***

We arrived back in UK two weeks after leaving the Yemen and set about organising ourselves – and our Sherborne home.

Joanna immediately contacted local primary schools and was soon being called out to fill in where teachers went absent – 'supply teaching', it was called. I did some practical work in house and garden but also pressed on with what I was writing. This routine – Joanna off and on at schools and me working on my 'novel' – lasted till just before Christmas, when my literary effort was complete. Unfortunately (perhaps fortunately), publishers did not bite.

After Christmas I began teaching in an 'Executive Language Centre' in Yeovil, to which European businesses or banks paid a lot of money for selected staff to receive one-to-one tuition in English. Joanna taught there too on an intermittent basis. It was non-contractual employment though more or less full-time for me. The Centre itself was a country house with pleasant grounds and, in good weather, teacher and student would wander outside and sit on a garden seat or even go for walks for teaching sessions. Formal dinner, in considerable style, was arranged for students each evening and teachers were encouraged to attend, bringing a guest if they wished, free of charge. It was a very agreeable experience which we both took advantage of.

This was 1989 – *annus mirabilis*, 'springtime of nations' in Central and Eastern Europe – and as the year progressed conversations with our sometimes distinguished clients turned more and more to what was happening in East Germany. We placed bets, verbally at least, on when the Berlin wall would come down. I remember a top German executive telling me, 'It'll be ten years at least.'

One-to-one teaching is intense and a thirty-hour week can be tiring; gradually, however, you learn to pace yourself. Once I had settled down I started on another writing project, the completion of my 'church in politics' book. A literary agent happily took it on that summer but finding a significant publisher was another story. As already mentioned, the book finally came out in 1993.

By 1990 it was becoming clear that I needed more stable and remunerative employment. I had toyed with the idea of working for the Church again. I put out feelers in UK but bishops and others showed little interest in someone who had been overseas for ten years – in secular work to boot. It quickly became obvious that I would have to consider employment in foreign climes once again. This was not, I should point out, at all unattractive to me.

The Sultanate of Oman beckoned. Our friends the Gordons were there, for a start. But more to the point I came across advertisements for two interesting though very different posts: an assistant professorship in English at Sultan Qaboos University and the Anglican chaplaincy in Muscat. I applied for both and it soon seemed likely that I would be offered the university position. I was set to accept as soon as the firm offer came but something wholly unexpected intervened.

I heard from the Chairman of the Protestant Church Council in Muscat that I had not been selected for the chaplaincy (due to my 'lack of recent experience') but, he added, would I like to become General Manager of a chain of bookshops? The Council Chairman himself, a Swede, was running the company at the time but he was keen to return home. After careful thought – and discussion with Joanna – I accepted this position, though having no experience in the world of business.

The bookshop company had the name 'Family Bookshop', being one of a number of sister companies spread around the Middle East. These were theoretically independent under local sponsors but in practice answered to a head office in Limassol, Cyprus. The Chairman and Coordinator working from this office were Lebanese.

A meeting with the Chairman in London fixed the terms of my appointment and in April 1990 I was flying, via Cyprus to tie off a few ends with the Coordinator, to Muscat. Joanna remained in

UK to see out the period of her teaching contract with a school in Somerset. She would follow me to Oman in August.

My other half found it very difficult saying goodbye to me this time even though she knew we would be together again within a few months. When I had left her to go to Sudan in January 1978 she had felt her spirits amazingly lift once I had gone. This was partly, no doubt, because she had so much to do, looking after two children as well as carrying on teaching. This time round it was different. She had a full-time teaching job, to be sure, but the 'children' were now young adults away from home, Edmund up at Oxford and Annabel at Roehampton, in London, about to finish a Surrey degree. Joanna possibly caught a whiff of the tension that was beginning in the Gulf region, with Saddam Hussein making threatening noises about the 'rich, small, vulnerable state' of Kuwait – though few in the West seemed to be taking any notice.

Needs must, and we both got on with life in our respective situations, Joanna keeping going as a teacher while I commenced my new profession as a company manager.

Family Bookshop Oman LLC (FB Oman) was the largest of the companies directed from Cyprus. They had all had small beginnings as Bible Bookshops and for this reason the Family Bookshop organisation as a whole was under the control of the Middle East Council of Churches. They still sold Bibles and related literature in a small way but had developed over the years into retailers of a wide selection of books, mostly secular, in both English and Arabic. The bigger companies, like the one I was running, were wholesalers as well as retailers, supplying books, newspapers and magazines to outlets other than their own.

FB Oman comprised a company office, a distribution centre and six retail outlets, of which the biggest and most successful was in a suburb of the capital known as Medinat Qaboos, where also the office was situated. Three others were in or near greater Muscat while two were situated in Salalah, five hundred miles or so to the south. As General Manager I had the responsibility of overseeing all these outlets, which meant visits on a regular basis. The company strength, with myself, was twenty-five. This included an experienced

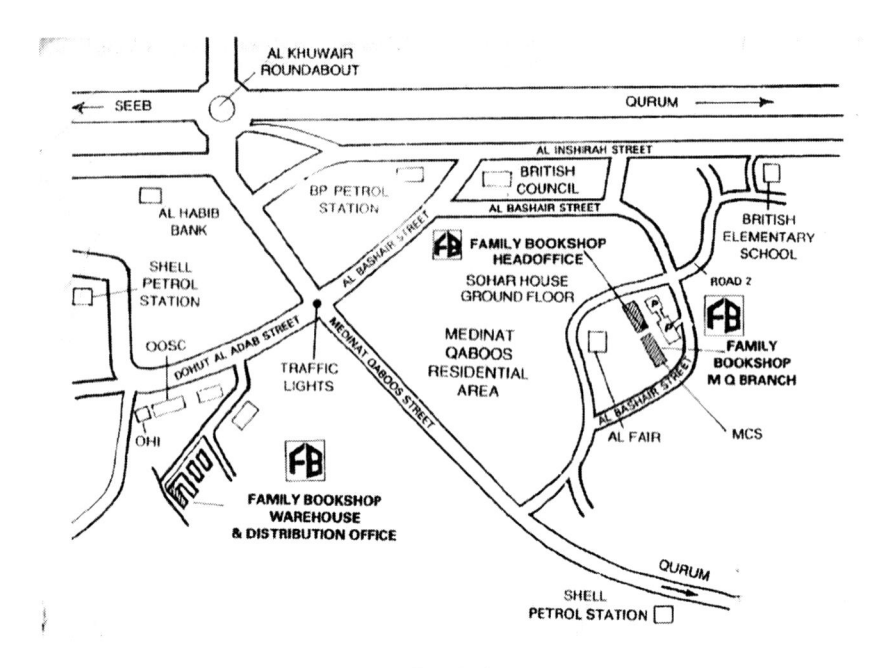

Map to advertise central Family Bookshop

Philip at FB Bookfair with Omani minister

bookbuyer and sales manager, an English lady whose husband (also working for us) was Lebanese. There was one other British member of staff, a Pakistani and two Omanis, but all the rest when I took over were from India – many hailing from Kerala, a region of the sub-continent where Christians are well represented. There may have been a preponderance of the latter in the company but overall it was a mix – Christian, Muslim, Hindu. The company sponsor, legally its owner, was of course Omani.

On arrival I spent two weeks learning the ropes from my Swedish predecessor. There was a lot to learn, starting from scratch as I was. (Selling parish magazines and organizing fêtes was the nearest thing I had to relevant experience.) By the time I took over I had just about got to know my staff and what went on in the company office, which was my place of work. Fortunately, I had not only the excellent sales manager but also a highly efficient administrative secretary – who would politely remind me of my duties – and an equally good chief accountant. Quite soon I was getting into a routine: arriving at the office at eight and working till one (which might include visits to outlets), going home for lunch and returning at half-past three to carry on till seven. With a half-day in the office on Saturdays, this made a forty-eight hour week. The shops had slightly different hours: nine to one and four to eight, Monday to Saturday. The working hours were long by UK standards but I personally found them acceptable as I no longer had to bring student assignments or exams home to mark – the considerable downside of teaching!

The two and a half hour break in the middle of the day gave time for a relaxed lunch – cooked each day by a Sri Lankan housemaid inherited from our predecessor – and a siesta, should one feel the need. Home itself was also inherited, a large house situated in a residential area built over sand dunes between the sea and barren mountains. A further inherited acquisition was a company car, a luxurious Toyota Crown, which I swiftly discovered had known better days.

Driving an automobile, reliable or not, was not the way I went to Salalah to pay my first visit to our southern branches. There was a perfectly good road, certainly, wending its way through the semi-desert terrain that separates the north of the country from the south. People used sometimes to drive to Salalah and it could even be done in a day though most broke their journey, staying the night half-way at a guest house. The norm, certainly for people on business, was to fly there – not Gulf Air, but Oman's internal airline. This I did, the flight lasting an hour. I was met by (Abdul) Aziz, the charming Indian who managed our fair-sized outlet in the town and a smaller one in Holiday Inn – which is where I stayed.

Salalah is very different from Muscat. Set on the edge of the Indian Ocean, with a range of low hills to the west, it has a micro-climate which includes a summer monsoon. Soon after the rains begin the hills are transformed almost overnight from a scratchy brown wilderness to soft green slopes – like nothing else in Arabia or the Gulf I had seen. They reminded me of the Wiltshire downs, or perhaps film shots I had seen of the Yorkshire dales. For someone living mostly in desert climes, walking the hills at their most lush (for the miracle is fleeting) was a joy, a dream. And I speak advisedly, for dreams of green, hilly countryside used to adorn my sleep quite regularly when I was in Sudan.

On a later visit to Salalah, when Joanna was with me, Aziz took us to see *a second* tomb of Job in those Dhofar Hills, as they are properly called. We entered the building that housed the tomb, which was draped in a green cloth.

'How extraordinary!' I whispered to Joanna as we stood gazing.

'Extraordinary?' she muttered. 'What's so extraordinary about it?'

We had now moved to the head of the tomb. 'It's so *long*. Do you think Job can have been abnormally tall?'

'Giants in those days, you mean? Possibly, I suppose. But there's nothing in the Bible to suggest it, is there?'

I shook my head. 'No, not giants as the norm. There was Goliath, of course.' The conversation was going nowhere so I drew a tangent. 'Job was a giant of a man in another way, one must remember. Maybe this elongation is a subtle kind of metaphor.' Joanna wasn't listening.

More pressing than the height of the tomb's occupant was the question of its authenticity. Did it, or the one in Yemen, house the bodily remains of the archetypal sufferer? Traditions of this sort – like the last resting place of Abraham in Hebron – should not lightly be dismissed; 'no smoke without fire' is not a bad rule of thumb. But in this case one of the traditions had to be false. We never settled the matter but became aware of a rivalry between the Yemen and Oman in matters historical. They both claimed Belqīs, Queen of Sheba, for example, as well as Job. Of course, today's unified Yemen Arab Republic and the Sultanate have an adjacent border, and as the precise extent of ancient kingdoms is unknown there can be confusion.

Oman is sometimes associated with the Magi, or 'Three Wise Men', who came to pay homage to the newly born 'king of the Jews' with gifts of gold, frankincense and myrrh. Persia is more usually cited as the provenance of these star-gazers but the Omani claim has some rationale – as we discovered when my colleague led us to a flat area near Salalah where frankincense trees flourish. Not so far from Salalah, too, is the ancient city of Ubar (until 1992, 'lost city of Ubar'), believed to have been the centre of the trade in frankincense. Most of the latter today, as well as myrrh, comes from Oman, the Yemen, or – just across the water – Somalia.

All this scenic beauty and accompanying history refreshed the spirits on that first visit to the Dhofar region, as also many times subsequently. Yet Salalah itself can also refresh.

On the eastern side of the town, near Holiday Inn, majestic palms flank and arch over the road, and having strolled beneath and a little beyond them you can suddenly find yourself in a green-fringed, almost English lane. There you may pause at a roadside stall to buy a coconut, fallen or picked from those same palms, and drink its milk – easily done as the vendor will have drilled a hole through the shell. All the while you will be aware of a low, rhythmic murmur from the sea to your south – much more than a murmur in rough weather – as ocean rollers break onto the beach of soft white sand, causing hundreds of little crabs to scurry into their holes.

After a couple of months, when I was more or less feeling on top of things, I was faced with annual stocktaking. This, lasting two weeks, was always the busiest time of the year as books and other items in every shop were counted and valued. My role was to do the rounds and encourage – picnic meals served to all were good morale-boosters – and then a great deal of checking and adding up. Finally, at the end of July, the report would go off to our Director and Coordinator in Cyprus. They would assess the 'state of the union' and make appropriate decisions relating to the Family Bookshop Company as a whole. The following month was normally reserved for the General Manager's home holiday, but not for me that year. Having been with the company little over three months I had not yet earned a vacation.

Two days into August the Iraqi war machine rolled into Kuwait. Resistance was quickly crushed and very soon the Iraqis were in control of the country. A limited conflict between the two countries had seemed likely to some but no one had predicted a full scale invasion and occupation – except the CIA, one day before it happened. The world watched horrified, wondering if Saddam Hussein would stop at Kuwait. Very soon the whole region was being talked of as a war zone.

This was hardly encouraging for Joanna, preparing to join me later that month. She had managed to get through our separation, though not without some emotion. I could say the same of myself.

'For I am your lady, and you are my man.' If I heard this song being sung by Celine Dion once, I heard it a thousand times. And whenever I did so a hollow feeling developed inside me as I identified with the melancholy male being addressed. Every now and then some acquaintance of mine would notice a sudden glazing of the eyes, perhaps as we sat together in a restaurant.

'What's the matter, Philip?' he would ask. 'It may never happen!'

I would come to with a start. 'I was recalling something my current way of life had pushed into limbo. It's nothing.' My companion would eye me doubtfully but tactfully change the subject.

Back in UK, the tension increased tenfold for Joanna as friends and relatives implored her not to fly out. (My mother, in her eightieth year, was not one of them.) One close friend of the family, who had been a naval chaplain, was wont to repeat the familiar mantra, 'In time of war, women and children should stay at home.'

The end of August finally came and Joanna willed herself onto the plane. It dropped down in Dhahran, Saudi Arabia, which worried her and a few others, for it was within range of Saddam's missiles. But though signs of military activity were visible, nothing untoward occurred and the plane took off again for Muscat. I should point out that she might not have made it at all to Oman if she hadn't had the best of friends accompanying her. This was Rosie Gordon, returning with her two children after a summer vacation in UK to join Philip ('The General') at his post. Rosie metaphorically held Joanna's hand during the flight and Philip and I met all four at Seeb airport.

Our daughter Annabel arrived off a flight from UK the next day. She had gained her Surrey degree and was set upon a career in the media. She was aware that you could not just walk into a good position; by one means or another you had to gain experience. The Sultanate of Oman, she was certain, would offer that opportunity. Negative counsel about travel to the Gulf grew more and more insistent, so she told her wavering parent, 'Look, Mum, I'm going to Oman whatever you decide. I can't pass up this chance.'

Having arrived, Annabel immediately picked up a job as an English news presenter with Radio Muscat, to which was soon added the planning and presenting of an entertainment programme. She then found a second opening: studio experience with a British Council video expert.

Once Joanna was safely in Oman she never looked back. Within a week or two she began teaching in the nursery class at the British School, Muscat, where she settled in quickly and was soon immersed in designing and implementing her personal style of instruction. There was the diving bell to plummet the depths of her fishy class 'ocean'; there were amusing drawings and diagrams posted on the walls; there were new and exciting books once she had pushed for and obtained a grant to set up a classroom library.

***

The year 1991 approached with everyone's attention focused on looming hostilities between an Allied Coalition and Iraq, to free citizens and others from a ruthless occupation. We watched as soldiers and airmen from the West arrived, some settling into the InterContinental Hotel, situated on the edge of a superb beach and offering many facilities – not least some smart shops, one of them an FB outlet. We began to enjoy the place, Joanna reading or sketching on the lawns, Annabel swimming in the Olympic-size pool and me, a little later on, playing squash. At one stage our daughter found herself sharing the pool with male members of the American military – which she didn't mind at all.

As the Coalition forces built up their strength towards the end of 1990 and into 1991, we watched large supply planes fly into and out of Seeb airport in regular waves. Then, when the Coalition air attacks had started on 17 January 1991, we followed progress through the media.

I and my family had ample opportunity for keeping up with news of any description because I took home every issue of all major British newspapers. These were copies that had been approved and stamped at the Ministry of Information (MOI), prior to our circulation of the issue around the capital. On occasions the ministry official would black or cut out some picture, report or article considered offensive. We then did the same with the rest before distributing them. Books, I might add, also needed approval before being put on sale. This censorship routine was the main reason for my visiting the MOI frequently – easy enough, as it was a quick drive from my office. In the end I got to know the personnel well, from the Director downwards, this being assisted by my knowledge of Arabic.

Those of us who followed the course of the conflict from Oman did not seriously fear an Iraqi missile or gas attack, unlike those in Saudi Arabia, Qatar and Bahrain, who felt distinctly vulnerable. We kept in telephone touch with our friends the Babikers, now in Qatar's capital city, Doha.

'Missiles have fallen on Bahrain, which is no distance from here,' Tricia told Joanna. 'There's a lot of tension around because we've been issued with gas masks. It's a waiting game, really.'

'Not very nice,' her friend sympathised. 'What about the kids? How are they finding it – the masks, especially?'

'Amani and the three older ones are fine. They don't make a fuss as they know what it's about. The two youngsters aren't so sure. We make a game of the masks, which helps.'

What Joanna and I did begin to notice in Oman was a degree of anti-Western – more precisely, anti-American/British – feeling. This, we assumed, was the explanation for the sudden arrival one morning of a dead rat on our doorstep. Cats, of course, quite often bring home as a kind of offering their mangled, half-eaten prey, but we had no cat at the time.

The Coalition air bombardment finally gave way to the ground assault, which commenced on the twenty-fourth of February. This lasted exactly a hundred hours, ending on the last day of the month (significant for me) when President George Bush (Senior) drew back from a 'turkey shoot' of Iraqi troops in frantic retreat.

A postscript to our experience of following the Gulf War from the vantage point of Oman was the visit I made to Kuwait some months later. This was to obtain distribution rights to some of the country's magazines and newspapers. I looked forward to this trip, hoping to find out for myself the impact the invasion, occupation and liberating war had had on the place. I made my most dramatic discovery, however, before the plane had even touched down. As we descended towards the airport we were suddenly enveloped in blackness; we had entered the band of sulphurous smoke that had been hovering over the country ever since the firing of oil wells by Saddam Hussein prior to the withdrawal of his troops.

Once landed, I booked into a hotel and spent three days pleasantly pounding the flat streets of Kuwait City, seeing how much destruction the Iraqis had inflicted – still very visible but not too extensive. I visited the Kuwait branch of Family Bookshop, just one big outlet, and made an appointment to see an appropriate ministry official. He received me graciously and after visits to one or two other offices – formalities in the Arab world are seldom simple – I came away with at least some new agencies, including one for a good-selling paper, *al-Watan* ('The Fatherland').

A spin-off of my position as General Manager was meeting some interesting authors, usually because they wanted to encourage

Philip, with Joanna and Simon Bouji, tackling General Sir Peter de la Billière

sales by having a book-signing session in one of our shops. For obvious reasons, the books normally had a local connection.

One such author was General Sir Peter de la Billière, Commander-in-Chief of British forces participating in the Gulf War and second-in-command to the Supreme Commander, General Norman Schwarzkopf of the U.S. Army. The role of the British in the ground offensive was code-named Desert Saber and de la Billière describes this and much else in his book *Storm Command*, which in 1992 we were selling and he was signing in our Medinat Qaboos outlet.

I drove him around – no longer in that Toyota Crown – and was with him throughout the signing session; I had wondered if I would feel overawed but in fact he was the easiest person to talk to.

'I have an idea we were in Khartoum together, sir,' I remarked on picking him up from the InterContinental Hotel. 'Weren't you in charge of the British Army Training Team there, and living in Omdurman?'

'I was, yes, until the end of '78. What about you?'

'I arrived in January of that year. So we overlapped for a while, though I don't think we met despite being briefly neighbours in Omdurman. How did you find it?'

'A very good posting, generally. A change from life on Salisbury Plain.'

'So you know the Salisbury area,' I said with interest. 'I spent much of my childhood there; army camps all over the place. In fact, a prisoner-of-war camp near us at first, which my father as local vicar used to visit. One of the POWs – Germans, they were – used sometimes to come to the vicarage and he made me a superb model Spitfire.'

So we conversed, exchanging thoughts and memories. I learnt something of his previous experience of Oman in the early 70s, for instance. This was for the Dhofar campaign, when 22 Troop SAS joined local forces in putting down militant, Yemeni-supported opposition to Sultan Qaboos – a fascinating episode. All in all, I found the general charming, modest, interesting, asking myself not for the first time why members of our armed forces are such straight, likeable characters. Something to do with being under orders and implementing them without question, I speculated.

Then I remembered the Roman centurion of long ago, for whom Jesus had nothing but praise.

A second author I met soon after my arrival was Tom Stacey. Some of his novels or short stories, most of them set in the Middle East, were on sale in our shops but it was as publisher that he visited FB Oman on a regular basis. His company, Stacey International, specialises in beautifully-produced titles about the Arab world – 'coffee-table' books you could call them – which were some of our best sellers. Joanna and I got to know Tom well at this time, coming to realise that we had quite a lot in common. Most notably, I discovered on reading *Decline*, his tale of personal and national collapse, that he felt almost as strongly as I did about the enormity of 'the church political'.

A third significant writer to come my way had no specific plans to promote the sale of his book. However, he was interested to know how many copies FB had been able to move so he turned up one day, unannounced, in my office.

'What can I do for you?' I said, rising from my desk.

'I've just been in your shop looking for my book,' he replied.

'*Your* book? So you're an author.'

'One book to my name, anyway.' He extended a hand, which I took. 'Cooper – Roger Cooper.' I gestured him to a chair.

'So did you find the book on our shelves?'

'I'm afraid not.'

'Oh, I'm so sorry. Should I know you? The name has a slightly familiar ring, but ...' I concentrated. 'No, it won't come.'

He smiled. 'If you read the British papers you could have come across it. The book is called *Death Plus Ten Years* and describes the time I spent in an Iranian jail – as a kind of hostage.'

'But of course!' I exclaimed, 'You were high profile in the press not long ago. A government minister went to Tehran to push for your release, if I'm not mistaken. Now you're here. Remarkable!'

He fumbled in his bag. 'I've a copy of the book with me. Please accept it. I'll add a signature.' He scribbled a message on the fly leaf and handed it over.

'That's very kind – and we'll certainly order some for the shops.

My book-buyer may have ordered some, in fact, and I never noticed.' I scanned the cover. 'It should sell well.'

'Indifferent sales to date. Not like the Beirut hostages.'

We chatted on for a while, with me commiserating over the all-too-frequent discrepancy between quantity of sales and quality of product.

My surprise visitor had been accused by the Iranians and was then convicted of being 'the British Master Spy' from 'the Intelligent Service' (*sic*). He was, in truth, a businessman and lover of all things Persian, including the language, in which he was fluent. Arrested at gunpoint on leaving his Tehran hotel in December 1985, he was incarcerated in Evin prison (where tens of thousands perished during and after the Khomeini revolution), to be finally released in April 1991. The title of his book records the sentence passed on him by the court, which refused him the services of a lawyer. A reviewer of his book in *The Independent* summed him up thus: 'Roger Cooper is perhaps the last of a distinguished line of Englishmen, from R. Burton and E.G. Browne to T.E. Lawrence and Wilfred Thesiger, whose romantic longing of ailleurs drew them to the Middle East where they found their spiritual home.'

I saw a good deal of him and we had some absorbing conversations – not least on religion. This led him to attend church one Sunday, when he heard me preach the sermon. I recall in particular a dinner party in our home where he was the most entertaining of guests. At one point, having opened a new bottle of wine, I was about to refill his glass.

'This is a different vintage, Roger,' I said. 'Would you like a new glass?'

'Of course I would,' he retorted immediately. 'Why do you ask?'

I was put to shame. (Asked the question myself at the time, I would probably have replied, 'Don't be absurd!')

Roger went on, 'Dining etiquette is important, Philip. It's the mark of a civilised society – indeed, of a civilised person. I did my best to inculcate some of its principles to my fellow prisoners in Iran. They had voted me chief chef and I took the responsibility very seriously.'

Our guest's experience in captivity not only stands as witness to his expertise in culinary art and manners. More importantly, it reveals his humanity: in his book he writes of his prison interrogator-cum-torturer almost with affection.

Probably the best known of the writers we met in Oman was another of that 'distinguished line of Englishmen'.

The maverick explorer Wilfred Thesiger came to the Sultanate to attend an exhibition in Muscat mounted in his honour. He had asked if we could, to coincide with this visit, arrange a book-signing session to promote his autobiography, *The Life Of My Choice*. We were, of course, most happy to oblige.

The exhibition, sponsored jointly by the British Council and the *Diwān* (council of state, or government), was a major affair, featuring numerous photos and memorabilia from Thesiger's trek across the Empty Quarter. Besides the explorer himself, guests of honour included one or two of his Omani companions on that adventure, most notably Sālim bin Kabīna, who had been a very young man at the time. We as a family were official guests at the opening ceremony and later at the lunch – Omani style, featuring a whole roast lamb served with biryani rice. There we met Thesiger and the companions, bin Kabina clearly proud at having been intimately associated with the famous Englishman, photos on display providing ample testimony to this. The now grizzled companion took me aside at one point.

'*Yā sayyed*, could I ask a favour?' he began – in rich Omani colloquial. I murmured my readiness to listen.

He continued. 'I was long ago faithful servant to the noble Englishman here, as everyone knows, but the British government has never recognised my services. Could you speak to your people and suggest they award me a pension?'

Needless to say, this took me completely aback. 'I fully appreciate your position, *yā sheikh*,' I replied finally, 'but unfortunately I don't have *wāsta* with the high and mighty in my land. Even if I gained a hearing, they would take no notice.' It took a bit more to convince the dear man but he eventually saw my point.

The book-signing was held in Medinat Qaboos. There was a crowd of people waiting in the shop for Thesiger to arrive and when

Philip talking with Wilfred Thesiger before his TV interview

I entered to be ready to welcome him one of them remarked to our sales manager, 'Perhaps that's him now.' (The sales manager relished telling me this later; being nowhere near an octogenarian, I was not exactly flattered!) As to the signing, it was a success in terms of the number of volumes sold but a customer was heard to murmur as she walked off clutching her book, 'Crusty old gentlemen, I must say.'

There was a further significant event related to Wilfred Thesiger's visit: an interview with him for Muscat Radio/TV, subsequently taken up by CNN. Annabel was assigned to conduct this as she had already performed such tasks for her employers. It was held at the British Embassy Residence in Old Muscat and I attended, sitting with Thesiger while technicians set up a makeshift studio.

'Is it a good experience, coming back here after all these years,' I asked him.

'I've been here several times since that journey across the empty quarter, of course,' he pointed out. 'But to answer your question, I'm not sure that this return is so good. I appreciate the way the Omanis have honoured me but find it distressing to see the old ways and customs being eroded. Western ways have had a devastating effect upon Arab culture and I for one regret it.'

It was interesting to hear from the lips of the man himself something of his feelings – doubts, mostly – about the way life was developing in the Middle East, as indeed more widely. The recording of the interview then went ahead, but we ourselves never saw it on the box. Friends of ours on holiday in China at the time, however, tuned into CNN and were amazed to see Annabel putting the questions to a figure of such renown.

***

Reference to Wilfred Thesiger's long association with Oman, as also to Peter de la Billière's early experiences in the country, makes it appropriate at this point to say something on the history of the Sultanate, especially in relation to its ties with Britain.

Oman – or Muscat and Oman, as the territory used to be called – has a long and interesting history. For some twelve hundred years, until the coming of Islam in the seventh century of our era, it was under the control of either the Persian Empire or the rulers of the Yemen. It was a valuable possession because its long coastline gave trading seafarers safe and easy access to Persia in the north, India in the east and Africa in the south. A century after the advent of Islam, however, Muscat and Oman developed its own form of elective theocracy, choosing an imam as spiritual leader. This lasted until 1154, when the Nabhanite dynasty of hereditary kings was established, to be maintained unchallenged for almost three hundred years. There then began a struggle between imam and king or sultan that continued until modern times.

Early in the sixteenth century the Portuguese started trading with India and to facilitate this took control of Muscat and the surrounding territory. For a century and a half they remained the dominant sea power of the region but in 1650 the imam Sultan bin Saif recaptured Muscat from its colonial rulers. At the end of the seventeenth century his son Saif bin Sultan began extending Omani influence and power by seeking to annex some East African coastlands, an important Portuguese garrison falling to him in 1698. Following this success, he was able to gain control of the island of Zanzibar – a centre of the slave trade – as well as the coastal regions north of Mozambique.

In 1837 Sultan bin Sultan placed the island at the heart of his empire by making it his main place of residence. At his death in 1856, however, the empire was divided – following strenuous British diplomacy – between his two sons, one inheriting Muscat and Oman while the other took Zanzibar and the Omani possessions along the east African coast.

Britain's interest in the affairs of Oman had commenced well before this development; that interest was formalised in 1798 when Oman became a British protectorate. A century later the Sultans were seeking British help against the imams elected by tribes of the interior around Nizwa, who were threatening the coastal territories. In 1920 the British, acting on behalf of the Sultan, negotiated the Treaty of Seeb, by which autonomy was granted to the Nizwa region. In 1954, however, a new imam, supported by a powerful tribal leader, initiated armed resistance to the efforts of the Sultan to extend his control into the interior. This insurrection continued until 1959, when with British help it was put down.

A further threat to the Sultan emerged in the 1960s when a newly-formed Marxist movement, the Popular Front for the Liberation of Oman, took up the cause of insurgents operating in the hills of Dhofar. This precipitated the palace coup of 1970, when Qaboos bin Sa'id, who had graduated from Sandhurst military academy in UK, ousted his father Sultan Sa'id bin Taymur – who was then exiled to London, where later he died. The new young Sultan turned his attention to the south and, after gaining help from Jordan, Iran and Britain, finally crushed the insurgency in 1975.

Since that time Sultan Qaboos has ruled Oman in royal style, retaining for himself the reins of power, though allowing himself a Council of Ministers and a Consultative Council (*Majlis al-Shūra*). The country's wealth remains its oil reserves, a national petroleum company, jointly owned by Shell, having been set up in 1967 to exploit this resource.

IX

Quite a Liberal Society

Such was the autocratic – though in some ways quite liberal – Arab state to which Edmund, having obtained his degree from Oxford (and completed three months as a waiter in a Sherborne hotel to earn some money), came in October 1991 to gain some experience prior to launching himself on the world as a journalist. He joined us and his sister in our residence in al-Khuwair, on the edge of Greater Muscat.

His aim was, as I say, to be a journalist. Like his father, grandfather and great grandfather before him, his degree was in theology, a subject he both enjoyed and performed well in. Yet he had no wish to take that discipline further – whether academically, or vocationally as a full-time servant of the Church. I advised against the latter and with Joanna encouraged the journalism idea as appropriate to his temperament and gifts. With this in mind we arranged for him to take a local course in typing. He also began learning Arabic, as we all felt that proficiency in the language would be a useful string to his bow.

As a follow-up to this, quite early in 1992 he went to Syria, the manager of the Family Bookshop branch there, at the request of our company Coordinator in Cyprus, agreeing to take him on while he continued his language study. In the summer he attended a course in Arabic at the Institute of Languages, Damascus University. On my way home at the end of July, I spent a few days with him – my first visit to the country.

I recall Damascus as a huge, meandering city. If any two things could be said to sum the place up for me – culturally, at least –

it would be coffee, its seductive aroma and the hordes of people sipping it, and backgammon, equal hordes playing it or watching it being played. The streets in the centre were packed; I was told the population at the time was six million, of whom I knew not a soul apart from my son. Which makes one experience I had remarkable.

Out walking – I think it was to find an airline office – I became lost and decided I must ask directions from another pedestrian. I was on an inner bypass and there were few around but a lone figure was walking ahead. I quickened my pace until we were level.

'Excuse me,' I began, 'but could you …' The words died on my lips as he stopped and turned. I knew the man!

'*Marhaban*,' he said. 'Good to see you again. How are you?' I gazed at him, unable to find words. I knew him as a former colleague, yes, but at that moment couldn't for the life of me remember where this had been. He, meanwhile, showed no particular surprise – imagining, I suppose, that I'd spotted him from over the road and purposely approached him.

'Ah, indeed, how am I?' I stuttered. 'Yes, er, I'm fine. And you? *Keif as-sahha?*'

'*Bikheir, al-hamdu lillah*. So you're now in Damascus. A wonderful city, you'll agree.'

At this point only could I place him as the Palestinian who had been Head of Arabic in the Language Centre at Sana'a University, his office right opposite mine. We exchanged some items of news before he gave me the directions I needed. Once we had parted, I tried to calculate the odds against randomly approaching a stranger in an unknown foreign capital only to find the 'stranger' isn't a stranger at all!

Edmund was lodging with a Syrian family in the Christian quarter of the Old City, near *Bāb Toma* (St Thomas' Gate), and I joined the family for the few days of my visit. I was captivated by the area, the narrow lanes and alleyways, overhung by bay windows and little balconies, on each side of you those heavy, padlocked timber doors behind which – you knew – lay charming courtyards, secret to all but those to whom the porter opened. I walked with Edmund down 'the street called Straight', thinking of St Paul, then

Edmund when AFP correspondent in Kuwait, with Annabel

became fascinated with the myriad small shops – window after window displaying a rich assortment of wares, both modern and antiquarian. Best of all, we stood at *Bāb Toma* and sipped a fruit cocktail to end all cocktails.

'This is amazing, unbelievably good,' I said, licking my lips. 'I'd give up alcohol if one of these was constantly available.'

Edmund would have none of it. 'You can't mean that, Dadio.'

I grinned. 'No, I suspect not!'

We had one trip together outside the capital, to a village in the foothills some twenty-five miles away called Ma'lūla. It was attractively situated in a narrow valley, the colourful houses climbing up a steep cliff and the barren hills surrounding it displaying some striking features, not least a rift or siq (reminiscent of the spectacular one at Petra) at the head of the valley. We walked to the top of an elevation to the west to see an ancient site, then descended and visited a tiny Byzantine church – one of the earliest in existence, we were told – built over what was probably a much older place of pagan sacrifice. But it wasn't so much the physical features of the village or its surroundings that appealed so strongly; it was the fact that in this relative backwater the locals – or more accurately, the older among them – spoke Aramaic, the language of Jesus. What had once been the lingua franca of the region had dwindled in usage over the centuries until just a handful of people in isolated pockets communicated in it. This visit to Ma'lūla was easily my most memorable Syrian experience. Which is why on another visit to the country years later Joanna and I made a beeline for it.

Perhaps I should say something about the Syrians, albeit relying on the most fleeting of impressions. A single word springs to mind with which to epitomize this ancient people: gentleness. What I have experienced of them since – not least in neighbouring Lebanon, where I write this some twenty years later – only confirms that initial judgement.

***

I have said that the Sultanate of Oman represented, in my experience, quite a liberal society. By which I mean primarily that whatever your status or background – sex, ethnicity, nationality, religion – you were generally free to pursue your career and interests without interference from the authorities. My career in Oman I have already talked about to some extent. I shall, however, have more to say about it shortly as an unexpected twist brought it to an abrupt close. As to my interests – or rather both Joanna's and mine, and how we pursued them – I shall sketch them now.

There were the many trips we made in our Land Rover into the interior. Like everyone else – expatriates, I mean – we did the drives to well-known destinations, locations of special scenic or cultural interest such as Jebel Akhdar, the highest mountain in the Sultanate, with its village near the top where locals wove rugs which they offered for sale. From this village you could walk to the edge of an escarpment and look vertically down a drop of several thousand feet. We had seen even more spectacular sights in the Yemen, however, so were inclined to be blasé.

We went to Sinaw, more or less in the desert, to experience probably the most ancient and distinctive Arab activity – camel trading.

'I don't believe it!' Joanna gasped as we watched some men trying to fit a hefty-looking beast into the back of a pickup. 'There's no way they'll get him in.'

'I shouldn't be so sure,' I countered. 'They're very determined, these dealers.'

Determined they were, cajoling and commanding, pushing and pulling, bending and roping up the legs until finally it resembled nothing so much as a giant chicken trussed and ready for the oven. Then, creaking and groaning, the animal was squeezed into the truck.

'That's cruel,' Joanna commented, in line with her feelings generally about the way domestic animals are transported.

'It's the way of the world,' I said a little wearily. 'But at least this specimen of the animal kingdom is not destined for the slaughterhouse. Once unloaded at the home of its new owner it will receive treatment fitting its status in this part of the world, I'm sure. The camel is, after all, the fountain of all goodness for Arabs – practically, culturally, even linguistically.'

'Linguistically?' My spouse looked doubtful. 'What do you mean?'

Entertainment for children

By A Staff Reporter

There are very few organisations or associations which have devoted themselves to the task of entertaining children, whose main source of amusement has remained television and video in recent times.

There is hardly any film produced with just children in mind.

Yet, one can't complain about the role played by theatre groups exclusively for children. At least not in Oman.

Two years ago, around 50 talented residents of the country collaborated to give the best of entertainment to the children, through Dramarama — a theatre group devoted solely to children.

It was the initiative of two enterprising women. Cassandra Bullock and Philippa Hogg, which made this dream a reality.

Since then they have presented six delightful plays with a moral or ecological message. The characters are visually engaging and the atmosphere definitely lively.

Recently the duo who are otherwise employed, presented *The Mermaid's Pearl* (a 20 minute play), for the pre-school class of the British School. It was written by a member of the theatre and its a pilot venture by Dramarama.

Dramarama which celebrated its second anniversary recently went public two years ago with the play *Golden Goose* at the Inter-Continental Hotel. It was adapted by Hogg who is back in her hometown now.

Speaking to *Times*, Cassandra highlighted the group's plans on presenting a children's western theatre, which may go on the floorboards some time in October. "This will be a children's dinner theatre," she pointed out.

Explaining the role played by Dramarama in the entertainment scene, she said, "It is important for children to experience live theatre. And it is heartening to note that we have been compared to a repertory theatre or a professional group of actors who are involved in theatrical performance of various plays (for short periods) in England which keep moving throughout the country. This is indeed praiseworthy for amateurs like us."

Their play *The Selfish Shellfish*, written by David Wood highlighted the need to protect marine environment and the damage done to sea life, while *Utter Garbage* by Les Ellison highlight the importance of recycling and the problems associated with garbage strewn around. For this play the characters were dressed up as rats and the garbage constructed for the play was larger than life.

This had a great influence on the children who were heard talking about the play and the characters long after the play was staged, she pointed out.

Joanna Blair, a teacher at the British School and a member of Dramarama designs the set. "We have used the medium of drama to enrich the lives of the children in a proper manner. We want to send them home contended after the show, not disturbed. That is why all our plays are light hearted," she explained.

Their major sponsors throughout have been BP and Jotun. "Jotun has always provided free paints for our sets," she pointed out. Almost 50 per cent of the set is done and painted by the members themselves, who are all involved in the entertainment game without any material gain.

The team takes six to eight weeks to put up a play. The successful ones presented by them include *Punch and Jud's – Life Size*, *The Troll's Revenge*, written by Alan Davies and Philippe Hogg and *The Tempest*, Shakespeare's play adapted by Brian Dean. For this play, which was presented at Al Bustan the hotel constructed a huge ship which was built on the stage itself.

Most of the members of Dramarama are also involved in the Muscat Amateur Theatre which is very active in Oman.

A scene from Utter Garbage

Children's theatre is well and alive in Oman, thanks to Dramarama – a theatre group solely for children

The Dramarama troupe

Joanna Blair and Cassandra Bullock – making Dramarama a success

Dramarama, a pleasant leisure activity

'You know what they say about Arabic, every word has three meanings: a general meaning; its opposite; and something to do with a camel. If you still doubt the linguistic influence, listen to the noises camels make – like the one we've been watching. Why do you think Arabic has all those guttural sounds Westerners find almost impossible to reproduce?'

She was convinced.

We visited Nizwa with its impressive castle and souq, both in process of being 'restored'; then beyond to the village of Bahlā', notable for its pottery kilns snuggling among the date-palms – this of particular interest to Joanna, an amateur potter herself, who bought a pot or two. We took the rough coast road down south to Sūr, passing Turtle Beach on the way, and saw how traditional Arab dhows were constructed. But remaining most vividly in the memory are the picnicking trips we made up the palm-rich wadis that wound between the mountains, sometimes featuring a stream of the clearest water, plus water for irrigation purposes running along a *falāj* (aqueduct), often cut into the mountainside. At times the stream would widen and deepen to become a pool into which you could dive from the surrounding rocks.

While trips into the country were probably our main recreational activity, Joanna and I – and Annabel when she was with us – were also able to pursue our theatrical interests. There were several dramatic or operatic societies in Oman and Annabel quickly became involved in a production put on by one of them, a sort of fairy story staged in the gardens of the InterContinental Hotel. Friends of ours happened to be leading lights in a group called Dramarama specialising in innovative theatrical ventures and they decided to present *The Selfish Shellfish*, a spectacular play for children with an ecological theme. Permission was obtained to stage it in the National Auditorium at al-Bustan – a magnificent venue for any production, having amenities and facilities as sophisticated as a West End theatre. Joanna designed an impressive set while Annabel organised the lighting, a skill she had developed in her college days. This production was well received and opened the way for a second such.

Utter Garbage was the original composition of a fellow expatriate, Les Ellison, and it had never been staged before. The Dramarama committee read the script, were impressed and set out immediately to look for a cast, set designer and team of workers. The National Auditorium was once again booked and rehearsals were scheduled. Joanna was again asked to design the set, which she did most imaginatively; its most spectacular feature was a hugely-magnified rubbish tip. I was also approached by one of the husband and wife directors.

'We think you'd make a very good sea captain,' Cassandra suggested. 'That's if you don't mind having a tail.' I looked a little askance. 'The tail is non-negotiable, you must realise, because you'd be playing Captain Horatio Rodent.' She eyed me quizzically.

'You mean, I'd be a rat.'

'That's it. Most roles are rats of some kind so you won't feel out of place. And Captain Rodent has a wonderful time, sailing the nether seas in a sardine tin.'

This was irresistible, so I accepted the offer and immediately began learning my lines. I was fitted out with a smart costume, tail included, but it had an unusual feature. The naval cap and jacket were wholly traditional but my lower half comprised breaches to the knees and then sheer-line stockings. To this day I have not been allowed to forget the latter, which at the time caused much amusement.

With two ex-professionals amongst the cast, the production – a world première, no less – was a huge success and it was no surprise when we heard sometime later that the play had been published by Samuel French.

Dramarama's next venture failed to get off the ground through lack of support. I meanwhile was asked by another society to fill in at short notice for an actor who had withdrawn and take the role of Grand Inquisitor (Don AlHambra Del Belero) in Gilbert and Sullivan's *The Gondoliers*. In my youth I had enjoyed choral singing so I managed to get my head and vocal cords round the solo or part-songs; meanwhile, the pantomime quality of G&S light opera was much to my taste. The whole experience was extremely enjoyable, not least because it reminded me of my father. From his university days he had been an ardent aficionado of G&S and it was this same much-loved opera that he chose for my introduction to the genre – as a boy of eight or nine – at a performance in Salisbury Playhouse. This was a day or two before I became a boarder at school and a snatch or two of its songs remained permanently in the memory – to be recalled always with a tinge of melancholy.

My adventure into opera was almost my thespian swansong – as *Utter Garbage* turned out to be Joanna's – but not quite; I was asked by the Protestant Church in Muscat to perform a couple of monologue sketches to illustrate New Testament stories. These were daunting in prospect but extremely rewarding in execution. Since then I have not – unless you count light-hearted antics at parties or in class – trod the boards. Every dog has his day, it is said. In a small way, I had mine.

Opera could be enjoyed in Oman at a more serious level. Our friends Roger and Yukari Barnard – who like us had come to Oman after serving in the Yemen – tried to educate us in 'real' opera; they took us to productions presented by visiting professionals. This was a first for both Joanna and me, but we certainly enjoyed the experience – though partly, it must be said, because of the company we were in. We saw the Barnards at other times, for beach outings and some memorable dinners, but once they had left Muscat they emigrated to New Zealand. There they remain and the two families have not met up since.

Our other good friends from the past, as already mentioned, were of course Philip and Rosie Gordon. We saw much of them and their trio of offspring, Timothy, James and Eleanor (the last being born while we were in Muscat), who were godchildren to Annabel, Edmund and Joanna respectively. We ate together, picnicked together, partied together.

We had a holiday trip with the Gordons to Dubai – a place I had also visited on business – booking into the luxurious Ramada Hotel. We spent our time looking round, enjoying in particular the famous creek with its Arab dhows, many in process of being loaded up with multifarious goods: second-hand cars and other vehicles,

The Gordon family celebrate a birthday

sometimes to be cannibalized for spare parts, as well as carton upon carton of household goods, mattresses, rolls of cloth and suchlike. We asked someone where his dhow was headed and he replied 'Iran'. Then Joanna noticed a pile of plastic jerry cans nearby labelled 'DANGER – CORROSIVE'. Intrigued, she looked more closely and made out the words in smaller script 'Pepsi concentrate'!

Talking of scripts: we were puzzled by several waterside restaurants with menus written in a form unknown to us. I thought it slightly reminiscent of Greek – and then the penny dropped. It was, of course, Russian. The post-Soviet nouveaux riches (code for mafia, you might say) had wasted no time in descending in considerable number on lucrative trading locations all round the world. Dubai was a favourite; Greek Cyprus was another, as I had already discovered on visits I made to the south of the island. These trips – sometimes with Joanna – were necessary to keep in close touch with my company Chairman and Coordinator.

Did we make any friends from among the locals, it may be asked. Not really. As a people the Omanis are inclined to be reserved. However, given more time we might have established a lasting relationship with one or two. Joanna and I both fondly recall a young couple whom we met towards the end of our time in the Sultanate and who seemed to take a liking to us. They asked us out for an evening meal in their home and we learnt more about them.

'We have recently returned from a holiday in Iran,' Osman remarked over dinner.

'Yes,' his wife Fātima chimed in enthusiastically. 'It was very exciting. There was so much to see.'

'Really?' Joanna responded politely. 'Can I ask what in particular you refer to?'

Fātima looked across at her husband, who carried on. 'We were looking at some very beautiful mosques, as well as ancient religious texts. Of course, we also saw a few remarkable ruins from the days of the empire.' He pondered for a moment. 'But it is Islamic history and thinking that really interests us.'

We found the kindness of this Shi'a married couple extremely touching, and began to realise how much their faith – not least the fact that it was *Shi'a* faith – meant to them.

***

I have said that one was generally free to pursue one's career in Oman. How free was I to do this? How free was I to learn about and develop a new expertise in business management? Not as free as my expatriate associates, is the short answer.

The trouble did not originate from the Omani authorities, it has to be said. Yet trouble there was waiting for me, and if Omanis were not the initiators some of them helped it along. My sideways move into the world of business, a little audacious perhaps, was brought to a speedy conclusion.

Family Bookshop, for long enjoying a virtual monopoly in its field, had quite recently found itself in competition with a new company called United Media Services (UMS). I soon became aware just how intense the rivalry between us was, both at the wholesale and retail level. With regard to the latter, we gained an advantage when, early in 1991, we opened a major new retail outlet in a burgeoning area of the Omani capital, al-Qurum. Once opened, it quickly developed a fast turnover and eventually became our most profitable branch.

Shortly after the opening of this outlet, the UMS distribution manager, an Indian, happened to see me in the street and approached me.

'I was thinking, Mr Blair,' he remarked, 'that it would be a good thing if you met my boss. Getting together on a friendly basis can only help the establishment of a happy relationship – so necessary for the future of both our companies.' I murmured something vaguely positive and left it at that.

Not long after this he got in touch with me and pressed me further about the importance of such a meeting, suggesting a time and date. I thought it wise to accept and awaited the day. Once in the Director's plush office high in some *'amāra* (tower block) in Ruwi – I remember the occasion vividly – I was ushered to a comfortable leather armchair and offered coffee and sweetmeats. A rather one-sided conversation then ensued.

'I hope very much, Mr Blair,' the UMS Director, a Bangladeshi, began, 'that our two companies can work amicably and constructively together.'

'That is indeed greatly to be hoped,' I responded prosaically. 'I can assure you that you have nothing to fear from my side. It would be completely against company policy to initiate anything that might militate against such an outcome.'

'This is so encouraging to hear,' my opposite number cooed. 'It would be a pity if any small misunderstanding got in the way of company growth – I mean, the development of our two esteemed companies. We are newer on the scene than Family Bookshop, of course, but you yourself are a newcomer to the Sultanate, I believe.' He looked hard at me. 'I assure you, Mr Blair, our meeting today fills me with confidence about the way you will respond to the challenge facing us both in our common field of business.'

Bullies, judging others by themselves, frequently imagine their victims have perceived and succumbed to an intended threat behind honeyed words because they respond blandly. In fact, such 'victims' may be in the habit of thinking the best of others and accordingly identify no threat to respond to; or else, if they do identify one, they do not respond in like manner because that is simply not their style. To this day I cannot decide which kind of victim I represented, but victim I most certainly was.

Nothing untoward occurred until the affair of our Land Rover quite a while later. On receiving it back from a routine service at an engineering company employing sub-continent workers, Joanna discovered a five-point star scratched on the metal of one of the seats positioned over the back wheels. It was hidden unless you removed the cushion, but she was cleaning out the vehicle at the time so she spotted it. We were preparing for a five-hundred mile drive to Salalah with two other vehicles over the Eid holiday.

We were puzzled by this star at the time but forgot about it until the accident.

On our second day of driving, all three vehicles left the tarmac as we went off-road to reach 'the lost city of Ubar'. I was at the wheel of our Land-Rover 110, laden with passengers and gear, and after covering some miles on the roughly-graded track we approached a bend. We were not going fast – about thirty miles an hour according to the passenger in the front with me – but as I turned the wheel we started fish-tailing. We rolled and the vehicle ended up on the edge of the track on its side. No one was badly hurt and we scrambled out through the front windscreen frame, the glass having fractured and come right out. As we were doing so the vehicle following us drew up nearby. After informing and meeting the police we ended up at our destination, Holiday Inn in Salalah, that same night.

On returning to Muscat, we decided to salvage our battered vehicle and have it rebuilt. I made the journey down with the breakdown lorry, which hoisted up the front of the Land Rover in order to tow it away on its back wheels. The lorry with its load began moving – but for a couple of hundred yards at most because one of the Land Rover's back wheels at that point fell off and rolled away. We checked the hub to find the bolts intact, the wheel-nuts having dropped off; the nuts on the three other wheels, meanwhile, were perfectly tight. While doing the checking I realised that the offending wheel was the one over which the star had been scratched. Since then we have tended to assume that the star was a cryptic sign – almost a signature – placed by an ill-wisher who had tampered with the wheel below, making sure the nuts were not fully tight.

We did not associate this incident and its suggestion of malicious intent with our rival media company at the time but subsequent developments, clearly incriminating the latter in another form of foul play, made such a connection credible.

A year or so later our UMS rivals stole some of our magazine distribution agencies. I say 'stole', and that's exactly what it was. We had agency documents from the companies concerned which we had cleared – as was necessary – with the Ministry of Industry and Commerce. One day, however, the Ministry of Information refused to approve the distribution of a dozen of our English periodicals – including *Hello*, nearly as profitable as the rest put together. They told us that UMS had now procured the agencies.

We protested, resubmitting our agency documents to the Ministry of Industry and Commerce. They said they would look into the matter – but nothing happened. After a while I and my Lebanese distribution manager mounted a kind of campaign, visiting the ministry offices again and again to argue and remonstrate. For month after month this went on until our patience was exhausted.

My distribution manager composed a letter in Arabic addressed to the Minister of Commerce and Industry which I read, approved and signed. It spelt out in forceful terms our dissatisfaction with the way we had been treated by the ministry officials insomuch as they had been unable, after a lengthy period, to explain why our commercial rights had been infringed. Having handed the letter in to the ministry office, we waited for a response.

It came the very next day. I and my distribution manager were summoned to present ourselves before the Director General of the Ministry of Commerce and Industry. On arriving at the ministry building, we were directed to this official's office. Brandishing our letter (it had evidently not reached the minister), he proceeded to rage and storm.

'How dare you address this letter to the minister,' he fumed, 'insinuating that members of our ministry might have acted improperly.'

My distribution manager protested. 'We have been trying, *yā mudīr*, to get to the bottom of a situation extremely detrimental to …'

'There can be no excuse for such slander,' the Director General cut in. 'If we bring you before the libel court, you can be sent to prison – and you will also be liable for expenses.'

This was by no means all he said; he continued for some time in this manner, stressing the heinousness of our crime. We were not arrested on the spot, I'm happy to say, and when we were finally dismissed and standing outside my colleague turned to me.

'We must tell our sponsor at once,' he advised. 'He'll have to negotiate the way out of this.' I needed no convincing and immediately informed him.

Our Omani sponsor had a certain amount of clout, working in the Diwan, and after listening to my story he said he would write a letter to the Ministry explaining the situation. A few days later he handed it in, to be told a reply would be quickly forthcoming. Now, however, there was a development on a quite different plane. Early in the morning a few days later the immaculate paintwork of the

Buick used by our sponsor's wife, parked every night at their home (very near ours), was found viciously scratched all over.

The next stage in this extraordinary affair was a meeting between our sponsor, with me in tow, and the Deputy Director General of the Ministry of Commerce and Industry. The latter declared that I and my distribution manager should be sacked and that, failing this, Family Bookshop would be 'blacklisted'.

Three days after this, I was working alone in our office premises later than usual when my phone rang – unusual for the time of day. I picked up the receiver and held it to my ear, but at first could hear nothing. Then a hoarse, almost sepulchral voice started repeating our sponsor's name. Let us call him Tāriq. '*Tā-ā-ā-āriq, Tā-ā-ā-āriq, Tā-ā-ā-āriq* …' the voice croaked slowly. There were more repetitions before the receiver the other end was replaced.

Coming in the wake of the vandalism on the car, the provenance and intent of this call were only too obvious: our commercial rivals were leaving no stone unturned in their efforts to discourage us from fighting for our legal rights in the matter of the agencies.

A few days later we were in receipt of the formal response from the Ministry of Commerce and Industry to the letter our sponsor had addressed to the Director General. For the time being, at least, the punishment inflicted on me and my distribution manager was to be limited to that of being prohibited from entering ministry premises. The news came as something of a relief and when, hard on its heels, another encouraging though wholly unexpected development occurred, we almost began to think in terms of victory.

On one of my regular visits to the Ministry of Information to do with distribution, a young clerk whom I knew called me over to his desk.

'I have something for you that could be important, *yā sayyed*,' he said very quietly. He rummaged in a drawer, pulled out a piece of paper and handed it over. I perused it and immediately looked up again.

'This is *very* important,' I murmured softly. 'You obviously know why and I can only thank you for obtaining it – at some risk, maybe.'

'It was my duty,' he muttered. He glanced quickly round the room and then added, 'I'm afraid a few people here accepted bribes

– free airline tickets – in return for what's in your hand.' He started busying himself with something on his desk and I took the hint, stowing the paper carefully in my pocket and walking away.

What he had procured for me was a copy of a computer sheet listing all the periodicals officially registered for distribution by our rival company. It had been crudely tampered with to make it look as if UMS had the right to sell twelve titles for which we were the legal agents. I handed a copy of it to our sponsor at the first opportunity.

A protracted 'negotiation' now took place to settle the whole sorry business, our Coordinator arriving from Cyprus to become involved. The final upshot was that no further steps against me and my manager would be taken so long as I left the country within six months. By any standards, it was an extraordinary settlement but I was in no mood – or position – to argue. I simply assumed that a number of agendas had been in play, the strict pursuit of justice being fairly low on the list.

There were a couple of postscripts. Firstly, all the stolen distribution rights were very soon restored to us. Secondly, I received a message from the Director of the Ministry of Information, who had been away for the entire period of the crisis, inviting me to call on him. I had always liked him and he received me with the utmost courtesy.

'You are a good man, Mr Blair,' he said earnestly. 'I'm so sorry to hear you are leaving. Is there anything I can do?'

I thanked him warmly but declined the offer, saying my departure was for the best. We then chatted pleasantly over cups of coffee about the Sultanate and our respective views on life.

I saw out my final six months in Oman with a spate of activity, implementing some important developmental changes for the company at the request of my Lebanese Coordinator.

As usual, Joanna left Oman for UK soon after her school term had ended at the beginning of July, leaving me alone in our large residence, apart from our Sri Lankan housemaid/cook. I supervised my fifth annual stocktaking – fairly adept at this by now – and for the last time compared notes and socialised with our Greek

Cypriot auditors. This behind me, the month of August was mostly spent tying off ends in the office and then entertaining and handing over to my successor as General Manager, a Lebanese businessman rather older than me. Of course, the question of my next career move sometimes occupied my thoughts.

My Cyprus bosses were concerned to see me happily placed and suggested I take over the management of the FB company in Bahrain, the position having become vacant. But while grateful for the offer I turned it down. The Bahrain manager had to double up as book-buyer, for one thing, and I did not possess the experience, knowledge or, to be honest, genuine interest to fulfil such a role. Besides that, however, it would mean being largely tied to Bahrain's big central outlet. There was no chain of shops requiring visiting, as in Oman, and I could not see myself enduring such a restricted way of life. I had never been a lover of office work, but in Oman this was alleviated by efficient managerial and secretarial staff.

There was some talk of my becoming a travelling representative based in Cyprus for the Family Bookshop operation as a whole and this sounded attractive, but nothing was certain and eventually the idea was dropped. Thus, at the end of August 1994, when I attended the farewell party organised by the Coordinator in my honour – which he also attended on a flying visit – my future remained in the air.

The following evening the Coordinator and a couple of others accompanied me to Seeb airport to see me onto a Gulf Air flight to UK. As well as my suitcases, I was carrying one or two generous parting gifts. The goodbyes were said and I boarded, settling into my seat with a sigh of contentment. (Air flights for me have always represented the ultimate haven because once on the plane no one can get at you.) Random pictures from my four years, four months, in the Sultanate flashed before my eyes: those remarkable Omani castles; the Sultan's Youth Orchestra playing in the National Auditorium; prize-bull fights further up the coast (bull push-of-wars, more accurately); the Syrian 'Basil Fawlty' who ran a restaurant in al-Khuwair.

The in-flight meal arrives, is consumed, and I stare lethargically at a film. Whither next?

X

Another Return

Cyprus it turned out to be. Not, however, with Family Bookshop, and not in the Greek south where the company had its head office.

Of course, on returning to UK both Joanna and looked for work, Joanna finding it immediately in the form of supply teaching in local primary schools while I found it once again in the Executive Language Centre in Yeovil. We slotted into these responsibilities smoothly enough and the months turned into a year and the beginning of a second year. By this time Joanna had again landed a short-term teaching contract but for me teaching had almost dried up. The Language Centre was pulling in fewer clients and therefore was less in need of teachers operating on the basis of weekly contracts – as the system for most of us was. Not unreasonably, the order of the day was last in, first out, so I was called upon less and less. As the year 1995 drew to a close it became clear that my days at the Centre were over, barring a sudden upturn in its fortunes; I needed something else.

I was lucky – or God was good. Sherborne School for boys, where my father had taught for nearly nine years following his 'retirement', had developed a new branch of its activities in the form of an International School, which was highly successful. I came to hear that it required a part-time English teacher in the New Year, applied and was accepted. So from January 1996 I began teaching English to young teenagers from all over the world.

The teaching went well for me and the school clearly appreciated my efforts. There was the possibility of a full-time position the following September and it seemed I would be a strong candidate for the position should it materialise and I decide to apply. But though I had no problem with the youngsters I felt increasingly that teaching them was not my forte. I had never felt inclined to be a schoolteacher, as it happened, despite my having become a teacher of sorts. I think this was something to do with my lack of enthusiasm for clubs and clubbing. Schools (especially boarding schools) are rather like clubs in being a world within a world, and those who function best in them are those who are content to live largely within such a microcosm. I have always been happiest working in an environment with wider horizons.

Fortunately for me, around April 1996 I came across an advertisement in an educational newspaper for assistant professors of English at Eastern Mediterranean University (EMU), Turkish Republic of Northern Cyprus (TRNC). I immediately sent off an application and within a week or so had received a call from a member of the university staff.

A British voice responded when I picked up the phone. 'Paul Larbalestier here, Deputy Head of the English Language Teaching Department. We at Eastern Mediterranean are considering your application and I thought a chat might be useful.'

'I'd much appreciate it. Was there something special you wanted to ask?'

'Well, we went through your very interesting CV, which shows you have a lot of overseas experience, most of it as an English teacher. I should stress that we're looking for people who believe teaching to be the priority, as also those who are used to a foreign culture. We've had one or two who left a bit quickly!'

'I should be able to satisfy on both those points,' I assured him, smiling privately at the second. 'So would my wife, who's also hoping to pick up a post, as I mentioned.'

'Ah, yes,' the voice came back quickly. 'I wanted to say, the university has its own secondary school, Eastern Mediterranean College. There's little doubt she'd get a position there.'

'This would be excellent. The double billing is important. For one thing, my wife Joanna can't stand being out of work, but in any case we need the two salaries.' I then remembered something quite different. 'I've been wondering where Gazimagusa is, the town given for your postal address. In the north, of course, but I don't recognize the name though I know the island. You will have seen I spent eighteen months in Cyprus at Her Majesty's pleasure.'

'We certainly noticed this and thought it significant,' the other replied. 'As to your question, Gazimagusa is simply the Turkish name for Famagusta. The university is on the ...'

'Famagusta!' I broke in, repeating a name I knew so well. 'That's where my camp was, or just outside it. Four-mile point, they called it, on the Nicosia road.'

'Still there, part of the sovereign base, on the old road. You can get a pass to visit it.'

And so the conversation continued, for a while focusing on the island and its situation. I then asked some questions about salaries, accommodation and the like, our chat ending with the virtual promise of a post for me, plus further reassurance about one in due course for Joanna. When the formal offer with a written contract arrived by post I signed and returned it without hesitation.

Another return.

**

At the end of August 1996 we flew to Ercan Airport, near Lefkoşa (Nicosia), TRNC, via Istanbul, as there were no direct flights into the country, unrecognized as it was as a nation by all except Turkey. Which immediately calls for comment.

A lot of water had passed under the bridge since I had flown out of Cyprus one September day in 1959. Ever since that day I had followed the fortunes of the island with interest through the media. It had not been inspiring: the country, newly independent in 1960, had followed a largely downward path for most of the thirty-seven years between my departure and – discounting a few quick visits to the south – my return that August. Let me now give a sketch of the island's history from earliest times until independence from Britain, and then an account of some important events thereafter.

During the Middle Bronze Age (1900 – 1600 BC), the island of Cyprus is apparently referred to in historical records under the name *Alasia*. There is evidence in this period of major pottery exports to the Levant and Egypt, as well as a measure of urbanisation. Around 1550 we find the sizable settlement of Enkomi – situated just outside modern Famagusta – being developed as a major port, to be abandoned some five hundred years later when its harbour silted up. (It is quite eerie to walk round its excavated remains today – streets, houses, temples, gates, even grassy outlines of jetties.) It was succeeded by the port city of Salamis, abandoned in the Christian era following a huge earthquake, though leaving some impressive ruins.

Around the middle of the first millennium BC the island came under the control of the Persians and then, following the conquests of Alexander the Great, of the Greeks. In 30 BC it became part of the Roman Empire. We hear of a visit to the island of Saints Paul and Barnabas in 45 AD, when the Roman proconsul was converted to the Christian faith, and in 116 a Jewish insurrection when up to 200,000 people died. In 330, when the Emperor Constantine made Constantinople the imperial capital, the Byzantine period commenced. This lasted, with ups and downs that included a brief period of Arab rule, until 1191 when King Richard I of England (the Lionheart) took possession of the island. He, however, sold his right to the island to the Knights Templars, who quickly sold it on to Guy de Lusignan, initiating the Frankish period.

The Lusignan dynasty lasted until 1489, when Queen Catherine ceded Cyprus to the Venetians. In 1570 the Ottoman Turks invaded the island and absorbed it into their empire. Ottoman rule continued until 1878, when under the Cyprus Convention Britain gained control of the island, though it remained nominally an Ottoman possession. On the outbreak of war with Turkey in 1914, Britain annexed Cyprus, and ten years later the new Republic of Turkey renounced all claims on the island.

In 1955 a militant campaign to achieve *enosis*, or union, of the island with Greece was mounted by EOKA (National Organisation of Cypriot Fighters) under George Grivas, code-named Dighenis, a Cypriot by birth who had served in the Greek army. Britain declared a state of emergency and in 1956 deported Archbishop Makarios III, who together with Grivas had founded EOKA, to the Seychelles. EOKA militancy lasted until 1959, when in January, at the London Conference, the parties concerned (Greece, Turkey, UK, Greek-Cypriots, Turkish-Cypriots) agreed on principles for the island's independence that excluded both *enosis* and partition.

The Constitution of the new Republic of Cyprus was a complex one. Executive power was vested in a Greek President and Turkish Vice-President, to be elected by their respective communities. They both enjoyed powers of veto and were supported by a Council of Ministers. Legislative power was vested in a House of Representatives of thirty-five Greeks and fifteen Turks, also communally elected, the Turkish members having a veto over certain forms of legislation. A Supreme Constitutional Court was also established to consider challenges to the validity of legislative or executive actions, and provisions were made for the Constitution to be amended in certain circumstances by the House of Representatives.

To guarantee the maintenance of the Constitution and the independence of Cyprus an international treaty was signed by Cyprus, Greece, Turkey and the United Kingdom. This stated that in the case of a breach of the Constitution, Greece, Turkey and the United Kingdom should consult together, with each guaranteeing power reserving the right to take independent action to restore the status quo where concerted action proved impossible. The treaty also allowed for two sovereign British bases on the island. Archbishop Makarios was in due course elected to the office of President of the new Republic while Dr Fazil Küçük was returned unopposed to the office of Vice-President. Elections were held to fill the House of Representatives and the official announcement of independence was released on 16 August 1960.

The first three years of independence were economically positive but politically negative. The provisions of the Constitution were much disliked by the Greek Cypriots but adhered to by the Turkish Cypriots, who used their veto to oppose anything questionable. Makarios accordingly proposed thirteen amendments – which, however, reduced the safeguards provided for the minority community. These were rejected by Ankara and, on 23 December

1963, fighting broke out between the two communities in Nicosia. On Christmas Day a cease-fire was agreed, to be formalised the next day, and from that moment the Cypriot capital was a divided city.

The above outline of what led to this outbreak of bi-communal conflict is somewhat misleading. 'The devil is in the detail', they say, so let us take a closer look.

As soon as the settlement for independence was agreed, Archbishop Makarios began talking about 'the glorious liberation struggle … which will continue to complete victory'. On 15 August 1962, in a sermon at Kykko Monastery, he stated, 'Greek Cypriots must continue to march forward to complete the work begun by the EOKA heroes.' Some of his Greek Cypriot cabinet ministers were similarly provocative, notably Polykarpos Yorgadjis, Minister of the Interior (and ex-EOKA militant), who stated publicly in 1962: 'There is no place in Cyprus for anyone who is not Greek.' On the question of the proposed amendments to the Constitution put forward by Makarios, Pierre Oberling writes, 'They were, of course, unacceptable to the Turkish Cypriots. The projected amendments would have deprived them of the veto power, which alone prevented the Greek Cypriot leaders from destroying the Republic and achieving *enosis* by legal means.' All this and much more – including evidence that Greek Cypriots were recruiting, training and organising a 'secret army' as early as 1961 – is revealed in Professor Oberling's book, *The Road to Bellapais: The Turkish Cypriot Exodus to Northern Cyprus* (Social Science Monographs, Boulder, 1982; distributed by Colombia University Press, New York).

It may seem out of place in a personal work of this nature to enter so boldly into the controversy (still not fully resolved, as I write) between the two ethno-religious Cypriot communities. Yet I do so as someone who was at the sharp end of the conflict for eighteen months and has closely followed its ups and downs since, visiting the island several times and finally living there a second time for five years.

I will now give a brief account of some important events occurring in Cyprus from 1964 to 1974.

The year 1964 saw a stranglehold placed upon the Turkish community, both political and social. According to Oberling (op.

cit., p. 126), 'As soon as the fighting started, during the 1963-1964 crisis, the Greek Cypriots took over the government and dismissed all Turkish officials. ... Turkish Cypriots became, to all intents and purposes, stateless persons without any civil rights.' Things were no better socially; by the end of the summer the number of Turkish homes destroyed or damaged ran into thousands, and many had lost any source of income. Official records state that up to 25,000 Turkish Cypriots fled their homes over the crisis of 1963-64, often leaving all their possessions behind and being reduced to living in small enclaves.

In 1967, under the leadership again of George Grivas, two Turkish Cypriot enclaves were attacked by police patrols reinforced by the National Guard and subsequently captured. Turkey called upon the United Nations to bring about a ceasefire and sent an ultimatum to Greece, backed by air sorties over her territory that showed she was in earnest: war with Greece was on the Turkish agenda unless the ultimatum demands were met. Greece responded by recalling Grivas from Cyprus but did nothing about the other demands.

The President of the United States, Lyndon Johnson, now became involved. A compromise agreement between the two countries was achieved and some of the Turkish demands were implemented, including the withdrawal of most Greek troops from the island. This crisis finally persuaded Archbishop Makarios that *enosis* could only be a distant objective. By now, indeed, most Greek Cypriots favoured indirect action, the applying of social and political pressure on the Turkish Cypriot community rather than the employment of naked force. Die-hards willing to fight for the cause had become a small minority, mostly political reactionaries such as priests, EOKA veterans and Greek-trained teachers and businessmen. Be that as it may, by the end of the decade the Turkish Cypriots, who ten years before had been scattered across the island, had been pushed into relatively few enclaves.

In 1974 Greece, ruled at the time by a military junta but remaining one of the three powers bound by treaty to guarantee the 1960 Constitution, fomented a coup in Cyprus designed to overthrow that Constitution. The coup operation, code-named

'Operation President', commenced after the morning rush hour on Monday, 15 July 1974. The plan to ambush and assassinate Makarios was bungled, however, allowing him to make his way unnoticed to Paphos, occupied largely by his followers. Despite this setback, the National Guard, having crushed resistance, supervised the swearing in of Nikos Sampson, 'the Butcher of Omorphita', as the new president. As well as the many supporters of Makarios killed in Nicosia in the wake of the coup, others were massacred in the vicinities of Paphos and Limassol.

Prime Minister Bülent Ecevit of Turkey issued an ultimatum to the Greek government with three reasonable demands, which were rejected. He then appealed personally but unsuccessfully in London to Prime Minister Harold Wilson for British cooperation in enforcing the Treaty of Guarantee, obtained a lukewarm response from US Secretary of State Henry Kissinger, who merely dispatched his deputy to London, Athens and Ankara to negotiate a settlement, and met opposition from both UK and USA to any condemnation of the Greek-sponsored coup by the United Nations. Only at this point did Ecevit, on 19 July, exercise his right of unilateral intervention under the Treaty of Guarantee and order Turkish troops to carry out a 'peace operation' (*barış harekâtı*) in the interests of protecting the rights (and lives) of the Turkish Cypriots on the island (Oberling, *op. cit.*, pp. 155-63).

***

When Joanna and I landed in Cyprus in 1996 the situation was as it had been twenty-two years previously, following the Turkish intervention: an island divided. In the south were the Greeks, apart from the mostly Greek-populated town of Dip-Karpaz at the far end of the Karpaz, or 'panhandle'; in the north were the Turks, apart from a handful who had remained in Limassol and a few scattered individuals elsewhere in the south. The two communities occupied, respectively, 64.4% and 35.6% of the territory, and each held roughly half of the historic capital, Nicosia.

As already indicated, we had flown via Istanbul since direct flights to the North from other international airports were impossible, indeed illegal, the Turkish Republic of Northern Cyprus being recognized as a state only by Turkey. By the same token we had already had to send mail for the North to a special address in Turkey (Mersin 10), from which it was forwarded to its true destination in TRNC.

We walked from the plane to the doors of the airport building while people lining a balcony waved and called to relatives and friends arriving with us. Once inside we passed quickly through security and customs to the arrival hall. The Deputy Head of my department had promised we would be met by a driver and we looked around confidently: there was no sign of anyone. We sat for quite a while but no one arrived and Joanna finally became thoroughly incensed.

'This is ridiculous! We've obviously drawn a complete blank in this Eastern Mediterranean place. What do they expect us to do? Hire a taxi? There probably isn't one. I feel like flying straight home.'

'The driver may have been delayed,' I volunteered.

Joanna was dismissive. 'All this time? A driver won't be coming now – if indeed there ever was one. We'll have to phone the university.'

'And get the person on the exchange, who'll know nothing,' I said wearily.

'What else can we do?' my spouse retorted. 'You'd better go and find someone and say we've got to make a call.'

I looked around and saw an office still open. It had a telephone and the fellow on duty helped me get through to the university. To my amazement, despite the lateness of the hour I was put in touch with an official of some kind.

'Car?' he responded to my inquiry. 'I not know about car to pick you.'

'Okay,' I said, 'maybe you don't know, but we *need* a car, a driver.'

'No driver now,' the voice said. 'Drivers go to home.'

I gritted my teeth. 'We are new teachers and have arrived at Ercan airport. Please find a driver and a car to take us to the university.'

The man at the other end suddenly relented. 'I send car, no problem. Please to wait.' The last instruction was scarcely necessary; we waited for perhaps an hour before the driver finally arrived. He then transported us and our luggage to the university.

Not a promising start, you could say. But in fact from that point onwards we were impressed by the arrival arrangements. We were put temporarily into a flat with fresh food for consumption in the fridge, and not long after were shown possible permanent accommodation. We refused a place in the centre of town but a little later a pleasant, more spacious apartment nearer the university became vacant and we immediately agreed to take it, happy that expatriate staff only had to pay a nominal rent.

I was soon in the classroom, giving lectures to cheerful (sometimes slightly bumptious) students, almost entirely a mix of Turkish Cypriots and mainland Turks. I quickly came to like and respect the Deputy Head, Paul Larbalestier, who was meticulous in attending to our further needs. He was furious about the airport pick-up fiasco.

'I specifically arranged for a driver to collect you from the airport,' he told us. 'I gave him the details and he wrote your name down. He should have been displaying it in the arrival hall.' He ran fingers through his hair, exasperated. 'It's strange as he's normally so reliable. I'll have to look into it.'

He did so, and a few days later reported back. 'Would you believe it? Some prat called "Mr Phillips" – I've yet to track him down – arrived on the same plane and hi-jacked your car. He insisted he was the one to be picked up. I can't blame our driver.'

We put the matter behind us.

Joanna very quickly found a position at Eastern Mediterranean College and before long we were enjoying the rhythm of teaching in our respective institutions. Both of the latter were on the fast-expanding university campus and within walking distance of our apartment, itself in a new residential district named Karakol, meaning 'police station'.

For me there was something slightly surreal about it. Nearly forty years before, while still a teenager, I had arrived on the edge of the same town, just one more British serviceman assigned to security duties as a new wave of EOKA violence shook the island. Not too much had changed. Famagusta Old City, always inhabited by Turks, I found to be largely as I remembered it: the many old churches; the soaring Gothic cathedral (reminiscent of the chapel at Lancing College, my old school), now a mosque; the narrow streets down which I and my service friends had sauntered to buy some small luxury, perhaps an item of clothing from one of the excellent tailors.

What both Joanna and I found especially poignant was the walk we took one Saturday morning not long after our arrival – frequently repeated thereafter – through no-man's-land to Dhekelia sovereign base, part of which ran alongside the Turkish Cypriot border. You had to drive two or three miles and then park your car before going the rest of the way on foot. As Paul had intimated, we were allowed onto the base as British passport holders – though strictly warned not to stray, by accident or design, onto Greek territory. Once through the Turkish and British security checks you came to a NAAFI canteen where you could have a slap-up English breakfast.

From this canteen you could walk a little way up a side road and stand outside the gates of an RAF signals station – my old camp – facing the guardroom in which I had so often been on duty. On one occasion I crossed a piece of waste ground to a lonely concrete post – all that remained of the entrance to a telex compound I had on occasions been required to guard. Looking closely I could make out the legend 'A1' scratched on it. This had been the number of my police tent on camp; some other SP, occupying that same makeshift billet, must have whiled away a few moments on duty inscribing the 'name' of his temporary home on the gatepost for posterity.

One thing struck me immediately in this vicinity, the absence of the orange groves that my dog-handler friends of long ago had patrolled. These had been extensive and healthy; now there was just the occasional lifeless tree. I soon learnt the reason: continuous extraction of water from wells in the area had so lowered the freshwater table that seawater had permeated the ground, killing off deep-rooted vegetation.

So here I was – now with a wife – back at the spot where my odyssey had begun. What would this divided island, which had once brought me both happiness and direction, bring the second time round?

XI

Second Time Round

A few months after our arrival at Eastern Mediterranean University we were abruptly reminded that the old scars were still sore; that fear and suspicion were still infecting people; that the 'emergency' on the island was not yet concluded. From seemingly nowhere erupted the 'missile crisis'.

In early January 1997 the media were in alarmist mode: the Greek Cypriot government had announced the purchase and forthcoming installation of a battery of Russian S300 surface-to-air missiles and Turkey had immediately issued a warning that if the deal went ahead they might respond militarily. Such missiles, of course, could not be deployed directly against the Turkish Cypriot north of the island but they could be used against planes sent by Turkey to intervene in some way to protect the north. In the months following there was an uneasy stalemate as neither side, despite a certain amount of political horse-trading, seemed prepared to back down. In June the tension heightened when Greek F-16s landed at Paphos Air Base in the south, as a part of expanding defence ties between the two nations, leading Turkey to moot the possibility of an air strike against Paphos – which would almost inevitably lead to confrontation with Greece.

Joanna and I were not too troubled by the crisis, having over the years lived through many such threatening scenarios. Yet some of our colleagues were genuinely worried, one in particular becoming obsessed with the idea that there was to be a new and bloody chapter in the bi-communal conflict. Efforts to reassure her failed and, being a US citizen, she left with her daughter for the States, leaving behind her British husband, one of my teaching colleagues. The uneasy stalemate continued, with Russia insisting the missile deal go through, for the rest of 1997 and into 1998, the general tension easing somewhat not because of tangible improvement in the situation but because the whole business was becoming tedious. Eventually, in December 1998, the Greek Cypriots agreed with Greece to deliver the missiles to the island of Crete. The missiles were to remain under Cypriot control, but this move effectively defused the crisis.

The protracted missile saga should not lead the reader to imagine that the Turkish Cypriot populace as a whole were constantly up in arms about threats from the Greek Cypriot south. Some were too concerned with, and busy about, promoting better relations between themselves and their southern counterparts to interpret the latter's every twist and turn as provocative. Such were our friends Ekrem and Günay Şehali. Günay was a teaching colleague of Joanna's, which is how we got to know them.

Ekrem was passionately concerned to bring about a total rapprochement with the Greek Cypriot community and thus lasting peace for the island. He belonged to a group of similar-minded people on both sides who met at regular intervals in Switzerland to share thoughts and ideas as they looked for the best way forward.

'Of course,' he once told us, 'I won't belittle the horrors of 1974. We, like so many others, had to get across from the south of the island to the north, which was coming under the control of the Turkish forces. It was a nightmare journey as it was necessary, driving in our car, to avoid gangs of Greeks who would happily have gunned us down. We made it, but there were some scary moments.'

'You're not bitter about all that – and the years that led up to it?' I asked.

'What's the point?' he replied, 'We have to move on, all of us. The main thing is for the two communities to get together – to meet, talk, listen, learn. Then mutual trust will return and old wounds be healed.'

***

When I had accepted the post at EMU we promised ourselves that we would complete at least one academic year but were not sure if we would stay longer. We wanted to see how we felt before committing ourselves further. Five or six months into that year we realised we were enjoying both the work and the island so opted for another contract. Towards the end of August 1997, therefore, after our summer vacation in UK, we were back in Famagusta.

Our friends Chris and Wendy Hutton, with their two daughters, Catherine and Anna, came to stay with us almost immediately, arriving on the afternoon of 31 August. It was a Sunday, and an unforgettable day – rather less, however, because of our friends' safe arrival but because in its early hours Princess Diana, together with her friend Dodi al-Fayed, were killed in that notorious car crash in the Alma Tunnel in Paris.

The rest of that day on BBC Radio World Service, to which we regularly tuned in, was devoted almost entirely to commentary on this devastating item of news. Together with the assassination of J.F. Kennedy and the Twin Towers atrocity of 9/11, the death of Diana is said to have had such an impact on people that they can recall exactly where they were and what they were doing when they first heard about it. This is certainly true for me: I was in the kitchen of our apartment preparing our usual simple breakfast, having just switched on the radio.

The two weeks of our friends' stay was a golden time – for us, certainly, but for them as well, it seemed. The word 'golden' is particularly apt in this context because of the visit we all made to 'Golden Beach', near the end of the Karpaz. This truly magnificent piece of coastline had in 1959 suddenly opened to my view minutes before I arrived – to visit a friend – at the RAF signals station situated on the cape. Thirty-eight years later it lived up to all it had promised from that momentary glimpse.

The huge, unblemished stretch of sand curved round a quiet, uninhabited corner of the coast, almost making a bay. Low hills fringed it on the landward side, except for a dip through which you could drive your vehicle to a group of wooden huts – a kind of encampment – that had been built (quite legally) by a pair of enterprising brothers. These were Turkish Kurds who had settled on the island. The biggest hut served as a restaurant and the smaller ones, set on the undulating edge of the sand, provided simple but quite comfortable sleeping accommodation. The beach, incidentally, offered nocturnal accommodation of a different kind to turtles. Once a year these would flop onto the shore by night in considerable number (having swum goodness knows how far), laboriously manoeuvre themselves up the beach to lay their eggs in the sand, cover them up carefully and return to the water to swim away. As the expected time approached nature-lovers would come from far and wide in the hope of witnessing this fascinating event; some, too, would return later to watch the young turtles hatch and then struggle down the sand and into the sea.

Joanna and I, together with our friends, had not booked ourselves in for the night. After enjoying ourselves on the sand and in the deliciously warm water, we wandered back to the camp for a meal. Tekin, the red-headed brother in charge, started a fire on which an assortment of meat was grilled and mountains of chips fried, while someone inside the main hut prepared the salad. As daylight was fading huge helpings were placed before the visitors – others besides ourselves, including several youths – together with drinks according to taste. It was a very convivial gathering.

'About time to be going, don't you think?' Wendy said looking at her watch, then at her girls, as the evening wore on. 'I mean, it's quite a drive back and we've got plans for tomorrow.'

'Oh Mum,' Catherine cried, 'the fun's only just beginning! Why can't we stay the night?'

Wendy looked across at us. 'Not on, is it, Joanna, Philip? A change of plan?'

'We've got the two cars,' I pointed out. 'If you Huttons want to stay it's not a problem with us.'

Catherine and Anna put their heads together and murmured something and then Anna piped up. 'Of course, you oldies could go back in one car and Catherine and I can stay on and drive back tomorrow in the other. Catherine's a very good driver.'

Wendy was doubtful about this idea until Tekin, whom we knew well and trusted, said he'd keep an eye on things and make sure all was in order. So in the end we adults went off in the car I had rented for the day while Catherine and Anna were left the jeep their father had hired for their holiday.

Next day the girls returned to Famagusta safely having had, they told us, a terrific time.

Talking of rented vehicles, I should mention that we had not returned to Cyprus on our renewed contract entirely alone; our Land Rover came as well. We had brought it to UK from Oman in 1994 and used it there for two years. We laid it up at home for our first year in Cyprus but for our second year – and, as we anticipated, rather longer – we decided to ship it to Famagusta. It arrived a month or so after us and getting it released from the port was a major operation. A young Cypriot offered to help me with the complex bureaucratic formalities, however, and after nearly a day on the job I drove it triumphantly through the gates and the couple of miles to Karakol.

The capacious four-wheel drive proved an ideal form of transport over the next four years. Nor was it expensive to run, for it gave little trouble and petrol on the island was considerably cheaper than in UK. Our one regret in bringing it was the fact that we would no longer be supporting Mr Benzinoğlu, proprietor of the garage in Famagusta from which we had rented cars – and whose daughter was one of Joanna's pupils. A jovial soul, who had given us reliable vehicles at a good price (unlike a scurrilous business just down the road), his surname is one I shall never forget. Meaning 'son of benzine [petrol]' it must have been adopted – perhaps by his grandfather – when Kemal Ataturk's new secular republic required families to have surnames, or possibly when the British colonial administration in Cyprus required the same. Whichever way it was, his great grandfather must also have been a garage man!

We explored every corner of the north of the island in our Land Rover, ranging from the farthest tip of the panhandle to the western extremity of TRNC in the Troodos foothills some way beyond Güzelyurt. Girne, better known as Kyrenia, a historic port centrally placed on the northern coast, with an attractive harbour and Crusader castle, was a favourite destination. Several times, to

Trip with friends up the Karpaz

Practicing Turkish with a local shopkeeper

have a break from life in Famagusta and at the university, we spent a night or two there in a hotel overlooking the harbour. On one such occasion we met up – after an interval of some thirty years – with the school friend who had been best man at our wedding. Quite early on in his career as a medical consultant, Michael Saunders had moved to Newcastle with Irene and the children, which I suppose explains how we managed to avoid seeing each other for so long.

Another favourite spot was Kantara castle, perched on the eastern end of the Kyrenia range of mountains. We regularly took our visitors to see the castle but when Joanna and I went alone we would usually stop short of the castle at a restaurant in the nearby village (mainly consisting of holiday homes), set among attractive woodland on a saddle-back of the mountain range. More often than not such outings would be in the winter because besides serving excellent food the restaurant boasted a log fire – very necessary at that altitude. Undoubtedly our most important visit to Kantara was the one on which Edmund came with his new girlfriend Rania – Lebanese, and like him employed at the time in Dubai. A fine photo of the two of them under an arch of the crumbling castle (taken, unusually, by me) records that occasion.

One of the bonuses of these outings was the chance they gave me to practise my Turkish. From the beginning of our time on the island I had been making efforts to master the local language – difficult, but grammatically regular, very old and, to me, quite fascinating. I was greatly helped by the fact that over thirty per cent of the vocabulary was borrowed from Arabic – though an 'academy' on the mainland was making strenuous efforts to root out such words and replace them with Turkish neologisms. I used a book in the Teach Yourself series and would many times peruse this over my lunch hour during term-time.

On our trips we would sometimes find ourselves meeting villagers who knew little or no English and I would seize the opportunity to get into conversation with them, if only briefly. As time went on I became reasonably proficient at speaking the language though never finding anything other than simple written statements easy to understand.

We organised a more ambitious trip beyond the bounds of the island for which we had to dispense with the services of the Land Rover. This was at the turn of the year when the university had a holiday and both Annabel and Edmund had come out from UK to be with us. The four of us flew from Ercan airport to Istanbul and booked into a comfortable hotel in the Sultanahmet district of the Turkish capital. It was extremely cold when we arrived and despite the fact that the Turks are virtually all Muslims the feeling engendered in us was most decidedly 'Christmassy'. The city centre was bustling with people clad in heavy coats, mufflers and often woolly hats, hot chestnuts were on sale at every corner, and streets and shops were aglitter with decorations.

We wandered around happily and on New Year's Eve joined others in a fashionable, though inexpensive, eating house almost under the walls of the Blue Mosque – which of course we visited, as also the breath-taking Hagia Sophia. (Joanna and I were touched to find we were granted free entry to these buildings by the man on the gate once we told him that we were teachers in Northern Cyprus.) We enjoyed listening to one or two vocal performers in the restaurant, though of course couldn't sing along with them as others did, and we cheered with the best when midnight came and went.

The climax of our short holiday was the drive we made to a region of Turkey that Joanna had long wanted to visit, the Dardanelles. Her reasons were entirely personal: her father had been wounded in the allied landings made at Gallipoli in 1915, and forty years later he had described in some detail – and recorded on tape – his experience. It was a long drive in our hired car along a fairly straight though undulating road, the edges of which were at times partially drifted with snow. We were worried more snow might fall as we were journeying but though the sky looked threatening this did not happen. We reached our destination in mid-afternoon, leaving us with less daylight than we would have liked.

We saw the beaches where the allied landings had occurred though we were unable to identify them by name – Cape Helles, Anzac Cove (Ari Burnu) or Suvla Bay. Nor, as it happens, could Joanna even remember the name of the beach where her father, chief

Edmund Joseph Norris, RN (Joanna's father)

engineer on a supply vessel of the Royal Navy, had been wounded. But she knew the story well, that he had been at the wrong end of a bayonet thrust to his neck from a Turkish soldier (leaving a permanent scar), lost consciousness and was picked up by a friend who got him back to their ship – where he regained consciousness. She also knew why, according to her father's somewhat whimsical narrative, he had, as a naval officer, been on the beach at all. Apparently the ship had had a cargo of donkeys to offload and as this was being effected he was knocked into the water where, in his own words, he 'held onto the tail of a donkey' to get to shore. (He was, apparently, a poor swimmer.)

Having seen – and found strangely moving – the quiet beaches and slopes above, we drove round and up to the memorial erected later by the Turkish government on the hill overlooking Anzac Cove. If the beaches stirred the emotions, so did this tall monument. On it, in the waning light, we read words of Kemal Atatürk commemorating the allied fallen:

> Those heroes who shed their blood and lost their lives ... you are now lying in the soil of a friendly country. Therefore rest in peace. There is no difference between the Johnnies and the Mehmets to us where they lie side by side here in this country of ours ... You, the mothers who sent their sons from far away countries, wipe away your tears. Your sons are now lying in our bosom and are in peace. After having lost their lives on this land, they have become our sons as well.

We motored away pondering the courage and nobility war sometimes evokes, but mostly its evils. The total casualties of the Gallipoli campaign initiated by the allies – Britain, France, Australia, New Zealand – were staggering, the Turks losing 300,000 men and the allies 250,000. In January 1916 the allied garrison, so expensively established on the peninsular, evacuated Gallipoli, so nothing was achieved for the war effort beyond acts of individual heroism. Joanna's father, caught up in the fighting by accident rather than design, was perhaps the recipient of one such act in Suvla Bay (the scene of his fall on the beach, as we later established), when allied landings took place there on 6 and 7 August 1915. But the opportunity for heroism can scarcely be weighed against the suffering the conflict caused. War, however, seems to be the lot of man on this earth – until 'the day dawns and the morning star rises in your hearts'.

Another trip we organised for ourselves during this Cyprus period was much further afield.

I had long wanted to go 'down under' to visit my uncle John and his family, most of whom lived in and around Perth, in Western Australia. The need to do something tangible about this wish had become pressing because John – also my godfather – was by now ninety-four years old and becoming increasingly frail. We therefore arranged to fly out from UK in late July, 1998, and spend ten days with them. We broke the journey in Dubai, staying for a few days with Edmund, and took another plane via Borneo to Perth. I recall us flying through an alarmingly strong cross wind, and wondering whether it was typical, before finally touching down. We were met by Mary, John's wife of over sixty years, and Margaret, eldest of their four children. They drove us to Guildford, a suburb of Perth, telling us on the way that John was in hospital, though not in a critical condition. We were to stay with my cousin David, who shared the family home with his parents.

David was a physicist – as I write, Winthrop Professor of Physics – at the University of Western Australia, where he and his team had constructed the world's first sapphire clock and then concentrated on the search for Einstein's elusive 'gravity waves'. He and his Chinese wife, Ju Li, also in the university physics department, welcomed us into their half of the house. At the first opportunity, needless to say, we were off to see my uncle.

John Blair, second of the three brothers, had taken up dairy farming near Albany, on the southern coast of Western Australia, after resigning as Resident in the British colonial administration of Nigeria. He stuck at farming for ten years but it became less and less remunerative, so he turned to teaching – the classics, which he had studied at Oxford – for another ten years in a boys' school. He thus had three distinct careers, establishing a kind of symmetry with my father's working life. Having retired – when he mastered carpentry, though almost blind – he decided his third career had been the best.

Yet as Joanna and I sat beside him in his hospital bed, my uncle quietly said, 'I consider my life to have been a failure – in all respects except one.' He smiled and inclined his head towards his life-long partner.

I was much struck by this confession because my father had said something similar the summer before he died. 'Does everyone feel like this towards the end?' I have since asked myself. (Enoch Powell, classical scholar and distinguished parliamentarian, once pronounced, 'Every politician's career ends in failure'. This narrower and oft-quoted aphorism is hard to dispute!)

We saw quite a lot of David's older sisters: Margaret, a good friend to me in childhood days, still devoting herself to the cause of Australia's native population; and Helen, a teacher and, like her father, skilled in the crafting of wood. Anne, however, youngest of the four, lived in Melbourne; she was a babe-in-arms when I last saw her.

We had some good outings: to Albany down south, where we glimpsed the one-time Blair farm; to a temperate rain forest, where we stayed in David's rammed-earth 'ranch', set among the karri trees, kangaroos and emus; to a vineyard, where we sampled the local wine. We also had much fun at a birthday party for David's son Lyndon (by Eve, his first wife).

'What on earth's that?' I asked my cousin when, in the midst of the festivities in the garden, he suddenly appeared lugging a long and obviously heavy cylinder.

'Oh, this,' he replied with a grin. 'It's liquid nitrogen. I've borrowed it from the university lab. I normally do for birthdays. It's amazing – just look at this!'

He did something with the 'gas', producing some spectacular effects, and then sprinkled it freely around. A few drops fell on us watchers.

'Hey, David,' Joanna called out. 'What are you doing? I felt some on my skin. That stuff's dangerous, surely!'

Philip's uncle and godfather, John

'Not really,' my irrepressible kinsman responded. 'It'll feel cold for a moment, of course, but a drop or two is harmless enough. And it's great for making iced drinks or ice cream. Come and see how it's done.'

And we did, queuing up for each of us to be given, as David poured a little of the 'gas' into the appropriate cup or onto a mixture, an ice-cold beverage or frozen, creamy preparation.

We left Australia both happy and sad: the former because of a great experience; the latter because we realised we would not see John again. My uncle died a month after our departure – and just two days after our son Edmund had, at the end of a lightning visit, also said goodbye. It seemed he had made a special effort to hold on till his great-nephew had come and gone – then slipped away. *Sic transit gloria mundi.*

***

Joanna and I were involved in the development of a Christian fellowship group in Famagusta. It had been formed shortly before our arrival, a major step being taken by the American professor of English whom I replaced in the university. He had requested permission from the university authorities for the group to meet in an ancient church in Famagusta named – very appropriately – St George of the Foreigner; the university had previously requisitioned it for theatrical activities. The authorities responded positively, granting permission for the group to use it for Sunday worship.

We were essentially a Protestant body, Roman Catholics already enjoying the ministrations of a priest who celebrated mass on the nearby United Nations camp. There was no Anglican or free church minister visiting Famagusta regularly so we elected a committee, with a chairperson, secretary and treasurer, to organise services and other activities. The committee took to meeting in a popular restaurant near our apartment run by a lady of Jamaican background. As well as providing us with excellent nourishment at a very reasonable price, she in due course became an active member of the committee.

For our Sunday services people took part on a rota basis as leader, preacher, or 'music maestro' – which meant providing instrumental

Marriage of Manga and Mirindra in Kyrenia (Girne) Anglican church

backing for the hymns. We sometimes had a visiting preacher, such as the Baptist missionary working in Lefkoşa or the provost of the Anglican cathedral in the Greek half of Nicosia. The system worked well, and our weekday meetings – with both social and spiritual aims – were appreciated. Our group was very international, its members hailing from USA, UK, Kenya, Ghana, Albania, China, and even Turkey, to name the most significant countries. I found the 'do-it-yourself' character of this church fellowship extremely satisfying, partly because it took me back to my RAF days when I had been involved in something similar.

One of the leading lights of our fellowship was a university colleague of mine who had arrived with us in 1996, Linda Bilton. She played the piano and was regularly 'music maestro', though often fulfilling a second role as well. She became a close friend, leaving when we did and moving to the Gulf.

Two other good friends from these times were Mangatiana (Manga) and Mirindra Robdera, who were from Madagascar. Manga arrived the year after us, very much a bachelor, and joined the university mathematics department. When he left for the following summer vacation, however, he announced that he would be returning with a wife.

'She's a very nice person and I'm sure you'll like her. We haven't seen all that much of each other but it's about time I got married.'

'Do you love her?' I inquired mischievously.

'Love?' Manga looked a little surprised. 'Well, what does that mean exactly? With my background I'm probably more into logic than love. But yes, she's attractive and seems right. I think she'll say yes.'

Sure enough, the following September he came back with a pretty young lady in tow – only it wasn't the one he (or we) had expected!

'It didn't work out with the one I told you about,' he confessed solemnly. 'In fact, it didn't even begin to. We agreed very quickly, the two of us, that we'd never make a go of it. *But* ... I have to be grateful to her because she asked if I'd like to meet her friend who, she insisted, was keen to get married.' He glanced at the young woman sitting beside him. 'I readily agreed – and the rest is history. Mirindra and I were introduced and … and we decided we had no time to lose. We were married in a civil ceremony ten days later.'

'*That's* what I call a whirlwind romance!' remarked Joanna, laughing. 'What have you to say about it, Mirindra?'

She looked appropriately demure. 'You could certainly say whirlwind but romance might give the wrong impression. It was very carefully thought out, you see. Manga's a mathematician and nothing's going to change that.' She allowed herself a smile. 'Love is important, but it's something else.'

'One more thing,' Manga said. 'We are going to have a church wedding. In fact, although we are legally married – Mirindra couldn't have accompanied me to TRNC unless we were – we do not consider ourselves truly man and wife until we have that Christian ceremony.'

The latter was arranged to take place in Kyrenia Anglican church, where there was a resident priest. Mirindra asked me to stand in as father and 'give her away', which role I was delighted to fulfil, and she hinted that Joanna could perhaps play the part of mother in the days leading up to the wedding. Joanna, of course, happily agreed. The ceremony itself, attended by members of the Kyrenia congregation as well as friends, and the reception that followed, were touching and great fun respectively. A little less than a year later their first child, Toky, arrived on one of those much-coveted dates: 9.9.99. We were asked to be godparents and naturally accepted.

***

In May 2000 my mother died. She was eighty-nine.

I received a message one Thursday from my brother, who lived with her in Sherborne. Apparently she had had a mild stroke but was recovering well; there was therefore no need for me to rush home. Strangely enough, my sister and brother-in-law, Lorna and Jolyon Carpenter, were flying out to have a short holiday with us – their first in Cyprus – the very next day. Yet I knew instinctively what I must do: book the first available flight to UK. I had failed to make it in time to see my father before he died; this wasn't going to happen with my mother. I made the appropriate inquiries and was able to book a seat for Saturday, two days later.

Lorna and Jolyon duly arrived the next day, the news from home remained good and we enjoyed a good dinner together enhanced by an excellent Turkish wine. It seemed unnecessary for them to return on the flight with me – if indeed that was possible. They therefore decided they would stay the weekend, when Joanna could drive them to one or two interesting places, but would fly home on the Monday.

My Saturday flight was uneventful and we landed at Heathrow at around midday. I took the usual coach to Woking and was on a train to Sherborne a little after two. The old Southern Railway Waterloo-Exeter line is no longer particularly fast – at least, not beyond Salisbury – and we were pulling into Sherborne at around four. I was met by our friend Joy (who had acted for years, and still acts, as our UK commissary) and we dropped briefly into a shop before driving to Yeovil hospital. It was there that my mother was, as I thought, making a good recovery.

I was disappointed. I arrived on the ward to discover my mother had suffered a relapse hardly an hour earlier and had gradually lost consciousness. Alive she was, however, and – recalling what I had been told, that those who appear beyond reach may be aware of people around them – I held her hand, talked to her softly and said a prayer. Nigel, my brother, came in soon after my arrival; he had not heard about the sudden relapse and it clearly hit him hard. We sat together for a while though, as the evening wore on, he became restless and left. A severe diabetic, he no doubt went home to inject himself before returning. As it turned out, I and my mother were alone at the end. I had been with her for some five hours and expressed my deepest feelings. It was enough.

What can I say about my mother? She was, above all, full of love for all who came within her orbit.

An image has always stuck in my mind. My parents were both – if I may put it thus – true socialists. In the years immediately after the war there was a certain amount of homelessness, not least in the three villages that comprised my father's parish outside Salisbury.

Philip's mother and father at time of marriage, early 1930s

We lived in a big vicarage and though we were a family of five my parents opened it up to those in need. At one stage there were three families living with us: one in the attic, another in the dining room and pantry, and a third in the scullery and 'coal cellar'. (The last was a room, cleaned out and roughly decorated, next to the scullery.) When my father relinquished this parish in 1954 to take another in Devizes, a farewell party was held in the parish hall. At the end of it the mother from the family who had occupied the scullery and coal cellar went up to my mother, threw her arms around her and hugged her. This is the way people felt about Honor Blair.

I stayed in UK for a week. Lorna came down as soon as she could after her return from Cyprus. We had a simple service at the crematorium and buried Honor's ashes alongside Harold's in his mother's grave in the local cemetery. We also arranged a memorial service in Castleton church, just down the lane from our house, to which various members of the family and friends were able to come. My sister read some words from a poem by Robert Bridges to commemorate our mother's artistic spirit, preserved in her many paintings:

> *I love all beauteous things –*
> *I seek and adore them;*
> *God hath no better praise,*
> *And man in his hasty days*
> *Is honoured for them.*
> *I too will something make*
> *And joy in the making.*

My sister also chose two musical pieces for the occasion, Honor having been a talented pianist in her youth. One was the chorale 'Wake oh wake, with tidings thrilling!' written originally in German by P. Nicolai and set to music by J.S. Bach. For this, Lorna played the viola while Tethys, her elder daughter, was at the organ. The other was a carol, written by J.M.C. Crum to an old French (Provençal) tune, with the poignant refrain, 'Love is come again, like wheat that springeth green.'

Love was indeed the theme of this 'thanksgiving to God for Honor Blair', as the commemoration was described on the service sheet. Perhaps the words printed at the end of that sheet best sum up the occasion – and even human life:

> *Love is not changed by Death,*
> *And nothing is lost,*
> *And all in the end is harvest.*

***

I have said little about our teaching during the years in Northern Cyprus. There is little I want to say. We had our ups and downs occasionally – particularly Joanna who worked very hard in Eastern Mediterranean College, helping to establish a school library among other things, but at one point found herself up against the wiles of a jealous (non-Cypriot) colleague. She moved to Eastern Mediterranean Primary School after two years, however, where she was extremely happy. I did my lecturing, mostly in general linguistics, plus thesis supervision for teachers of English working for their MA. I encountered few problems until our fifth year, when a new Head of Department arrived from Turkey and it soon became clear that his appointment was a lot to do with clearing out Western expatriates – or at least discouraging them – and replacing them with Turkish staff.

That fifth academic year of 2000 – 2001 was, as it happened, highly productive for us both. Joanna studied for and obtained an MA in English Studies from the university's Department of English Literature, which meant she could embark on teaching at university level. I myself wrote most of a new book. At the end of 1999 my second book, *Watching for the Morning*, had come out; it considered, from a Christian perspective, the state of the world and where both it and mankind were heading. This new book, entitled *God's Credentials*, was my third serious study. It was designed to confront a wave of atheistic publications which, as I saw it, employed arguments based on highly questionable assumptions. My literary agent wrote enthusiastically to me, 'I can't imagine a book more crying for publication and promotion'; however, the major publishing houses he tried, both general and religious, were not interested. In the end a very small Christian operation called K&M Books brought it out early in 2007.

For various reasons – my new Head of Department, the Turkish economy and plunging lira (which had reached 2,000,000 to the pound), the sense that we had experienced and perhaps completed something worthwhile – we decided to move on. I did not seek a renewal of my contract and Joanna resigned from her position at the primary school, to the distress of her colleagues. We had collected some happy memories: evenings full of laughter with our friends John, Rod, Bill, Daphne and others in our flat; tasty meals at Pizza San Marina just over the road, run by hospitable Abdul Rahim and his brothers; picnics in the ruins of a Byzantine basilica set in the prettiest surroundings some way up the Karpaz; concerts in Bellapais Abbey, where on one occasion Joanna received a friendly nod from the President of the Republic, Rauf Denktaş; visits to Lefkoşa bazaar, where we once almost collided with the same gregarious, amply-proportioned Denktaş, out doing some shopping like us.

We decided to drive home. We disposed of everything we didn't want, bundled the rest into the Land Rover and set out around midday at the beginning of August for Kyrenia. We had booked ourselves and our vehicle onto the late afternoon ferry to Turkey. The weather was perfect as we drew away from the port. We stood at the rail and saw the island slowly receding from view, and then turned to watch the declining sun. There was scarcely a ripple on the glowing water until a shoal of flying fish broke the surface and skimmed along beside us.

It was a good way to be leaving. Not for the first time we had no idea what lay ahead. Coming to Cyprus five years previously had seemed like full circle and I had tended to think my appointment at Eastern Mediterranean University would be my last. Events – for the most part – ruled otherwise.

How much of life lies in the waiting? Once again we were casting off, to float adrift until we found some other haven.

XII

A Drive Home – and 'Dilmun'

On arrival at the port of Taşucu, on the southern Turkish coast near Silifke, our main concern was to get our vehicle insured. The TRNC insurance was no longer valid because on leaving Cyprus permanently we were 'exporting' the car and therefore had to hand back our number plates. Before setting out we had therefore fixed back onto the Land Rover the British plates it had displayed on its arrival in Famagusta, but this slightly confused the Turkish authorities. What we wanted was the international 'green' form of insurance that would enable us to drive legally across Europe to England. We had not been able to obtain this in the Northern Cyprus Republic because, of course, it was not internationally recognized as a state. Nor was this cover available at the port, we were informed, but they could give us temporary cover for use of the vehicle in Turkey. We had no option but to accept and were finally able to drive away.

A hotel presented itself immediately and we had a long and refreshing night's sleep followed by a good breakfast to fortify us for a day of driving. The terrain in the area is undulating and after setting out in high spirits we were soon climbing some hills. Near the top of a rather steep ascent our V8 engine began to falter – as did our spirits. Surely we weren't going to break down so early in our cross-continent drive! We managed to keep going, however, and crested the hill. Once we reached more level country there were no more hiccups. To be on the safe side I stopped by the side of the road and peered under the bonnet in case I could identify a fault. Nothing was apparent so I thought I'd just check the oil.

'Goodness, Jo, the sump's empty!' I said in dismay having looked at the dipstick. 'I suppose that's why the engine was jumpy on that hill.'

She groaned. 'That's a pity. No service station close at hand.' We considered our situation for a moment or two and then noticed a car approaching.

'It's a taxi, isn't it?' I suddenly cried. 'I'll flag it down.' I did so and it drew to a stop. I asked the driver if he could take me to find some oil and he nodded.

'Are you just going off and leaving me with the Land Rover?' Joanna said doubtfully.

'Well, you're on a main road and petrol stations seem pretty plentiful in Turkey. I shouldn't be long.'

She glanced up the road, noticed someone a little way off and announced, with some asperity, 'If you think I'm staying here with complete strangers around, you can think again. We'll go together – and that's that.'

I hadn't a leg to stand on, of course, so immediately agreed. Off we went in the taxi, to find a place a mile or two further on as I had hoped. We bought the oil, returned quickly and paid off the taxi. A few minutes later, having poured in the precious liquid, we were on our way again – though halting periodically to check the level.

Our destination was Bodrum, on Turkey's western coast, and our drive thereafter – relieved by a couple of pleasant stops in amazingly cheap hotels, one owned by the parents of a student from EMU – was punctuated by frequent visits to petrol stations to buy and pour into our engine litre after litre of oil. The head gasket had split. I had indeed noticed a little oil leaking onto the ground just before leaving Cyprus, but Land Rover spares were not readily available in the north of the island and had to be brought out from UK. There was little option but to set out on the assumption that the leak would not quickly worsen.

We arrived in Bodrum safely – or, more specifically, in Gölköy, an attractive village set beside a nearby inlet of the sea. We had arranged to stay a few days with friends from our Yemen days, Cem and Semra Clissold. This was an Anglo-Turkish couple, as the names might indicate. (Turkish 'Cem' could be construed as a

Turkish version of English 'Jim'.) Apart from the pleasure of seeing our friends and our enjoyment of the idyllic spot in which they were living, those few days were essential to get our vehicle fixed. We managed to find a car mechanic in Bodrum who specialised in Rover vehicles but he did not have the gasket to hand. He therefore sent off to the main agent in Istanbul, asking for delivery within twenty-four hours – which was achieved, to our astonishment. He put in the new gasket and on the fourth day after our arrival we were able to set off for Izmir, where we intended to take the ferry to Italy.

There was still a problem, however, the question of international insurance cover. We had phoned an insurance company in Izmir from our friends' home and been reassured about its availability but when, on arrival in Izmir just two hours before our ferry was due to leave, I visited their office there appeared to be an insuperable difficulty. Apparently their computer would not accept our vehicle because it had not been registered in Turkey. We were in a catch-22 situation – emanating ultimately, of course, from our having been residents of a 'non-existent' state, the Turkish Republic of Northern Cyprus. I explained the dilemma and pleaded with the official to help – and, to my everlasting gratitude, she did.

'Has your car been at a Turkish address?' she inquired.

'Well, yes, I suppose it has,' I responded. 'We spent a few days in Gölköy, near Bodrum.'

She seized on my words. 'Ah, then we can enter it as a Bodrum-registered vehicle. Now let me see, what is your car number?' I spelt out the English registration details and she screwed up her eyes. 'Yes … that might satisfy.'

She entered everything and we waited anxiously while the electronic wheels turned. I looked feverishly at my watch: it was scarcely an hour before our boat would be sailing.

'Allah be praised!' the lady suddenly cried. 'It's okay. We can issue the international cover, which will have fourteen days validity.'

I pressed her, almost incredulous. 'You're quite sure, are you? I mean, if we have a problem, will the company honour this agreement.'

She looked mildly shocked. 'Certainly! What do you take us for?'

The documents were printed out, I paid the money and rushed down the stairs and into the road, where Joanna had been waiting in the Land Rover. Needless to say, she had been getting increasingly anxious, and was hugely relieved to know that we were not going to have to drive across Europe illegally, or – as we had half-contemplated – sell the car and go home by some other means.

The three-day voyage to Venice was delightful. We had a small but comfortable cabin and ate in the dining room where waiters served you at table. We met and conversed with friendly fellow passengers but mostly relaxed on deck, or in the lounge with a book. Going through the Corinth canal was interesting, bringing back memories of thirteen years previously, when during our holiday in Greece we had driven over the road bridge crossing the canal. The only slight downside of the trip – affecting my stomach rather than Joanna's – was the storm and consequent rough seas as we approached Italy.

We stayed two nights on the mainland opposite the 'city of marble ... paved with emerald', beneath which 'the unsullied sea drew in deep breathing, to and fro, its eddies of green wave', as John Ruskin once effused. We walked round, forked out a prodigious sum for half an hour in a gondola (we had promised ourselves this luxury) and experienced the most anaemic pizza I can remember in a restaurant overlooking the Grand Canal. But of course it was all great fun.

From Venice we motored north, over the Brenner Pass into Germany, where quite soon we stopped and stayed a night in a guesthouse. We set off again the next morning but not long after skirting Munich an ominous red light began to shine on the dashboard. We were climbing a hill at the time in stifling weather and decided to take no chances. We took the first turning right off the autobahn, which led us to the town of Pforzeim, on the edge of the Black Forest. We found a very reasonably-priced hotel, parked the Land Rover there and went out for a meal.

The next day, after making a few inquiries, we drove to a vehicle workshop where a pleasant young German was in charge.

'The problem's electrical,' he informed us. 'Your alternator – that is, the dynamo – is giving out.'

'Ah,' I said, turning to Joanna. 'So *that* is why we faltered on the hill in Turkey. I should've realised. It wasn't the oil at all.' I turned back to the young German. 'So what's your advice?'

'Well,' he replied, 'it might last the rest of your journey. On the other hand it might not.'

We had no wish to risk a breakdown so asked him to put in a new one. He didn't have the right kind in stock but could order one from Frankfurt, requesting quick delivery. 'Two days at most', he told us.

We were content, and decided to make the most of this unplanned interlude in 'Gold City', as Pforzeim is commonly called. It is famous for the manufacture of exquisite gold filigree jewellery. The two days, however, stretched to four. We learnt from our mechanic that the lorry bringing our new alternator had got 'lost'. (Yes, he really said this!) Not quite up to Turkish standards, we privately joked.

Make the most of our time we did, anyway, in the beautiful weather the country was enjoying. We had a convivial meal or two in a (very German) beer garden; we took a train into the Black Forest and ended up at a kind of health resort for third-age citizens who ate and drank ferociously before getting up to dance; we visited a nearby town, one-time home of Philip Melancthon, who had been Martin Luther's associate in the setting up of the Lutheran Church following the great reformer's protest against Rome. The town had a museum featuring items from the lives of the two men and it was a thrill for me – Luther being yet another of my heroes – to see, for example, a sixteenth-century copy of Paul's Epistle to the Galatians with marginal annotations in the reformer's own hand.

The day came when our vehicle was supposed to be ready and we went to pick it up.

'I'm extremely sorry, sir,' the German mechanic immediately informed me, 'but the alternator they sent is the wrong specification. It's a genuine Land Rover part but it's for a right-hand drive vehicle, not left-hand. It doesn't fit.'

I could hardly believe my ears. 'So what's to be done?' I managed to say through clenched teeth. 'This has become an extraordinary catalogue of errors.'

The mechanic looked suitably mortified. 'It is most unfortunate, sir, certainly, and I have to say, unusual. But I have a second-hand Ford part which I can try. It will probably work.'

It did, and we were able to resume our journey across Europe later that day. We had no regrets as our full four days in Pforzeim had turned out to be restful, entertaining – even educational. But it amused us to think we could have been on our way with just a day lost if the Ford spare had been fitted immediately.

The remainder of our journey was – much to our relief – wholly uneventful. From Germany we crossed into Belgium, and thence into France, where we spent a night in Calais prior to taking the ferry to Dover. We arrived in Sherborne with just three days validity remaining for our 'one-off' vehicle insurance policy.

***

What to do now?

It is the same well-tried routine: Joanna looks for supply work in local schools; I try to find casual employment as a language teacher. Joanna, as always, succeeds; this time, I don't.

But I wasn't going to be at a loose end: there was work to be done in the garden – major work. A gate had been constructed at our request by a builder in the back wall of our garden, leading onto the car park of a new estate. The estate filled what had been a field – often containing a friendly horse who would look over the wall at us. We, together with some neighbours, had arranged with the owners of the estate, a housing association, to be granted vehicular access to the public road through their car park. But the level of the park was three or four feet higher than that of our garden. We had had some hard core delivered to our garden to form the base of a raised parking space and had procured two estimates of the building cost. These were seven and eight thousand pounds respectively – which seemed to us extortionate. I was willing and able: building the parking space accordingly became my winter task.

In the end it was not a space but a drive, sloping down from the new gate to our lawn. I paved it with stone tiles that had once been on our roof.

'You see, darling,' I told Joanna triumphantly when after four or five months it was finished, 'I have in fact *earned* that seven or eight thousand pounds through hard labour.'

She smiled. 'Fair enough. Men aren't totally useless!'

There were one or two other things to occupy me. Firstly, I managed to fit in some writing, but that – another attempt at a novel with an Arab world flavour – still awaits completion. (A retirement job, perhaps – only we keep postponing this step.) Secondly, from the spring of 2002 we took in one or two foreign students who wanted tuition in English in the context of an English home. Joanna looked after their domestic needs and we shared the teaching.

But this way of life could not last. I applied to the University of Bahrain for the position of assistant professor of English, mentioning that my wife was also a qualified English teacher and would be available to take up a post. We were both offered contracts, to which we readily agreed, and in late August found ourselves once again packing our bags and flying off to foreign parts. We were more than happy about this. After so many years wandering the world – or more precisely, the Middle East – we were finding we got itchy feet if we were back in UK for very long.

Bahrain, as my reader may have guessed, is Dilmun. Let me explain, drawing my information mostly from the classic study by Geoffrey Bibby, *Looking for Dilmun* (Collins, 1970; Stacey International, 1996).

First of all, it should be pointed out that the small island of Bahrain today has an extraordinary feature that strikes every visitor. (I will mostly use the term 'island' though in reality Bahrain is an archipelago of islands – now fully interconnected with fill-ins or bridges.) There are some 85,000 burial-mounds stretching across five percent of the undulating, partially desert terrain. Until relatively recently most local Arabs wrongly considered them to be graves of the Portuguese, who established garrisons on the island in the sixteenth century of our era. A more realistic theory is that the mounds and their internal chambers were built in the second millennium BC by nomad tribes living on mainland Arabia, the island serving solely as a burial ground. A third theory, which once gained considerable currency, is that they were constructed by the Phoenicians, whose maritime adventures expanded from the beginning of the first millennium BC. I myself, on seeing these mounds for the first time, was reminded of the 'barrows' you see around Stonehenge, in Wiltshire, where I was brought up – but I formulated no theory as to the origins of Bahrain's 'barrows'.

The name 'Dilmun' was lost to mankind for some two and a half millennia, until it turned up in a translation of the annals of the kings of ancient Assyria, published in France in 1861. These records were discovered in the late 1840s during excavations of Nineveh, the capital of Assyria; they were inscribed on alabaster tablets in the Accadian or Assyrian languages, using the wedge-shaped cuneiform script which took some time to be deciphered. On the publication of a translation of the annals, people were mostly interested in the fact that they confirmed the accuracy of references made by Isaiah in the Old Testament to a king of Assyria called Sargon. In passing, however, they made reference to one 'Uperi, king of Dilmun, whose abode is situated, like a fish, thirty double-hours away in the midst of the sea of the rising sun'.

Nearly twenty years later, in 1880, the archaeologist Sir Henry Rawlinson wrote the following about this hitherto unknown kingdom: 'Let it be understood then, that throughout the Assyrian tablets, from the earliest period to the latest, there is constant allusion to an island called Niduk-ki in Accadian, and Tilvun or Tilmun in Assyrian, and that this name ... undoubtedly applies to Bahrein.' Rawlinson's identification was not at the time supported by much evidence; it was more a matter of intuition. The book by Geoffrey Bibby cited above, however, is an exhaustive study of the question by an archaeologist who concluded from his field research in Bahrain that Rawlinson's verdict was well grounded.

We turn now to something a little less obscure. Most people have heard of the ancient Mesopotamian text – sometimes described as the oldest story in the world – called *The Epic of Gilgamesh*. The way this text came into our hands, and what it is about, is worth a brief mention before we move on to what it tells us about Dilmun.

The unearthing of monuments inscribed in cuneiform from the palaces of the kings of Assyria – Sargon, Sennacherib, and Assurbanipal – in Nineveh, introduced modern man to that kingdom's history. The associated discovery of thousands of baked clay tablets, also exhibiting the cuneiform script, in what turned out to be the library of Assurbanipal, opened up to us the literature of early Mesopotamia, especially the creation narratives and epic poems of Babylonia and Assyria. In the year 1872 translations of some very significant texts from the vast number of these tablets held by the British Museum were published. They told of a king of Uruk (biblical Erech; modern Warka) who embarked upon a search for immortality. Described as semi-divine in the narrative, he is today considered a real king who reigned around 2700 BC. He is mentioned as the fifth king of Uruk after the flood in another extant text, the Sumerian King-List. He is, of course, Gilgamesh, whose quest covers much of the Epic bearing his name.

Once again, popular interest in the narrative revolved chiefly around the relevance it had for biblical studies, for its eleventh 'chapter' told of a visit the king had made to one 'Utu-nipishtim', who had been granted immortality after surviving a flood in which 'all mankind was turned to clay'. Utu-nipishtim explains to Gilgamesh the manner of his survival, how he had, on the advice of Enki, the god of the waters under the earth, constructed a huge boat and – together with his family, a few others and 'the beast of the field both wild and tame' – boarded it and thus escaped being drowned. He concludes by explaining how Enlil, chief of the gods, had given this promise: 'Hitherto has Utu-nipishtim been mortal. Now shall he and his wife be like the gods; and they shall dwell in the distance, at the mouth of the rivers.'

What precisely, you may be asking, have Gilgamesh and Utu-nipishtim to do with Dilmun?

In 1914 the text of a damaged clay tablet found in lower Mesopotamia at Nippur, whose patron god was Enlil, was published. This gave the last third or so of the Sumerian flood story

– enough to show that it was the same in essence as the story given in the Epic of Gilgamesh, of later Babylonian provenance. Most importantly, the end of the story was intact and from it we learn that the survivor of the flood, in this case named Ziusudra, was, like Utu-nipishtim, granted immortality. The narrative reads: 'Anu [father of the gods] and Enlil cherished Ziusudra, life like a god they give him, breath eternal like a god they bring down for him. Then Ziusudra the king, the preserver of the name of vegetation and of the seed of mankind, in the land of crossing, the land of Dilmun, the place where the sun rises, they caused to dwell.'

The remarkable parallels these flood narratives exhibit with that given in the biblical book of Genesis can, incidentally, hardly be coincidental. Scholars today usually argue that the biblical account is a later and refined version of the Sumerian/Babylonian account, this principle applying also to the respective creation accounts. D.J. Wiseman, however, formerly professor of Assyriology at London University, has another idea. Speaking of the Babylonian creation account *Enuma elish*, he writes: 'Any similarities with the Genesis record have to be rescued from the overlaying extraneous matter which forms the bulk of the poem; such can best be explained as due to both versions going back to common primary facts.' This reconstruction, of common primary facts lying behind narratives that show some similarity, can be applied also to the respective flood accounts. A third possibility, however, turning the usual argument of scholars on its head, is that both the creation and flood accounts of Sumeria/Babylonia are bizarre, half-remembered versions of the original accounts preserved in Genesis. Abraham, it should be remembered, migrated with his family to Canaan from Ur, in Mesopotamia, in around the twentieth century BC. He had a distinguished lineage and would surely have carried his family records and related traditions with him – inscribed on clay tablets. These may have included the accounts of creation and the flood that later became part of Hebrew scripture.

But let us return to Dilmun, the 'land of crossing … the place where the sun rises'. What made Geoffrey Bibby, and what makes most archaeologists today, so confident that Dilmun should be identified with the island of Bahrain?

We turn first to the Sumerian flood story. Bibby concedes that the ambiguous phrase 'the land of crossing' tells us little but he considers the description 'where the sun rises' highly suggestive. The Sumerians and Babylonians, he informs us, used often to refer to the Arabian Gulf as the 'sea of the rising sun', so that an island anywhere in that sea could be described as 'the place where the sun rises'. Secondly, there is the discovery made by Bibby and his fellow-diggers at Barbar, in Bahrain, of a Sumerian-style temple, concealed under an extensive mound. Artifacts unearthed on the site, also Sumerian in style, were dated to between 2500 and 1800 BC, testifying to a close relationship between the island and Sumeria during this period. A further intriguing argument presented by Bibby relates to the account of Gilgamesh, on the instructions of Utu-nipishtim, picking from the seabed the Flower of Immortality, restorer of lost youth when consumed; he delayed eating it, we are told, allowing a snake to snatch it from him, together with its blessing. Did this episode, our author speculates, have its origin in the Bahraini practice of diving to collect pearls – the precious 'flower' of the seas – from oysters? He tells how a shell-heap on the south-west coast of the island was discovered to be a pearl-fishers' encampment, the shells being almost entirely of pearl-oysters; mixed up with those shells were fragments of pots similar to those found in the temple at Barbar, dated to the third-millennium BC.

Perhaps the most persuasive piece of evidence in favour of the identification of Bahrain with Dilmun relates to the very word *bahrain*. It is of course Arabic and means 'two seas', almost certainly referring to seas on a vertical, not horizontal axis. I will at this point cite a passage from Bibby's book: 'The Sumerians believed that the earth and the sea rested upon another sea, the *abzu* [from which English gets its word 'abyss']. Unlike the ordinary sea, which is salt, the *abzu* is of fresh water, and the two are kept quite distinct, both in belief and in actual fact, the bed of the salt sea preventing the two from mixing. The Sumerians believed that the *abzu* was the source of all fresh water, rivers finding their source in the underground sea, and wells and springs being holes, artificial or natural, reaching down to it. And Enki was the ruler and guardian of this fresh-water sea.' Does this idea somehow correlate with Bahrain? It does indeed. The island has always been famous for its springs, fresh water from which has welled up on land and at sea, divers in the past collecting it from the shallow seabed off the coast in receptacles made from skins.

To show the connection of all this with Dilmun we now turn to another ancient text found, like the Sumerian flood story, at Nippur. It was discovered in around 1900 but only published in meaningful translation in 1945, when scholars entitled it 'Enki and Ninhursag' (the latter being the great earth Mother). The events recounted in this myth take place in Dilmun, and lines in the poem extol the virtues of that land:

The land of Dilmun is holy.
Holy Sumer – present it to him [Enki?] …
The land of Dilmun is holy, the land of Dilmun is pure …

The goddess Nin-sikilla, guardian goddess of Dilmun, then asks Enki to supply Dilmun with water, and we read on:

Father Enki answers Nin-sikilla his daughter:
'Let Utu [the sun god] stationed in heaven
bring you sweet water from the earth, from the water sources of the earth …
let him make Dilmun drink from the water of abundance …
In Dilmun … the lion kills not, the wolf snatches not the lamb …
The sick-eyed says not 'I am sick-eyed' … its old man says not 'I am an old man'.

So Bahrain, with its countless burial mounds, its temple, its age-old traditions like pearl-diving, was once – I for one am fully persuaded – the kingdom of Dilmun. As such, it was 'the eternal home of the immortal ancestor of all mankind', in the words of Geoffrey Bibby. Whether known as Utu-nipishtim, Ziusudra, or Noah, this settler could not have been more illustrious. In the Hebrew story, of course, he was not granted immortality after surviving the flood, but he received God's blessing and lived for a very long time.

And what, you may ask, of the good man's enormous boat? It rests far away on 'the mountains of Ararat', the Bible tells us, or according to the Qur'ān on the mountain al-Judi, known to the Assyrians as Mount Nippur. The Jewish historian Flavius Josephus claimed that it could be seen in that vicinity, citing Berosus the Chaldean (c. 290 BC): 'It is said there is still some part of this ship in Armenia, at the mountain of the Cordyaeans, and that some people carry off pieces of the bitumen, which they take away and use chiefly as amulets for the averting of mischiefs.' How remarkable that in our day a boat-shaped object of the precise length of the biblical ark, covered with mud and lava and more or less fossilised, has been identified in eastern Turkey at an altitude of around 6,500 feet on the slopes of Cudi Dağı (Mount Judi). This location lies within the territory of ancient Urartu, mentioned in Assyrian sources from 1300 BC. As for the form 'Ararat', it is simply a different (and later) way of adding vowels to the consonants 'RRT', which stand alone in the Hebrew text of Genesis.

When Joanna and I touched down at Bahrain International Airport in August 2002, we had no idea what a special place we had come to!

XIII

A Surprise or Two

We were met at the airport and driven to an apartment near the main campus of the University of Bahrain, which was on the southern edge of the densely-populated area of the island kingdom. All distances are minimal, of course, because the country is so small. By far the largest of the islands making up the actual archipelago is Bahrain Island, just thirty-four miles long and eleven miles wide.

Our apartment was in a pleasant complex which, like most others, had a swimming pool, which we put to good use. But we were told that we would soon be moving to one of the new villas being built for faculty members on campus near the wooded university perimeter. When we were first taken to see 'our' villa, a very spacious, comfortable-looking place, Joanna could hardly believe her eyes.

'Well I never,' she exclaimed, 'I've finally achieved my teenage desire – a home in suburbia!'

The campus as a whole, huge in extent, had some imposing modern buildings, with more structures and an intricate system of roads on the drawing board. It looked set to become something of a world within a world.

Not everyone was impressed, however. 'This could become a prison,' an expat cynic was heard to mutter. 'They simply want to keep us under observation.'

We were welcomed by our Head of Department, a Palestinian, who showed us to our offices, we met future colleagues, including our friend Linda from Cyprus days, and we were acquainted with the teaching facilities available. Then bureaucracy took over: medical clearance, the obtaining of work permits, bank accounts, driving licences, followed by a number of minor bureaucratic formalities. Within a week or two we were in the classroom. Most of the English teaching – to students of business, for example – involved very basic language skills, but I was assigned some more advanced instruction to graduate students.

'This place seems quite promising,' I remember saying to Joanna quite early on. 'Good salaries by our standards and a surprisingly efficient administration. They actually seem to believe in looking after their foreign staff.'

'Not bad,' responded my more cautious wife. 'It's the teaching that concerns me most and on that score things do look reasonably positive. Behaviour in class leaves something to be desired but I suppose you can't have everything.'

We hired a car on a long-term basis and were soon exploring. We started with the capital, Manama, particularly its extensive bazaar – no more than half an hour away by car, except in rush hour. You could get everything there at very reasonable cost: foodstuffs, spices, clothes (made-to-measure, if required, by good Indian tailors), kitchen utensils, bedding, jewellery and watches, mobiles, plus stall after stall of gimmicky novelties. Ours were mainly household needs, to supplement the basic furnishings provided by the university for our villa, which we moved into some three weeks after arrival. Such necessities were quickly accumulated and we were soon feeling comfortable at home, as well as happy with the way things were going at work – just a short walk away. There was, sensibly, a general store on campus and this looked after most daily needs. Life became a pleasant routine, not least the short trips we often made in the evenings to shop, buy a take-away, or eat out at a restaurant.

We attended Sunday worship at the Anglican cathedral in Manama, where a new Provost had recently been appointed. The building did not boast the dimensions of most cathedrals – at some point it had been elevated from the status of 'church' to that of 'cathedral' – but it was large enough to accommodate the mostly expatriate congregation. It was *very* Anglican, which we didn't mind, but we sometimes missed the warmth of the fellowship we had enjoyed in Famagusta.

It took little time to gauge the political and social situation in the country. Over the main entrance to the university three huge posters, featuring members of the royal family, were suspended: in the centre was the king, Hamad bin Isa al-Khalifa, on his right was the prime minister, his brother; on his left was the commander-in-chief of the armed forces, his uncle. Set a little back from the road as you approached the entrance there was a hoarding on which **'98%'** was displayed in mega-digits. On looking more closely, I discovered that this was the level of public support, according to a plebiscite, for *al-mīthāq al-waṭanī*, 'the national charter'. Loyalty to king, his family and country was clearly the first duty of the young people attending the nation's most prestigious academic institution.

The somewhat autocratic rule by the 'royals' was illustrated by their tendency – as we gradually became aware – to requisition attractive areas of the country for their personal use. There was a stretch of low-lying land beside the road near the university which was well stocked with small trees and which began to sprout patchy grass in the spring. It was a favourite picnicking spot for the locals, whom we would see parking their cars in the shade of the trees, lighting fires and laying out trays of food. One day we were surprised to see this land fenced off. In due course we heard that the king was renovating one of his palaces nearby and at the same time extending its land to incorporate this greenish area. Later on, too, a pleasant stretch of beach just down the road from us was commandeered.

Other aspects of the social scene were also forthcoming.

'I suppose you know the police and army are mostly imported,' a friend informed us one day. 'The Shi'a are very much in the majority here while the royals and therefore the government are Sunni. So they bring in Sunni Muslims from Yemen and elsewhere to fill the ranks of the security forces.'

'So they can rely on them,' I murmured.

'Yes, of course,' our informant snorted. 'You must know that there was something near an uprising by the Shi'a-dominated opposition some years ago. If the security forces were largely Shi'a they would probably side with the protesters.'

We began to realise that the outwardly peaceful kingdom of Bahrain might deliver a surprise or two. Dilmun of the twenty-first century was not quite the Dilmun of Sumerian times.

***

Two months after our arrival we found ourselves in Beirut for an important wedding. We had made attendance of this wedding a condition of our acceptance of the posts at the university and those responsible had readily agreed. It was important because it was family: Edmund had finally proposed to Rania, his Lebanese friend, and she was prepared to throw in her lot with this roving Englishman. It was to be a 'church wedding'; indeed, if they were to be married in Lebanon, as tradition demanded, it could be no other.

As I write, there is no such thing as a civil marriage in Lebanon, though the issue is increasingly debated. Those who want one have to go elsewhere – to Cyprus, for example. According to Lebanese law, marriage can only be solemnized by the various sects of the recognized religious authorities, Christian, Muslim, Druze and Jewish. So, for example, Christians have to be married according to church rites and Muslims according to Islamic law. The latter allows for 'mixed marriages' between Muslim males and Christian (or Jewish) females but a non-Muslim male has to convert to Islam to marry a Muslim female. As for the various Christian bodies in Lebanon, they only allow the marriage of baptized Christians, so a non-Christian has to be baptized before being married in church. Lebanese law follows these religious rulings though diverging from Islamic law in allowing conversion out of Islam. For Edmund and Rania, happily, the position was very straightforward, both having Protestant Christian backgrounds.

The wedding was fixed for the second of November – which caused wry amusement in Rania's family.

'You realise what we've managed to do,' Edmund explained to us smiling. 'We're getting married on the anniversary of the 1917 Balfour Declaration, which expressed the support of the British

Marriage of Edmund and Rania. From left to right, Joanna, Mary (Rania's mother), Edmund, Rania, Philip, Annabel, Rita (carrying Michael), Rami (Rania's brother and Rita's husband)

government for the establishment of a national homeland for the Jews in Palestine. Mary – Rania's mother – isn't really Lebanese, she's Palestinian, having been born in Palestine and brought up there till she was eighteen. Her father, Syrian by birth, was an evangelical pastor in Tiberias until May 1948, when he and his family had to leave in a hurry – like so many others.'

'You mean the *nakbah*, the "disaster" as the Palestinians call it,' I said, knowing well the event in question. 'So many fleeing when the Jewish National Council proclaimed the establishment of the State of Israel, after we Brits had terminated our ruling mandate.'

'Absolutely,' my son said with feeling. 'We don't come out of it very well. But as I keep telling Rania, our wedding means that at last *something* good is happening for a Palestinian on November two. What's more, a Brit – yours truly – is at the centre of it!'

Mary's family was a large one. She had six brothers and when she and her parents, Abdullah Yusif Sayegh and Afifa Batrouni, left Tiberias all six of them were away working or studying. One was in Jerusalem, one in Gaza, three in Lebanon and one in USA. Lebanon was where the Sayegh parents and Mary came, expecting to return home in a few weeks. Some sixty-five years later, Mary still lives in Beirut.

The wedding was held in the National Evangelical Church, founded by Congregational missionaries and situated beside the *Saraya* (parliament building) in central Beirut. The ceremony was traditional, Rania, radiant in full-length white, being given away by her brother Rami (their father sadly diseased). The setting was beautiful, the aisle transformed into an avenue of white lilies. A white Jaguar took the bride and groom to the restaurant in Ashrafiah for the reception, where the courtyard had become a kind of hanging garden – white predominating again – for the international crowd of guests.

So much for appearances. Transcending all was the message given in church by the pastor: handing the couple a lighted candle, symbolising Christ, he told them to 'keep it burning' throughout their married life.

***

It required something of an effort, having returned from Beirut, to get back into the swing of teaching in Bahrain. Deeply emotional occasions take their toll. I think we recognised that after our many years living in the Arab world a kind of Rubicon had been crossed: we, and not just Edmund, had become a part of that world; grandchildren from this union, after all, were going to be half-Arab. To me this seemed an almost inevitable consequence of long-past decisions.

But there was little opportunity to contemplate our new situation in repose because the voices of battle were loud around us: the signs were that we would shortly be plunged into another Gulf War. The New Year celebrations having come and gone, the tension increased week by week. Some reminders as to the provenance of that tension are called for.

Following the attacks on the World Trade Center in New York on 11 September 2001, United States President George W. Bush began to talk of a possible Iraqi connection with the Islamic organisation al-Qaeda, responsible for those attacks. The Iraqi president, Saddam Hussein, was known to have encouraged terrorism, offering rewards to families of young men who became 'martyrs' by acting as suicide bombers. At the same time the US government – indeed, nearly every government – became convinced that Iraq possessed Weapons of Mass Destruction (WMDs). The possibility of these falling into the hands of terrorists seemed all too real.

The United States, supported initially by the United Nations Security Council, during 2002 dispatched military forces to the Gulf in considerable strength, backed by some from Britain, and Saddam Hussein thought it expedient to allow UN weapons inspectors back into the country. (They had left, expelled by Saddam, at the end of 1998.) By early 2003, however, it became apparent that Iraq was not fully cooperating with the inspectors and the US and British forces in place prepared for a conflict. On March 17 President Bush gave Saddam Hussein an ultimatum, requiring him and his sons to enter into exile or face invasion. Encouraged perhaps by the stance of France, who strongly opposed military intervention, Saddam refused; accordingly, on March 19 the invasion began. Front-line American troops wore rubber suits, expecting to be targeted by the chemical weapons Saddam was known to have used against his own people.

It is unnecessary to plot the course of this Second Gulf War involving a coalition of forces led by USA, or to discuss in depth its legitimacy – though to this day the latter is hotly debated, not least in relation to the conduct of George W. Bush and British Prime Minister Tony Blair, his ally. The root causes, however, are clear: the incomplete nature of the First Gulf War, which had stopped at the liberation of Kuwait, leaving the Iraqi dictator in power to further terrorise his people and destabilise the region; the swaggering stance of that dictator, convincing the majority that he was sitting on WMDs of some sort and was probably still pursuing – or would quickly seek to reinstate – a nuclear weapons programme.

Back to ourselves, at the University of Bahrain.

With the initiation of hostilities in Iraq, hastily-prepared leaflets and notices were spread around the campus by students – placed on desks or posted on windows, walls and doors. These were anti-Western, or more precisely anti-American and anti-British, and pleaded solidarity with 'our brothers in Iraq'. (Some wondered why the latter sentiment had been lacking when some of those 'brothers' were being cruelly oppressed by their own leader.) Joanna and I did not, meanwhile, feel personally threatened by all this as we had excellent relations with our students; off-campus, however, we were occasionally made aware of popular disapproval.

In a mall on one occasion, a young girl – no more than six, probably – detached herself from her parents, ran up and clumsily struck at me. Her father came over at once and apologised.

'I'm very sorry, sir, my child should not have done that.'

'Please don't think about it,' I said. 'It's completely understandable.'

I meant it. If anything, I admired the child. I was also touched by her parent's generous response to the situation.

There were student demonstrations within the university from time to time, impromptu marches and speeches, and as the war progressed people's feelings understandably intensified. One Iraqi colleague and friend, however, who had years before left Iraq and made a home in England, took an independent stance.

'Life under a ruthless dictator could hardly be worse,' he explained. 'It's not just that there's no democracy; it's the uncertainty, the fear that you – or members of your family – might somehow do the wrong thing and become the target of the security people. I have to say, I'm happy that Saddam's safely out of the way.'

'So you don't think the invasion was wrong,' I commented.

'No, it wasn't. But I think the Americans, British and others should withdraw as quickly as possible.'

Once the war proper was over, our friend's mother was able to leave her home in Baghdad and come to Bahrain to visit him, which would have been impossible under Saddam. We had a memorable beach picnic with the whole family – our friend, his mother and (English) wife, plus two children – when the above exchange about the conflict took place.

Having implied that the local populace – certainly its youth – was opposed to the military operation, I should point out that Bahrain was officially behind the war. The island nation provided the Coalition with a crucial facility, that of a base for the US Fifth Fleet – which in 1971 had superseded the British Royal Navy as the naval presence. I was made particularly aware of the American presence one Sunday in Manama during the early stages of the conflict.

'May I introduce a visitor to our cathedral,' a voice said in my ear as we stood sipping coffee after the service. 'He's off one of the ships.' I looked up to see a church regular standing next to a smart, smiling young man. The latter promptly proffered a hand, which I took.

'How do,' he said. 'My name's Bush.'

I stared at him for a second, before responding with a return smile, 'That's most interesting. My name's Blair!'

We laughed and fell to discussing the hostilities further north. 'Lieutenant Bush', as I will call him, turned out not to be a 'fighting sailor' but a kind of counsellor, giving advice to those on the naval vessel who wanted to share a problem with a sympathetic listener.

We talked for a while, realising we had quite a lot in common – not unlike our better-known namesakes.

On 15 April, Saddam Hussein's hometown of Tikrit fell and at that point the Coalition declared the conflict to be effectively over. In the University of Bahrain the tension quickly evaporated, the leaflets and stickers disappearing. The attention of staff and students turned to matters closer at hand – like what was going on just outside the southern fence of the campus perimeter.

***

The construction of Bahrain's Formula One circuit was a huge and spectacular project and we were made fully aware of this by the noise emanating from it. Joanna and I would sometimes drive out and approach the main seat of operations – the grandstand overlooking the start-finish line. It had an attractive design, incorporating canvas roofing resembling a series of nomadic tents.

Nearby was the observation tower, or 'waste-paper basket' as it was irreverently nicknamed because of its shape. It became the model for the trophy presented to the winning driver; it also caused a woman to faint when, during preliminary celebrations to the first Bahrain Grand Prix, a Gulf Air jet dipped so low that it looked for a moment as if 9/11 – still fresh in the memory – might be repeated.

It was fascinating to watch the winding, undulating circuit develop until it was finally complete. By 4 April 2004, the day of the race, all was prepared and that morning we and our friend Joy – whose visit from UK straddled the date – were sitting in one of the stands. Our friend, an F1 fan, had generously bought tickets for us all.

The race got under way and for us novices to the experience the main recollection is the deafening whine of cars endlessly circling – notwithstanding the earplugs we were using. Michael Schumacher, reigning world champion, predictably took the chequered flag but a young British driver was on the podium with him, having finished third.

'I know him, of course,' Joanna said carelessly.

'Never!' Joy exclaimed, unbelieving.

'But I do,' Joanna repeated, trying not to smile. 'I'll tell you how.'
'We're all ears,' I murmured.

'When we returned from the Yemen in 1988,' she explained, 'I became a supply teacher for primary schools in Somerset. I went to a school some way out of Sherborne on one occasion – I forget where, exactly – and there was a boy in my class who I found difficult because he was always playing with cars.' She paused, before adding. 'His name was Jenson, and as far as I know Jenson Button comes from Somerset.'

Joy remained doubtful. 'You remember this clearly?'

'Of course I do,' Jo insisted. 'I remember that school precisely because of the unusual name Jenson.'

We later checked Button's background and discovered that he was indeed from Somerset, having been born in 1980 in Frome, a town some fifteen miles north of Sherborne. Joanna's young pupil in 1988 and the skilled driver we watched in Bahrain may not have been one and the same, but even a tenuous personal connection with a household name adds flavour to the following of his or her fortunes. It undoubtedly increased our enjoyment of that April day in 2004, as also five years later watching the Brazilian Grand Prix, when Button was confirmed world champion.

The kings and captains of F1 having departed for a season, the Bahrain circuit was by no means out of commission. Other motor-racing events were organised, and on one occasion it opened for charity purposes, when I hired a bicycle and was able to pedal right round the track.

We enjoyed a number of other recreational activities. Horse-racing, for example, took place on the racecourse just down the road from the university and we sometimes took our place in the crowded stand.

We would, as expatriates, be ushered into the VIP enclosure, where we were served with canapés and juices. We could then go down to the 'paddock' and assess the form. There was, of course, no (official) betting but we enjoyed predicting the possible winners. There were usually foreigners – that is, Westerners – among the jockeys at the line-up, all of whom sported distinctive colours. At the end of the day prizes would be awarded in front of us all, as often as not both to and by royalty.

A regular pastime was taking walks with friends over the white, dusty interior of the island. These perambulations led us through some striking landscapes, particularly where a barren valley or *wadi* looked as if it had once been a deep river, the water subsequently receding to leave 'beaches' at various levels on the banks at each side.

We made the statutory visit to a huge thorn tree in the middle of a mini-desert. This the locals had christened 'The Tree of Life' – perhaps recalling Dilmun and the upper and nether 'seas' perpetuated in the country's name. We also trekked through more lush areas on the west coast, where there still languished a few palm groves. Most of these had been neglected and allowed to die off, or had been grubbed up to make room for the relentless process of urbanisation.

'It's a shame,' I was told by a fellow-walker, probably the Englishman with a Bahraini wife who had lived for years in the kingdom. 'The country used to be called "the land of a million palms".' A Bahraini idiom I learnt also reflects the country's former character. In English we say 'over the moon'; the parallel Bahraini expression is *fawq an-nakhal*, 'over the palm trees'.

We explored famous sites, both ancient and modern. Among the former was the Sumerian-style temple at Barbar already mentioned, some nearby steps leading down to a 4,000 year-old well. Among the latter was the causeway to Saudi Arabia, in the middle of which was an 'island' featuring twin towers, one on each side of the frontier. We ascended the tower on our side, to enjoy a superb all-round view, Dhahran on the Saudi coast being clearly visible. You could look down, too, on the countless cars passing to and fro, Bahrain being a popular Arab 'watering hole'. The causeway with its tower became a fairly frequent destination as we usually took visiting friends there.

We were certainly not bereft of friends while living in Bahrain. There was, of course, our erstwhile Cyprus colleague, Linda, but we also formed lasting friendships with an Indian couple from

Mumbai, Siva and Shaku, as well as Saswati, an Indian from Assam. Perhaps my family connection with India helped to consolidate these relationships but much more important, I feel sure, were our shared values.

Finally, the Anglo-Lebanese couple who had served under me in Family Bookshop Oman suddenly turned up. Simon and Anne Bouji had been respectively my distribution manager and book-buyer/sales manager. They had been relocated by the company to the FB operation in Bahrain, Anne having been appointed General Manager. We were delighted to renew acquaintance with this husband-wife team. Not long after they arrived, they invited us to dinner in their home – a sumptuous Lebanese meal, as always.

'An important company to be leading, FB Bahrain,' I said, congratulating Anne on her appointment. 'The shop's slipped a bit recently, I've noticed, but you and Simon should soon put that right.'

'To show you just how important,' Simon observed, smiling, 'just take a look at this.' He handed me one of his business cards.

A moment later I was exclaiming, 'Amazing! P.O. Box No. 1! How on earth did Family Bookshop get the very first number?'

'Because,' Simon explained, 'FB used to be a Bible Bookshop, as you must know. As such it was the first commercial company here, so of course it got the first P. O. number.'

'A fascinating detail of history,' I told him, 'which should be recorded somewhere.'

My thoughts turned to my own days with Family Bookshop, under bosses from Lebanon. How much that little country had in various ways entered our lives, I found myself musing.

***

One aspect of the island kingdom of Bahrain constantly impressed: the speed with which it had progressed in the latter part of the twentieth century relative to the long centuries of European development. Yet it would be wrong to suggest that there had not been significant development – interesting experiences, certainly – in much earlier times. I will therefore run through the country's history after its earliest and arguably most distinguished incarnation as the 'land of Dilmun' and up to independence from the British in 1971.

An early settlement discovered in Bahrain suggests that Sennacherib, king of Assyria from 707 to 681 BC, took possession of the Bahrain islands when he attacked north-east Arabia. From the sixth to the third century BC it was part of the Persian Empire under an Iranian dynasty. The Greeks at the time of Alexander the Great called it 'Tylos', referring to its flourishing pearl trade. From the third century BC to the coming of Islam in the seventh century AD it was under two more Iranian dynasties, those of the Parthians and the Sassanids.

The Bahrainis were among the first outside Arabia to embrace Islam, doing so in 629 AD. The prophet of Islam, Muhammad bin Abdullah, ruled Bahrain through a representative until his death in 632; thereafter Muhammad's successors (caliphs or *khulafa*) sent further representatives or governors. During this period the country largely relied on trade, especially with Mesopotamia. When in 750 the seat of the caliph moved to Baghdad there was an increased demand for goods, particularly from China and South Asia, which led to increased Bahraini prosperity. The country also at this time became something of a centre of Islamic learning and philosophy.

Early in the tenth century a rebellion in Bahrain led by a messianic Ismaili sect originating in Iraq resulted in the formation of the Qarmatian Republic, the goal being the construction of a society based on reason and equality. Around 1058 there was another revolt, weakening Qarmatian power, and in 1076 the Uyunids, an Arab dynasty, took over and remained in power until 1235. From the latter date until 1330, when the islands of Bahrain became tributary to the rulers of Hormuz, there was a time of instability, with various Persian or Arab kingdoms involving themselves in Bahrain's affairs. The traveller Ibn Battuta, visiting Bahrain in around 1331, described the Arab inhabitants as 'extremist Shi'a' but noted also the considerable wealth of the area from the pearl industry.

In the mid-fifteenth century the dynasty of the Bedouin Jabrids, who ruled most of eastern Arabia, wrested control of the islands. In 1489 the Arabian navigator Ahmad bin Majid visited Bahrain and gave a vivid description of what he saw:

In Awal [Bahrain] there are a hundred and sixty villages and fresh water can be found in a number of places. A most wonderful al-Qasasir, where a man can dive into the salt sea with a skin and can fill it with fresh water while he is submerged in the salt water. Around Bahrain are pearl fisheries and a number of islands, all of which have pearl fisheries, and connected with this trade are a thousand ships.

In 1521 the Portuguese invaded Bahrain and established themselves there, though the first Portuguese traveller to visit the islands was reputedly Duarte Barbosa in 1485. The motivation for this piece of colonial aggression, which followed in the wake of Vasco de Gama's voyages of exploration when the Portuguese battled the Ottomans right up to the Gulf, was control of the pearl trade.

The Portuguese ruled the islands with an iron fist until 1602, when an uprising sparked by the governor's orders to execute some rich Bahraini traders drove out the colonialists. The vacuum thus created was filled by the Persians, Bahrain becoming part of the Safavid Empire. The Safavid period saw a flowering of intellectual activity in the theological seminaries, the new rulers using the clergy to buttress their authority among the people.

In 1717 Oman invaded Bahrain, ending the Persian hegemony, and there ensued a period of political instability during which various external rulers took control, causing widespread spoliation of the country. Eventually the Omanis sold the islands back to the Persians but the latter were now too weak to maintain their authority and Huwali tribes seized power.

In 1736 Nadir, Shah of Persia, recaptured Bahrain with the help of the British and Dutch, and from 1753 the Arabs of the al-Madkhur family ruled in the name of Persia. All this almost constant warfare, however, led to much economic distress and Persian power was soon on the wane again.

In 1789 the al-Khalifa family, a clan of the Bani Utbah tribe, settled in Bahrain, their first ruler being Sheikh Ahmad al-Fatah. Following a second invasion of the islands by Oman in the early nineteenth century, the clan enhanced its influence and power by entering into a treaty relationship with Britain, by then the dominant power in the region, and this granted the al-Khalifa the title of Rulers of Bahrain. (In 1872 the islands became nominally a part of the Ottoman Empire, in coordination with the British.) The new treaty, like those made by the British with other Gulf principalities, specified that the ruler could not dispose of territory except to the United Kingdom and could not form a relationship with any foreign government without British consent. In return, Britain promised to protect Bahrain from all aggression and, most importantly, to support the rule of the al-Khalifa.

The peace Bahrain now enjoyed, making greater trade possible, brought the sheikhdom prosperity. Indeed, it became the most prominent trading centre in the Gulf. At the same time, it initiated the process of transformation of the country into a modern state – this being facilitated by the influx of Persian, Huwala and Indian merchant families. The last group brought with them many cultural features of the sub-continent, in style of dress, in cuisine and in education.

Between 1926 and 1957 a programme of social reform was carried out, under the *de facto* rule of Charles Belgrave, the British advisor to Sheikh Hamad Ibn Isa. Significant among these reforms was the abolition of slavery. Meanwhile, the economy was boosted by the discovery of reserves of oil on the islands in 1932, making Bahrain the first country in the Gulf to sink oil wells. This offset the collapse of the pearl industry, which occurred as a result of competition from cultured pearls produced in Japan.

During the Second World War Bahrain fought alongside Britain against Germany, becoming a key base for the allies in their efforts to safeguard oil supplies from the region.

In the 1950s and 60s there was severe pressure upon Britain from a leftist nationalist movement and, after that had been pronounced illegal and broken up, from its offshoots. These organised strikes and occasional riots. In 1965, an uprising broke out against the British presence in the country, the March *intifāda*. Finally, in 1968 the British government announced that it would end its treaty relationships with all Gulf sheikhdoms.

After attempting, in concert with the Trucial States, to form a union of Arab emirates, Bahrain sought independence as a separate entity. In December 1971, that independence became reality when the State of Bahrain formally declared its existence.

***

'We cannot accept this thesis,' announced the internal examiner, one of my departmental colleagues, as soon as Salāh al-Dīn had left the room in which he had been defending his MA thesis. 'We are agreed on this, I think,' he added, turning towards the external examiner.

The visiting member of the panel of three examiners – internal, external, and thesis supervisor, myself – nodded in confirmation.

'Not acceptable?' I responded cautiously. 'What precisely do you mean?' I allowed myself this slight disingenuousness. 'Of course, there is always room for improvement in any piece of research. This is no exception. I imagine you are saying Salāh will have to carry out some adjustments, or maybe additions, before we approve his work and award the degree. I can certainly continue to supervise …'

'You mistake me, Dr Blair,' my colleague interrupted. 'What you say is not what we mean. We're talking about outright failure, not a "pass" subject to revision, nor can he do further work and resubmit. He must not be awarded a degree, though he will be eligible to receive a diploma. As we made clear during the defence, apart from its other shortcomings we believe Salāh has manipulated the data to suit his views on the value of the formal teaching of grammar.'

'That last proposition is preposterous,' I retorted. 'For a start, as Salāh's supervisor I can vouch for his integrity. Secondly, there is absolutely nothing in the text of his thesis to justify such a conclusion.'

'Please don't argue,' the internal examiner responded blandly. 'Whatever you say, we are convinced of this from our reading of his work.'

'This is unprecedented. Do you totally discount my judgement? Who else has suffered such treatment? No one, I believe.'

'Ah,' my colleague persisted, 'but didn't you receive the report I sent you? It explains our position in full.'

'You mean the document I received yesterday?' He nodded.

I might at this point have mentioned that, having started to read this single-spaced, eight-page critique of my student's thesis, conveyed to me at the last minute, I was so disgusted at the scorn expressed in it for Salāh and every aspect of his research that I had thrust it aside. (In due course I consigned it to the dustbin.) I decided now to focus on the key issue.

'You say your report clarifies why Salāh should fail outright. From what you say now it seems your conclusion rests mainly on this charge of academic dishonesty. That is a very serious accusation.'

'We make it, nevertheless, with confidence.'

I was getting nowhere. My position in the matter was not helped by the fact that despite being the student's supervisor I had been required to chair the proceedings – an odd irregularity.

My fellow examiners had other criticisms of Salāh's thesis, I recall, though not of great significance. Two points I failed to mention, unaware of one at the time and failing to think of the other: firstly, the fact that his MA course work had been excellent, an 'A' grade awarded for almost every module, three of them by none other than my examining colleague; secondly, the fact that Salāh had come to no single conclusion in his study as there was a measure of ambiguity in the data. This made nonsense of the charge of manipulation.

My opposing examiners were going to concede nothing, it was obvious, so having reiterated my utter opposition to their stance, I fell silent. Salāh was thereupon called back into the room, the next stage in the proceedings. He had acquitted himself well in the face of a savage onslaught during the defence, I felt, but what he would make of the grade of outright failure I hardly dared think.

The majority verdict was duly announced by the internal examiner with no elaboration. What followed was painful to witness. Salāh simply slid to the floor with the faintest moan and there remained. After a while we called the Head of the English Department (HOD), who murmured something to the crouching figure about making an appeal. The latter, huddled pathetically against the wall, seemed hardly to hear.

The HOD then presented us with a document, written in Arabic, which he asked us to sign. I explained that I totally rejected the announced grade but he assured me it only confirmed that we had, as examiners, attended the defence. I skimmed through the text, and straightened up.

'Sir,' I said, 'what you say is not true. The rubric clearly states that by signing this form I assent to the grade awarded. I do not so assent and therefore will not sign.'

So the scene ended, with my HOD and fellow examiners taking their leave while I helped Salāh to his feet and led him to my office. After a while he became less distraught and we were able to take the first steps in planning a strategy to get the appalling injustice rectified.

The above accurately records – give or take the odd verbal difference in the dialogue – what transpired at the end of Salāh's defence in December 2004. (I should point out that I have changed my student's name for this account.)

In some respects it reflects what was happening at the time in our department on a wider scale under its Head, a Bahraini who had succeeded the Palestinian who appointed me and Joanna. The new leader was obsessed with two things: getting the right statistical 'curve' in class results, and showing his seniors that he was leading the battle against 'grade inflation'. To this end he put pressure on teachers to manipulate their overall class results to get 'acceptable' statistical curves and to lower student grades they had already submitted.

One young Bahraini colleague, a co-teacher on one of my courses, was so distressed by this pressure that she offered her resignation in protest. I took up her cause with the HOD – before the fiasco of Salāh's defence – arguing that she had awarded accurate grades. (She had consulted me about them beforehand.) I was wasting my breath.

The preoccupation with grade inflation was not the only reason for the enforced failure of my student, however; in due course it became clear that there were other factors. Once he had more or less recovered from what had been a real trauma, Salāh made inquiries among fellow MA students, as well as some of my teaching colleagues, and became convinced that the decision to fail him had been 'political'. One possibility was that the deed had been done because Salāh was Shi'a whereas the HOD was Sunni. This might have been a contributory factor, but I could not believe it was the main reason. I began to think the whole affair was as much about me as my student. This seemed confirmed when one of Salāh's informants told him the HOD had been heard to say that, one way or another, he was 'going to get rid of the oldies'. I subsequently came to hear that a Syrian professor of about my age had suffered the same treatment as me, having a supervisee's thesis unconditionally failed. This added weight to my interpretation of events.

While the Head of Department may have been the guiding force behind this extraordinary affair, he obviously had to have the cooperation of my fellow examiners. I cannot believe the external examiner was formally party to a plot to fail Salāh; external examiners, however, take their cue from internal examiners as to departmental policy and standards required, so the examiner in this case would have been sticking to protocol in following my colleague's advice. The latter was, I know, working with the HOD and though he may conceivably have convinced himself that the outcome he engineered was 'for the common good', his actions breached elementary principles of justice.

I fought the verdict for the rest of my time in Bahrain, appealing up to the top, which meant to our lady President, who was from the al-Khalifa family. I met obstacles at every turn, my request for a special committee to reconsider the case falling on deaf ears. In the end it became clear to both Joanna and me that we could not go on working in such an academic environment. We began to look for posts elsewhere, finding them fairly quickly.

Oddly, a meeting was arranged in our last few days at the University of Bahrain by one of the vice-presidents, a professor hailing from Lebanon, to discuss a report I had composed in Arabic and forwarded to the President. The professor, with one or two other academics, listened with apparent sympathy to what I had to say, which included the claim that Salāh had been failed for non-academic reasons. For a moment I wondered if, at last, there was a softening in their stance.

'So, Dr Blair, is it on the basis of the case we have been discussing that you and your wife are terminating your contracts?' the vice-president finally asked.

'Yes, essentially,' I replied.

He went on. 'Please realise that should you wish to come back you will be more than welcome.'

No softening, then; merely acceptance of our decision to leave, coupled with a piece of easy flattery. There was of course no turning back; indeed, I couldn't wait for us to take up our new appointments.

XIV

Holy Hill of Balamand

'All our politicians should be thrown in the sea.'
Even after making due allowance for the Levantine tendency to make sweeping statements, the vehemence of this remark, addressed to us by the driver sent to take us to the educational establishment where we would be working, took me by surprise.

Joanna and I had arrived in Lebanon on a direct flight from Bahrain. We had spent our first night at the central Beirut home of Mary Sayegh, mother of our daughter-in-law Rania, who, being pregnant, was also there. (Alexander, our first grandchild, was born the following November.) Mary's house was virtually on the civil war 'green line' of the seventies and eighties; it was also near the spot of a massive explosion some six months earlier, targeting and killing the former Prime Minister Rafic Hariri. The glass in her windows had been shattered, Mary herself being fortunately in Cairo with Edmund and Rania at the time. The proximity of the still-very-evident destruction caused by the Hariri atrocity was, we discovered later, in a bizarre way rather appropriate to our arrival in the country.

The next day the driver turned up at Mary's door. We set out, taking a route past Martyrs' Square as we headed northward for Tripoli, the country's second city. Our specific destination was a little short of Tripoli – the University of Balamand, an Antiochian Orthodox foundation situated near the top of a precipitous hill overlooking the Mediterranean. The name of the university reflects its location, for 'Balamand' is a Lebanese rendering of the French word 'Belmont'.

As we motored along the coast on the 'autostrade', the nearest thing Lebanon has to a motorway, we got into conversation with our driver and the word 'politics' had hardly escaped my lips when he came out with the above devastating indictment of his national leaders. It was in some ways a fitting introduction to the diminutive yet politically pivotal country we had come to live and work in. So many times, subsequently, local people responded to some remark I might make about their government with something like, 'What government? We haven't got a government in Lebanon. We do very well without one.'

As I say, we had flown to Beirut direct from Bahrain. This was in late September, 2005, after we had been on holiday in UK and then flown back to the island kingdom to pack up our bags and leave finally. We had applied for our new university positions just before leaving Bahrain for the summer vacation at the end of June and been offered them a month later. Having accepted the offers we contacted the Bahrain University authorities and told them of our decision. They were good enough to let us go without financial penalty.

It had been an eventful, sad summer in Sherborne. About three weeks after our arrival home my brother was rushed to Yeovil hospital with diabetic complications, his condition critical. The doctors and nurses, by dint of blood transfusions and intravenous medication, were able to revive him but it soon became apparent that this could only be short-term. For the next few weeks he received many visitors – my sister and other relatives, as well as friends and acquaintances associated, most of them, with the lecture network he had founded, the Wessex Research Group. I personally visited him two or three times a week, sometimes conducting a brief Communion service for him.

Towards the end of August, when he was very weak, he was transferred to the smaller hospital in Sherborne, a quarter of a mile from the cottage in Acreman Street where he had lived since joining our parents there in around 1980. On the following evening, as the darkness closed in on a wonderful sunset, Nigel died. Joanna and I, plus a lady friend of his, were with him at the time. We had a quiet service of committal in Yeovil Crematorium and, ten days later, a memorial service in Castleton church, near our home, which

Nigel (left) in Sherborne, with (left to right) mother, Uncle Jim, father; early 1980s

was attended by a wider public. Meanwhile, my sister and I had begun the task of sorting out his cottage, which among other things housed his huge library – ten to fifteen thousand books, at a guess.

My younger brother was in some ways a strange fellow; he certainly had some strange ideas. He was not the healthiest person, though tall and strongly built, having suffered from severe asthma as a child. Intellectually gifted, he was a compelling speaker and very determined. For some ten years, following graduation from Oxford, he taught history with considerable success at the secondary level. It was early on in this period, however, that he developed (in highly traumatic circumstances) the diabetes that thereafter dogged him and, partly because of this, no doubt, he found it increasingly difficult to cope with the stress involved in teaching at a boarding school. He resigned from his post and sought refuge in Sherborne, hoping to make a living by working part-time. This never properly got off the ground, however, and soon he was totally dependent on our parents.

I think now of Nigel as a wounded soul. He could be infuriating, yet also amusing, winsome, lovable. I feel that the last month in hospital gives the truest picture of him: patience, faith, and profound serenity. Almost all those who visited him came away commenting in some such terms.

***

Joanna and I flew back to Bahrain on September 15, three days after the memorial service, to carry out the necessary protocol for leaving the university and to make arrangements for the transportation of our possessions to Lebanon. Ten days in the country gave us the chance to say goodbye to our friends, as well as for me, the very day before we were leaving, to attend that final, fruitless meeting with the university vice-president and others about my woefully abused MA student.

Lebanon, from the outset, proved to be a different experience for us in almost every field of life. Let me begin with the country's geophysical features.

Some of the scenery was almost as spectacular as that of the Yemen, which had so enchanted us nearly twenty years before. The university we were joining is, as I have indicated, in a magnificent position on a virtual cliff-top some eight hundred feet above sea-level and overlooking the strip of flattish land, about half a mile wide, running along the coast. The apartment to which we were assigned, one of a number built for faculty members, was a hundred feet higher than the university proper and boasted stunning views of the campus spread out below against the backdrop of the sea.

It wasn't long before we were taking trips into the interior, first in a small hired car and then in a Pontiac Bonneville, 1987 vintage, which was very comfortable, powerful, built like a tank (necessary in view of the driving habits of some Lebanese) and above all cheap to buy. We were strongly advised to 'go American' in this way by our helpful Head of Department, Lloyd Precious. He pointed out that a second-hand German car of the same specification and age would cost anything up to three times as much. (As I write, this still holds, the Bonneville having given up the ghost and been exchanged for another cut-price Pontiac, a 2004, 3.8, turbo-charged 'Grand Prix'!) We found ancient Greek or Roman temples half-hidden among trees at a lower elevation, or else prominently placed on the top of lofty escarpments. Going up the Kadisha valley, not far from our new home, the vistas became more and more spectacular, the valley becoming a deep ravine, high along the side of which we would drive until we reached Bcharre, famed as the birthplace of Kahlil Gibran, poet and author of *The Prophet*.

Bcharre is a small town above the winter snowline, so though the road to it was daily cleared of any obstruction, when going at that time of year you had to choose your day carefully for fear of blizzards. If you go beyond the town, as we usually did, you climb higher until the famous cedars are reached. You see some very ancient specimens – forty or fifty, perhaps – and a lot more younger ones, efforts having been made in recent years to restore the population. The greatest of these trees, we were told, is three thousand years old and contemporary with King Solomon, who built Israel's first temple from cedar-wood imported from Lebanon. It stands next to the road, spreading over a timber-built restaurant and some small shops selling gifts and trinkets – most of these fashioned from cedar.

Beyond this great tree and its cousins you can drive higher to a ski-slope. At this point the mountain road becomes so deeply embedded in snow in the depths of winter that it is not kept open. The rest of the year you can drive up to the pass at the top and spiral down to the Bekaa valley the other side.

A quickly-developing hobby on these drives was finding a new restaurant to lunch at, usually on a Sunday after having attended morning service at the abbey church, just off-campus. (The monks of the Orthodox monastery, from which the university had effectively grown, worshipped there seven days a week.) We would frequently come across a suitable eating-place in a mountain village, strategically situated to enjoy a magnificent view, or else half-hidden in the depths of a ravine, next to – virtually under, at times – a waterfall. One such served fresh trout, bred in tanks constructed alongside the descending stream. At other times we would look for a place beside the sea, so would take the winding coastal road to the south – the only direct route to Beirut until superseded by the autostrade – and end up at a fish-restaurant on the edge of the beach. Whether in a mountain or seaside location, however, we would enjoy delicious Lebanese fare at a very reasonable price.

Talking of seaside locations, we early on became absorbed in some casual research into an item of industrial archaeology. This was the railway line, long closed, that ran along the coast from Beirut to Tripoli, criss-crossing the old main road between the cities. We would stop to look at bridges – road over rail, rail over road or chine – and sometimes walk along a section of the track (none of it had been pulled up), having on occasions to push our way through thick undergrowth and bushes. The latter became necessary to discover the southern entrance to a tunnel cutting through a spur of mountain not far from Balamand and which came out just below the old road on the very edge of the sea. We were fascinated to see initials, placed in relief above this northern entrance, reading 'S.A.E.C., 1942', which in due course we found stood for 'South Australian Engineering Corps'; the latter had been a component of the British and Free French force that occupied Lebanon for a while during the Second World War. In built-up areas the line seemed to follow streets or lanes, the track often showing through the tarmac; we wondered if this was intentional, to keep open the option of one day using the line again. Last of all we found the Tripoli terminal alongside the port and gazed over a fence at rusting steam locomotives and rolling stock.

We went south, of course, beyond Beirut to Saida and Sour (ancient Sidon and Tyre), exploring the labyrinthine covered *souq* in the former and the Roman forum in the latter. Saida was a favourite with us when we had a visitor to show around – like our friend Joy, who so liked Lebanon she came to stay four times. This was chiefly because Saida had a government Rest House overlooking the sea that served excellent food. Further attractions were climbing the hill of seashells piled up by the Phoenicians after extracting the famous purple dye, or entering the house visited (the notice on the door informed us) by Jesus of Nazareth.

Baalbek, in the Bekaa valley to the east of us, was naturally a must so we took the route over the mountains to get there. We wandered round the 'Sun City' of the ancient world, gazing up at the massive columns of the Roman temple, and then had a picnic in a grassy spot behind it. At which point my spouse became more interested in the landscape than in ruined monoliths and proceeded to sketch a line of poplars instead of pillars. This picture now graces our home at Balamand.

More could be said about the scenic beauties and archaeological treasures of Lebanon. We had experienced spectacular terrain and interesting sites elsewhere in the region but somehow our new country of residence seemed to combine, in small compass, the best features of them all – except, perhaps, for the magic of the Sudanese desert.

What else about Lebanon spoke to us?

From my father's library I inherited a handsome volume, with hand-cut pages and copiously illustrated with watercolour sketches, entitled *The Holy Land*. It was first published in 1902, when the Ottoman Empire, though waning in power, still covered most of the Middle East and more specifically the nations or areas we know today as Jordan, Israel, the West Bank, Gaza, Lebanon and Syria.

For the author and illustrator, respectively John Kelman and John Fulleylove, all these were simply 'Syria', the name used for the region by the Ottoman Turks, who also coined the term 'Greater Syria'; all its people (apart from a few Jews) were referred to in the book as 'Syrians'. The whole of it was thus 'The Holy Land', so Joanna and I as residents of Lebanon were living within the hallowed territory. I found this exciting.

I was not stretching a point, I satisfied myself. When you consider the fact that Lebanon is mentioned in the Book of Genesis as part of the region promised by God to Abraham, the many references in the Old Testament to Lebanon and its cedars being a place of beauty and fragrance, supplying timber to the covenant people, and, finally, the fact that in the New Testament we read of the visit Jesus made to 'the coasts of Sidon', when he ministered to a 'Syro-Phoenician' woman, the epithet 'holy' seems well earned.

As the years of my working life had worn on and it became obvious that my career was inextricably linked with the Middle East and all things Arab, I had begun to muse on the idea that we might end up in the heart of the region; in other words, in this 'Holy Land'. Apart, perhaps, from our brief sojourn in the Yemen, we had lived on the peripheries of the Arab world – just outside it in the case of Turkish Cyprus. The more I thought about a move to the 'centre' the more attractive, the more likely even, this development seemed. Our sudden and unexpected translation to Lebanon was a fulfilment of this hope and semi-premonition.

But what of this 'Holy Land', this 'Greater Syria' we had come to?

Seven years later, at a time when the nation of Syria had become the despair of all as it tore itself apart in a brutal civil war, Kevin Connelly, a BBC correspondent, sent home a thoughtful report. The presenter in London summed it up thus: 'Syria's unsettled history has been provoking foreign interest and intervention for centuries.' Those words, as I heard them one morning sitting with Joanna at our breakfast table, reminded me irresistibly of the book I had inherited from my father. Mr Connelly might well have talked of 'millennia' rather than 'centuries'. The second of the three parts into which my book is divided is entitled 'The Invaders', the author

Lebanon's famous cedars, national emblem

proceeding – in a simplification of the actual 'foreign interest and intervention' – to describe these invaders under five heads: Israelite, Roman, Christian (peaceable, in this case), Muslim, Crusader. What a vortex of peoples, struggles, *history* this 'holy land' has represented, even if one entirely neglects modern times.

So Joanna and I were settling into what was once no more than a province of this Arab heartland, as I have defined it. And what I must say about this micro-state, this Lebanon, is that to us and many others its history, especially its recent history, is a kind of mirror of the whole; the tensions, conflicts, catastrophes of that whole are somehow writ small in the tensions, conflicts and catastrophes of a minor part of it.

***

It was 'foreign intervention', almost certainly, that was responsible for the huge explosion in central Beirut on 14 February 2005, killing Rafic Hariri among others, the destructive legacy of which Joanna and I witnessed on our arrival in Lebanon. It is perhaps appropriate at this point, therefore, to sketch the history of this strip of Mediterranean coastland – about half the area of Wales – which is now a nation at the heart of the region's social and political life.

The country's cedars, as I have said, play quite prominently in the Bible; they also appear in the ancient Sumerian text already referred to, the *Epic of Gilgamesh*. The eponymous hero, king of Uruk, makes a journey with his friend Enkidu to the 'Land of Cedars'. He wants to earn a glorious name and does so by hewing down cedar trees in defiance of the 'watcher of the forest', Humbaba, 'he at whose voice Hermon and Lebanon used to tremble'. When confronted by the latter, the friends hew him down as well.

In the second millennium BC the area was populated by Canaanites, a Semitic people who clustered along the coastal plain where maritime trading cities developed: Tyre, Sidon, Berytus (Beirut), Sarepta (Sarafand), Gubla or Byblos (Jubail). These people created the oldest-known 24-letter alphabet, which developed into the Phoenician alphabet, related to those of Hebrew and Aramaic. The term 'Phoenician', and thus 'Phoenicia', came from the Greeks, who thus referred to these Canaanites and their land because of the purple (*phoinikies*) dye already referred to that they marketed.

The Pharaoh Thutmose III invaded Syria in the fifteenth century BC and incorporated Phoenicia (Lebanon) into his Empire, but by the beginning of the twelfth century the territory had regained its independence. The Assyrians conquered Lebanon early in the ninth century, to be replaced by the Babylonians in the seventh, followed in turn by the Persians in the sixth. The latter were defeated by Alexander the Great in 333 BC and, following his early death, his empire was divided amongst his generals. Lebanon fell to Seleucus I, founder of the Seleucid dynasty. Seleucid rule ended in 64 BC, when the Roman general Pompey added Syria and Lebanon to the Roman Empire. There ensued a flowering of economic and intellectual activity, the inhabitants of Tyre, Sidon and Byblos being granted Roman citizenship.

In 395 AD the Roman Empire was divided, the eastern or Byzantine part having its capital at Constantinople. The cities of Lebanon continued to flourish until a series of earthquakes in the fifth century demolished the temples of Baalbek and largely destroyed the city of Beirut, its famous law school levelled to the ground and some 30,000 killed.

Arab conquest and rule of the area brought Islam to Lebanon soon after the death of Muhammad in 632 AD. By then, however, the Maronite Christians had established themselves in Mount Lebanon and its coastlands, so the area remained predominantly Christian while Syria became largely Muslim. In the eleventh century, the Druze settled in South Lebanon and adjacent parts of Syria, clashing periodically with the Christians thereafter.

The Crusaders were active in Lebanon from the late eleventh century, finding support from the local Christians. Frankish nobles occupied the area as part of the south-eastern Crusader states, southern Lebanon forming part of the Christian Kingdom of Jerusalem established in 1100. Muslim forces regained control of the Holy City in 1187, and though it was restored to the Christians by the terms of a treaty it fell again to the Muslims in 1244, as did most of Palestine the following year. Muslim control of Lebanon was re-established later that century, when it fell into the hands of the Mamluk sultans of Egypt.

In 1516 the Ottoman Sultan Selim I, after defeating the Persians, invaded Syria and eliminated Mamluk resistance. Through judicious networking, the Emirs of Lebanon were able to meet the Sultan and persuade him to grant them semi-autonomous status. The result was indirect Ottoman rule through two feudal families, the Maans and the Shihabs.

In the first decades of the nineteenth century there were rival leaders in Lebanon, both called Bashir. Bashir (Shihab) II, a Maronite Christian enjoying Maronite support, had been elected Emir and ruled under Ottoman suzerainty as *wali* or governor of Mount Lebanon, the Bekaa valley and Jebel Amil. Bashir Jumblatt, a wealthy magnate with feudal backing, drew support from the Druze community. Sectarian war, including several massacres, broke out and this lasted until 1825, when Bashir II defeated Bashir Jumblatt in battle and promptly executed him.

The conflict was over but sectarian and feudal rifts deepened as Druze isolation and Maronite wealth increased. In 1841 armed conflict between the Druze and Maronites broke out again, a fearful massacre of Christians by the Druze occurring at Deir al-Qamar. The Ottoman solution was to divide Mount Lebanon into two districts, Druze and Christian, but this gave powerbases to each party and the conflict reignited. The intermittent sectarian war finally developed into open Maronite opposition to Ottoman power, the situation being exacerbated by French support for the Maronites, leading the British to back the Druze. Ottoman attempts to restore stability failed and, in 1860, Napoleon III of France sent troops to Beirut to help impose a partition. De facto control by the Druze was recognised and the Maronites were forced into an enclave, these developments being ratified by the Concert of Europe in 1861.

The rest of the nineteenth century saw a period of relative calm though acts of violence, breeding on continuing resentment, erupted from time to time. In general, Maronite, Druze and Islamic groups now focused on economic and cultural development. A major step was the founding of the American University of Beirut (AUB) in 1865, which helped to make Beirut a centre of reform movements, aimed not least at liberalisation of the Ottoman Empire. The outbreak of hostilities in Europe in 1914, however, changed everything.

In the course of the First World War the Ottoman Empire disintegrated and after the armistice of 1918 the League of Nations granted France the mandate for Syria. The French, however, proceeded to separate Lebanon from Syria, creating a new state over which they could have direct control. This created some discontent, Muslims wanting independence within a wider Arab body. In 1926 the mandate was given a republican constitution involving a balance of power between the various religious groups. The president, who had power of veto, was nevertheless required to be a Christian (in practice, a Maronite).

During the Second World War the French Vichy government controlled Lebanon until a British/Free French force invaded and occupied the Lebanese coast. The Free French pronounced the Lebanon an independent republic, elections were held in 1943 and independence became a reality on 1 January 1944.

In 1948 Lebanon, a member of the Arab League, declared war on the newly-formed state of Israel, though doing little of the fighting. A wave of Palestinian refugees arrived as a result of this conflict, another wave arriving following the Six-Day Arab-Israeli war of 1967.

Lebanon's civil war between Christians, Muslims and Palestinians commenced in 1975. Following an intervention by Syrian forces, requested by the Christian Lebanese president to halt Muslim and Palestinian advances, a cease-fire was implemented in October 1976, but the conflict resumed in 1977. In March 1978 Israel occupied South Lebanon in response to guerrilla attacks mounted from the region by the Palestinian Liberation Organisation (PLO), remaining until June when a UN peacekeeping force officially took over; the latter, however, was unable to control the activities of Lebanon's Christian militia, whom Israel thereafter encouraged and supported. In June 1982 Israel invaded Lebanon, primarily to eliminate PLO guerrilla bases, after which 7,000 Palestinians were deported. In

1983 the Israelis withdrew to a buffer zone on the border, where for the next seventeen years they maintained a garrison.

The internal struggle dragged on, with assassinations (President Bashir Gemayel, 1982; Prime Minister Rashid Karami, 1987; President René Moawad, 1989), massacres (1,000 Palestinians by Christian Phalangists in the wake of the Gemayel assassination, 1982), terrorist bombings (241 US marines and 56 French paratroopers killed in Beirut, 1983), hostage-taking (John McCarthy, journalist, 1986; Terry Waite, Anglican envoy, 1987).

In 1991 all militias apart from Hizbullah were dissolved, the Lebanese army defeated the PLO in Sidon and an amnesty was granted for certain war crimes. Syrian troops remained in the country, however, until 2005, when, following the assassination of Rafic Hariri on 14 February and the 'cedar revolution' of 14 March, they were finally forced to depart.

At which point I shall end my sketch of Lebanon's past, which is perhaps enough to give a taste of its richness and diversity – as also to illustrate the phrase 'unsettled history' which, as indicated, epitomises to me both the country and region in which I now live and from which violence has yet to be eradicated. (As I type these very words, in a restaurant at three in the afternoon on 19 October 2012, the television screen in front of me flashes the 'breaking news' of a massive explosion in the Ashrafiah district of Beirut.)

***

So much, then, for our country of residence; what of our university of residence? What, in particular, of the university posts obtained by the two of us?

I was to assist in the setting up of a new Master of Arts programme for teachers of English. I was well qualified for this, having taught English, and the methodology of teaching English, in the Sudan, the Yemen, Cyprus and Bahrain. In all but the Yemen this had involved the instruction of experienced teachers working for a Diploma or MA degree – as in the case of ill-fated Salāh al-Dīn in Bahrain. (He eventually found, I'm happy to say, a good university position after I had written him a cracking reference.) Joanna, meanwhile, was deputed to teach on the Intensive English

Course for pre-university students or freshmen, as I was initially as one of my subsidiary responsibilities.

'We're so happy to have you with us,' said the Head of Department (HOD) as we sat in his office on one of our first days. 'You're joining important programmes. The Intensive Course, running now for years, is at the heart of the university's mission, which is to graduate students with a good level of English as well as their major. As for our MA programme, very much my baby, I confess, we have high hopes for it. Of course …' he turned to me smiling '… the more successful we are, the better for our department and the university – new faculty, more money!'

A positive response was called for. 'Sounds most interesting,' I told him. 'Indeed, you've issued us with a challenge.' I looked at Joanna, before continuing, 'I have to say, it's good to hear how pleased – relieved, almost – you are to have us here. Were you short of applicants?'

'Not when we first advertised your post, Philip. But perhaps you didn't know, we advertised twice.' He glanced at me. 'We offered the post to an American early in the year and he accepted, but then there was the Hariri bomb. You've heard about *that*, I presume.'

'Yes, and seen its effects.'

'Anyway, the fellow promptly withdrew and, at that stage, it's true that people weren't exactly queuing up to come.'

'So you re-advertise – in June,' I said slowly, 'I apply and, bingo, get the job, with one for Joanna thrown in.' I thought for a moment. 'I shouldn't say this perhaps but it's an ill wind that blows no one any good!'

'Look,' the HOD responded quickly, looking worried, 'we didn't hire you just because we were desperate. I phoned your boss in Bahrain – your first boss, that is – and he gave you both such glowing reports that we snapped you up at once.'

So it was that Joanna and I learnt how the Hariri bomb atrocity in central Beirut had played a crucial role in our coming to Lebanon.

In my second year I was asked, alongside my other duties, to do some teaching on the Cultural Studies Programme, mandatory for all students. The President had come to know that I had a degree in theology and, after he had read and enjoyed my book on the nature and role of the Church, suggested I taught a group from the multi-section course on religion. This involved an introduction to the three 'Abrahamic' faiths: Judaism, Christianity and Islam. I accepted with alacrity; it was the fulfilment of another wish I had had for years – though by this time all but abandoned – to go back to my academic roots and teach theology.

But it was hardly the theology of my degree, which had focused exclusively on the Judaeo-Christian tradition. I was to teach Islam as well, about half my students being Muslim, not Christian or having some sort of Christian background. I could manage Islam, having studied the religion, but could I cope with a class of youths divided between two different, often antagonistic faiths? The answer, almost to my surprise, turned out to be 'yes'. I made two things clear at the start of each semester: firstly, that I would as far as possible present the three faiths objectively and in traditional form; secondly, that a university was a place for questioning and honest debate, where differences of opinion and faith should be openly faced and discussed, with individuals drawing their own conclusions. Where conclusions differed, I emphasised, individuals should simply agree to differ without rancour. The formula worked well – and has yet to fail.

But there were, once or twice, inter-faith problems within the university, the following being the most serious. In an English literature class a newly-appointed expatriate lecturer gave as a reading the passage from Dante where the prophet of Islam is pictured roasting in hell. It was a big mistake; his argument was, I believe, that in literature anything goes – and must in all circumstances be allowed to go. A worried student of mine, himself named Muhammad, showed me the text in question. 'This sort of thing appears in old poems,' I explained. 'I should forget about it. Dante is long dead!' He went off, apparently satisfied.

Official apologies were offered to the relevant students but this was not enough because the next day there was talk of threats – some said bomb threats – from Islamicists in Tripoli. High tension prevailed for a while, hardly lessened for us when the second day after the incident we watched an army helicopter hovering over the university, presumably to deter possible assailants. Nothing dire occurred, however, but sometime later the offending teacher, who in other ways was proving to be very high-handed, was dismissed from his post by the President.

As the years passed at Balamand, I was asked to do more on the Cultural Studies programme, teaching about ancient civilisations as well as religion. It ended up with my doing no English teaching at all apart from the supervision of MA theses. Joanna, meanwhile, became increasingly creative on the English programme, developing and coordinating a highly successful multi-section course utilising drama and simulation.

From all this it should be apparent that Joanna and I had unexpectedly found a satisfying professional niche fairly late in life. Any employment can have downs as well as ups so it would be wrong to suggest that there were no personal stresses for us at the university. In our first year or so a few students put us through the wringer; there were some very disturbed individuals among the new intakes and they could be extremely disruptive in class. One would desperately look for a strategy to contain them, not always with total success. Such individuals, happily, became increasingly rare; perhaps, we speculated, we had seen the last of a generation traumatised by civil war.

***

A ship is as good as its captain.

What I appreciated most about the University of Balamand was the attitude of service that was encouraged and which to a great extent prevailed, the sense that we were on a mission to the locality, to the nation, to the region. Such altruism emanated from the highest level – namely, from the President.

Elie Salem, I decided early on, was of that rare breed that combines energy and drive with profound wells of imagination. Too often it is one or the other, Martha or Mary – to cite the sisters who respectively typify the two qualities. When they are combined in a single soul, great things can happen. And when a third quality is added, small miracles can occur. That third quality the President also displayed, it seemed to me, a deep-seated, almost childlike transparency and integrity. The way these three attributes played out in Elie Salem's life is illustrated in his touching memoir, *My American Bride* (Quartet, 2008).

Dr Salem was elected to the presidency of the University of Balamand in October 1993, just five years after its foundation by the Antiochian Orthodox Patriarch, Ignatius IV. He had had a distinguished background both as an academic and politician, having been Dean of the Faculty of Arts and Sciences at the American University of Beirut, after which he became Lebanese Deputy Prime Minister and Minister for Foreign Affairs in the 'crisis' Lebanese government formed in 1982 by Amine Gemayel. He held this position for six years. The role he played in 1987 in drafting the Taif Document, an essay on reform adopted at a Peace Conference held in Taif, Saudi Arabia, and which in 1989 brought to an end the civil war, was particularly significant.

In his memoir Dr Salem described the post he took up at Balamand as one he filled 'with a great deal of passion and commitment'. The claim had substance, as can be gauged in various ways. Firstly, one can cite the remarkable growth of the student body at Balamand, some eight hundred students in 1993 becoming over five thousand by 2012. Secondly, there was the expansion of the main campus through the addition of fine buildings offering enhanced facilities and, just as important, attractive 'spaces', allowing students and staff alike to relax in the open air. These areas were often paved, with strategically placed seating, interspersed with flowers, shrubs and trees – all this enhanced by the magnificent natural position of the university, set on its 'holy hill of Balamand' (a presidential phrase I immediately warmed to). The term 'main campus', by the way, witnesses to the fact that subsidiary campuses were being established in Beirut and elsewhere. Thirdly, there were the presidential circulars and speeches, which would invariably underline the objective of creating an institution dedicated to the service of Lebanon and beyond. Words written by Dr Salem in one of his beginning-of-year messages to the 'UOB community', spell out that objective:

'We have a mission to translate the goals of the university to the goals of our people. We need to prepare citizens who assume civic responsibilities, who believe in freedom, in justice, in service, and in promoting good governance. Education liberates, ensures employment, provides for good health, and purifies the moral content of our lives. It is our destiny to lead and to share with other universities in the building of a new civilisation moored on the foundations of our rich and diverse historical legacy.'

A prophetic voice once pronounced: 'Where there is no vision, the people perish.' The institution where Joanna and I were working did not lack such vision.

XV

State of Disunion

At around 2300 hours on Wednesday, 12 July 2006, the Iran Air passenger jet took off from Rafic Hariri International Airport, Beirut, the last plane to leave that day. It had been delayed some three hours and one person on board, in particular, was extremely relieved that she was at last on her way. This was a young mother, who with her eight-month-old son was flying back to Tehran to be with her husband, who was working there as bureau chief to an international news agency. Three or four hours later a wave of Israeli warplanes was bombing the airport she and her son had just left, destroying its runways and causing incoming flights to be diverted to Cyprus. About five hours after take-off, mother and child touched down safely in Iran, to be welcomed by husband and father. The reunion was a happy one, naturally, but it was the more so when it became clear how close it had been to not taking place at all. Meanwhile, members of an older generation, on hearing what a tight run thing it had been, could only be thankful that the two had made it home.

Which cast of characters denotes: Rania Abi Aad and Alexander Jad Blair (mother and son); Edmund Alexander Blair (father); Mary, to whom daughter Rania had said goodbye in Beirut before flying off, and Joanna and I, who two weeks earlier had flown to UK for the summer vacation (older generation).

That Wednesday in July marked the commencement of a thirty-four-day war between Israel and – depending on your point of view – the sovereign state of Lebanon or the militant Hizbullah organisation, whose supporters effectively comprised a 'state within a state' in southern Lebanon. Early on that day, the latter fired diversionary rockets and mortar shells over the border into Israel, targeting military posts and settlements. At the same time a ground contingent entered Israel and attacked a patrol of two Israeli Humvees, killing three soldiers and kidnapping two others. The intention was to use the captives in a prisoner trade-off with Israel. An Israeli tank, armoured personnel carrier and helicopter were immediately dispatched across the border to rescue the kidnapped soldiers but the tank hit a landmine, killing its crew of four. A fifth soldier was killed while attempting to recover the bodies.

Hassan Nasrallah, leader of the Hizbullah movement, had been threatening such an initiative for over a year and he duly labelled it 'Operation Truthful Promise', claiming that Israel had broken a previous deal to release four Lebanese citizens they were holding. Prime Minister Ehud Olmert of Israel, however, immediately branded the seizure of the soldiers an 'act of war' by Lebanon, which at the time had two Hizbullah ministers serving in its government. He promised a 'very painful and far-reaching response'. Lebanese Prime Minister Fouad Siniora, however, denied prior knowledge of the Hizbullah raid and said he did not condone it. Accordingly, on 16 July, an Israeli communiqué modified the nation's stance, declaring: 'Israel is not fighting Lebanon but the terrorist element there, led by Nasrallah and his cohorts, who have made Lebanon a hostage and created Syrian- and Iran-sponsored terrorist enclaves of murder.'

The Israeli bombers had put Lebanon's only international airport out of action because, as Israel claimed, Hizbullah used it to smuggle arms. The Israeli Air Force also blockaded Lebanese air space while its Navy imposed a maritime blockade on Lebanese seaports. Having dealt with the airport, the air attacks focused on bridges and roads in Lebanon to prevent the transportation of the two abductees; they also targeted Hizbullah's missile and rocket stockpiles, said to number 13,000. Many of these were destroyed in the first few hours but this did not stop a barrage of over a hundred missiles a day falling on Israeli territory for the length of the conflict, many reaching the port city of Haifa and causing damage and civilian casualties. The Israeli newspaper *Haaretz*, meanwhile, described Hizbullah as a skilled, well-organised and highly-motivated infantry equipped with sophisticated weaponry emanating from Syria, Iran, Russia and China. As soon as they closed with Hizbullah fighters, Israeli soldiers confirmed this judgement.

Rocket, missile and artillery attacks were continuously traded as the days passed, with civilian targets on each side of the border suffering most damage. Israel's strategy was primarily to cut off Hizbullah from its suppliers and allies in Syria and Iran. The air strikes against Lebanon's infrastructure were one way of implementing this but they may have had a secondary aim, that of convincing the Lebanese that Hizbullah's presence only brought disaster. Such an aim, true or not, was not achieved since support for Hizbullah steadily increased among Muslims in Lebanon while Christians began blaming Israel for purely punitive destruction. Israeli ground attacks were few and those there were aimed at neutralizing threats near the border. The one major ground assault, carried out by Israeli commandos, targeted Baalbek in order to root out individual Hizbullah leaders. A United Nations ceasefire, agreed by all parties, commenced on 14 August.

What had been achieved by those parties?

The Lebanese Armed Forces did not engage in direct hostilities, though once or twice they fired anti-aircraft guns at Israeli aircraft and attempted to disrupt landing operations. Hizbullah guerrillas, on the other hand, established themselves as a fighting force to be reckoned with, not least in successfully targeting the city of Haifa with rockets and thus subjecting Israeli civilians to attack for the first time since the Six Day War of 1967. Israel achieved little, failing in its objective of rendering Hizbullah impotent. What the war proved above all was the helplessness of the Lebanese state to defend, or even fully to control, its own territory.

Joanna and I flew back to Lebanon on 15 September, the airport runways back in commission. Driving into the centre of the capital from the airport, we were confronted with huge hoardings featuring the satisfied features of Nasrallah alongside the words, in mega-letters, 'The Divine Victory!' A little later, driving north on the autostrade, our taxi was diverted several times to go round wrecked bridges, prolonging the journey back to Balamand. In due course we heard about, rather than saw, other examples of aerial bombardment, like the destroyed Hizbullah headquarters in southern Beirut.

We settled down again to teaching at our university, where life was quiet enough. One expatriate colleague had left Lebanon in a hurry the previous July, taking advantage of US evacuation arrangements. By September, however, there was no reason to fear further Israeli aggression. Our friend Linda from Cyprus and Bahrain days braved our 'war zone' – as many Westerners still seemed to think it – in order to stay a few days with us in October. It was then the countdown to Christmas.

There was an eleven-day break for students and teachers over the festive season and we decided to enjoy it in UK for a change. We were invited to stay a couple of nights over Christmas in Kent by my sister and brother-in-law and this we did, the occasion becoming something of a family reunion.

It had been our custom in Cyprus, Bahrain and now in Lebanon to visit UK during the break between the two semesters in February; having already been home this time round, we decided to spend a week in Syria. We took a taxi across the border to Aleppo, where we stayed two nights in the Old City, visiting in particular the Citadel – Muslim stronghold against the Crusaders – and the Baron Hotel. The latter establishment, built in the early twentieth-century, had quickly become a popular destination, attracting visitors like Charles Lindbergh and Amy Johnson, famous aviators, Theodore Roosevelt, former US president, Agatha Christie, crime writer (she began writing *Murder on the Orient Express* there, Aleppo being the famous train's eastern terminal), and finally – almost inevitably – T.E. Lawrence. Before urban development encroached, the hotel had had a terrace overlooking a swamp and from this vantage point guests would let fly with shotguns at the local duck population!

From Aleppo we took a train for the nearly two-hundred mile journey to Damascus, paying just three American dollars each for our first class seats in the rather austere, second-hand Bulgarian coaches. The Syrian capital seemed overflowing with people on our arrival and, eschewing the five-star hotels, we procured a cheapish room in a place near the centre. After a nocturnal walk round the Old City we turned in, to spend a not-so-comfortable night in rather unprepossessing accommodation. The next morning we decided to forget about the capital and take a taxi to Ma'lūla – the village in the foothills some forty-five miles away that had captivated me when Edmund, studying Arabic in Damascus fifteen years before, had taken me there. It similarly captivated Joanna the moment we arrived. We booked in at a hotel, set at the head of the deep mountain valley around which the village is spread, and spent two fascinating days in and around this historic location.

Syria, oh Syria! It is impossible to write of the country as I do now, towards the end of 2012, without a prayer that the days of her self-inflicted suffering will quickly end.

***

Early on the morning of Sunday, 20 May 2007, Joanna and I were both awakened in our apartment at Balamand by the crackle of gunfire. It seemed to be fairly near at hand.

Joanna rolled over in bed. 'That doesn't sound like people shooting birds,' she murmured drowsily.

'That's what I was thinking,' I agreed. 'It's more like automatic rifles.' We lay in silence until I added, 'Maybe the local males have found a more efficient weapon with which to gun down the sparrows. Anyway, I'm getting some tea. Time to get up if we're going to the abbey.'

Having washed and dressed, we were soon sitting at table having a simple breakfast. This was always a pleasure as we could, through the big double windows, enjoy the panoramic view over the campus and to the sea beyond. Sometimes there would be spectacular cloudscapes and occasionally, early in the morning, a rainbow would arch perfectly over the university and monastery buildings – the symbol of divine blessing, I would romantically remind myself.

We cleared up the breakfast things and set out walking, past some other faculty apartments and down the hill. A security official was coming up and he approached us.

View one evening from our Balamand apartment, over university to Mediterranean

'Where are you going?' he asked.

'To church,' I said, 'at the monastery.'

'Go back home and stay there, please,' he ordered us politely. 'There has been some trouble locally.' He said no more but we weren't going to argue. We turned round and walked back up the hill, wondering what was going on.

The next few hours were interesting. Perhaps half an hour after we had returned we heard the throb of a helicopter. It was approaching us and, having reached the campus, started circling. Peering at it through a side window as it flew low over us – something told us not to make ourselves conspicuous through the front window – we could make out a gun mounted inside, the man behind training it at the ground.

'They're looking for someone,' one of us said. 'Someone armed.'

We went on watching discreetly and the flying – up and down and round and round – went on for a long time. When this airborne gunship finally cleared off it was past midday and, relaxing a little, we had a pick-and-scratch lunch.

By the evening we had learnt that the 'trouble locally' was the killing in the adjacent village of four Lebanese soldiers by unidentified gunmen, that the latter were on the loose and that they could be hiding somewhere on our partially-wooded campus. Further, a rumour was going round that one of the gunmen had approached a local and asked where he would find 'foreigners'. The blood ran cold on hearing this and we needed no further encouragement to stay glued to the flat until further notice.

The 'further notice' came sooner than expected. The next day all expats, who numbered about ten, were required to meet the President in his university office. He had two things to tell us. Firstly, that the army helicopter had been circling above us the previous day at his request. This we had already guessed. His second point was more subtle.

'You know something,' he said suddenly, 'I'm reminded of my time as Foreign Minister during the civil war, when you found yourself doing some very odd things.' He smiled broadly, and I imagined he was about to recount some humorous anecdote. 'You could never go anywhere without being stopped, of course,' he went on. 'There were road blocks everywhere. You tried to take routes avoiding them but of course this was sometimes impossible.' He smiled again. 'You may not know why the Lebanese are not good at observing traffic lights. Because they got used to jumping road blocks. By heaven, it didn't do to stop because if you did you might find the fellows in charge were your enemies, who would dispatch you to a higher realm without a second thought.' He gave a cheerful laugh. 'All pretty crazy, you must agree!'

He was holding our attention in this autobiographical excursus into recent history but it hardly seemed a laughing matter. At any rate, we weren't laughing with him – nor, for that matter, at him. The President carried on.

'Another thing, someone advised me never to go out without at least three hundred dollars in my wallet. How much do you usually carry, by the way?' He looked round at us all. 'Good of course to be ready to meet any eventuality but in those days that was a lot of money. Most people don't take too much with them to avoid spending it – ha, ha, ha!' His laughing subsided and he became silent for a moment. 'Memories, memories! An extraordinary time it was. But anyway, I took the advice and always had the bucks with me.' The meeting meandered to its end with a bit more talk and we all filed out.

Walking home I remarked to Joanna, 'Our President's certainly a character. That was quite a performance.'

'It was *clever*,' Joanna corrected me. 'Don't you see, he was warning us. But he didn't want to worry us unduly so he mixed it up with all that rather forced jocularity.'

'You mean …'

'I mean, he was telling us to be on guard against road blocks, or being flagged down. Basically, not to stop or we could end up being kidnapped – or worse. And always to have decent money in our pockets to be able to pay someone off if we end up in a tight spot. You get the idea?' I did.

The university closed down that week and we didn't move off campus. I remember deciding, once we started going out in the car again, that if we found ourselves threatened by someone on the road we'd put our heads down and drive on, crashing through any obstruction. I made sure I had those dollars in my wallet, too.

All of which was a prelude to the prolonged stand-off between the militant movement Fatah al-Islam ('the triumph of Islam') and the Lebanese army.

The Islamic movement was suspected of having links with al-Qaeda and Syrian intelligence. It had for some time before been using the Nahr al-Bared Palestinian refugee camp, situated some nine miles north of Tripoli between the coastal road and the sea, as its base. Its leader claimed, the following June, that the group's objective was simply the reform of the Palestinian refugee camps in Lebanon in accordance with Islamic law.

The news that we were soon getting was rather different. We heard that the militant movement had designs to set up an Islamic state in northern Lebanon, and that they had intended to destroy the tunnel thirteen miles south of Tripoli on the main road to Beirut, effectively sealing off the north from the south. At the last moment, however, they had been frustrated as a result of an almost chance discovery by police of a group of Fatah al-Islam militants in a private house in Tripoli. This was early on the morning of Sunday, 20 May. Their fighters, who were taking up strategic positions, had accordingly brought forward the operation and started firing at any soldiers they saw. A number of Fatah al-Islam fighters had been surprised by a Lebanese army contingent in the village of al-Qalamoun, on the coast just below Balamand, and several of them had made off up the hill towards the university and the village of al-Qalhāt. There they had encountered and killed four soldiers – this being the incident Joanna and I had heard from our flat early that same morning.

Once Fatah al-Islam had started targeting the army, the latter responded vigorously. Clashes occurred in downtown Tripoli and then in the vicinity of the Nahr al-Bared refugee camp. The army brought in tanks and artillery to shell militant positions within the camp but found itself under fire from militants operating on the camp outskirts. By the end of May, however, the camp was surrounded and under siege.

Joanna and I, from our Balamand apartment, could almost track the progress of the conflict. Relentless thumping to the north of us continued on a daily basis; indeed, when we moved onto our balcony we could see smoke mushrooming into the sky from the shelling.

At the beginning of June the army attempted a ground offensive but after forty-eight hours this was repelled. On 9 June the military mounted another attack, only to be driven back after suffering heavy casualties, and on 19 June a third offensive occurred, supported by helicopters launching missiles. Two days later the Lebanese defence minister reported that all enemy positions on the edge of the camp had been taken or destroyed. On 24 June fighting broke out again in Tripoli and four days later the military discovered and engaged a group of militants in a cave in the mountains south of the city, killing five of them. This was probably the group responsible for the deaths of the four soldiers in our village.

By now, however, the university spring semester was over and on 30 June we left the scene for our summer vacation, to return on 17 September. By then the conflict was over.

It had taken three further army offensives over the period 12 July to 24 August, when a truce was agreed to allow the families of militants to leave. The evacuation of Palestinian civilians who had not already fled was also arranged, leaving the army to make its final assault on 30 August. Two days later the remaining militants attempted a coordinated breakout of three groups taking different escape routes, one only of which got away safely. It was later learned that the Fatah al-Islam leader, Shaker al-Abssi, had left the camp the day before the breakout. On 7 September, the Lebanese government officially declared victory.

At least four hundred and forty-six people, including one hundred and sixty-eight soldiers and two hundred and twenty-six militants had been killed during the hundred-and-five-day siege of the camp, with some five hundred soldiers wounded – one of them a student I had taught. Two hundred and fifty militants had also been captured. The thirty or more thousand Palestinians who had fled the fighting ended up in other camps across the country.

As I write, Lebanon is believed to be playing host to over four hundred thousand Palestinian refugees, over half of them living in camps. As already indicated, they arrived in two waves, following the 1948 Arab-Israeli war and then the 1967 conflict. Never granted Lebanese citizenship, they and their descendants became stateless persons, which meant no access to other Arab countries. In 1969 an Arab accord required that host countries should not interfere with the internal running of the camps. Though officially annulling this accord in the mid-1980s, the Lebanese government remained reluctant to enter the camps, encouraging their use by armed groups as safe havens.

***

While in the north the Fatah al-Islam episode was being played out, further south more far-reaching developments were under way.

The end of the year 2006 witnessed a wave of protests led by groups opposed to the government of Prime Minister Fouad Siniora. The main opposition groups were Hizbullah, led by Hassan Nasrallah, Amal, led by Nabih Berri, Speaker of Parliament, and the Free Patriotic Movement, led by ex-general Michel Aoun. Most Sunni Muslims and Druze supported the government and most Shi'a Muslims supported the opposition, but Christian loyalties were divided. According to estimates, the population of Lebanon at this time was approaching four million, of which fifty-four per cent was Muslim, five per cent Druze, and forty-one per cent Christian.

There was, of course, a background to the protests.

On 21 October 2006, the United Nations had submitted to the Lebanese government a draft proposal for a Special Tribunal to try suspects – including several Hizbullah supporters – for the assassination of the former Prime Minister Rafic Hariri. Nabih Berri duly called for a resumption of the 'National Dialogue' conference while Hassan Nasrallah warned of 'street demonstrations' if the latter failed to produce a unity government – in which, he added, his party and its allies should be granted powers of veto. Despite these strong-arm tactics and a subsequent walk-out of five Shi'a ministers, the cabinet in due course approved a draft accord for the Tribunal and forwarded it to the UN Security Council for endorsement.

On 21 November Pierre Gemayel, Industry Minister and outspoken critic of Syria, was assassinated by gunmen in Beirut, bringing the cabinet closer to the nine empty seats needed to ensure its collapse. The Security Council promptly accepted the draft accord and a little later the Lebanese government gave it the official stamp of approval – though pro-Syrian President Émile Lahoud declared the vote invalid due to lack of Shi'a representation. As good as his word, Nasrallah called supporters out onto the streets.

Joanna and I, on one of our weekend trips, found downtown Beirut effectively under siege. Below the parliament building several thousand people had set up tents for a sit-in. Streets we were accustomed to drive down were blocked, soldiers were on every corner, and the church where we sometimes worshipped was all but inaccessible.

The Hizbullah leader had spoken of 'peaceful' protests but in early December violent clashes erupted between pro- and anti-government groups. A few days later, in answer to the call for 'a historic and decisive' demonstration, around a million protestors thronged the capital. Into another year and towards the end of January the protestors were burning tyres on major thoroughfares to enforce a general strike; a semblance of order was finally restored.

The rest of 2007 saw relative calm but the tents stayed in place, causing the shutdown of some two hundred businesses and thousands of job losses. Meanwhile, total deadlock had developed between the ruling coalition and the Hizbullah-led opposition. Most notably, the country was without a president since no replacement had been found for the now-departed Lahoud.

In the early summer of 2008 things reached a climax. Early in May unions enjoying Hizbullah support called for a general strike. This followed closely on the announcement by the government that it intended to close down Hizbullah's secure telecoms network and dismiss the head of airport security because of his links with the militant movement. The next day five were killed in gun battles between government and opposition supporters and on 9 May Hizbullah gunmen took over West Beirut. They blocked main streets and drove out government supporters, eleven losing their lives. The government accused Hizbullah and its allies of aiming 'to return Syria to Lebanon and extend Iran's reach to the Mediterranean'. On 10 May, however, Fouad Siniora backed down, announcing that it now lay with the army to deal with Hizbullah's demands. The movement accordingly agreed to withdraw its troops from the streets and two days later Beirut was quiet. The period of violence had claimed eighty-one lives, with many more wounded.

The Doha Agreement, signed by government and opposition leaders on 21 May, finally defused the crisis. This provided for the election of a new Lebanese president, General Michel Sleiman, and the formation of a national-unity government. It did not, however, make provision for the curbing of Hizbullah's growing power, not least in relation to its huge arsenal of weapons. All the movement's demands were effectively met, leading a political commentator in one international Arabic newspaper to conclude, 'Hizbullah now governs Lebanon.'

***

Something much more important happened at this time in Beirut as far as Joanna and I were concerned. William Sari Blair, our second grandson, was born to Edmund and Rania in the American University Hospital in Beirut on Thursday, 29 May 2008. Edmund had flown in from Tehran earlier and was with his wife for the birth; we two grandparents plus Mary, the third, were close at hand. Thus began what became for us a very active summer.

We stayed in a hotel near Mary's home for a couple of days before returning to Balamand for the remainder of the university term. Baby and mother were soon out of hospital and William – assigned the name immediately – the centre of attention. This did not altogether meet the approval of two-and-a-half-year-old Alexander, of course. We returned to Beirut the next weekend for our new grandson's Birthday Tea Party and, to keep things fair, were back a fortnight later to attend end-of-term celebrations at Alexander's playschool. By then Edmund had returned to Tehran and, a day or two later, we ourselves flew to London.

As always on our return to UK for the summer vacation, the first two weeks were spent taking things easy, apart from going through the mountain of mail that had been delivered to St Martin's and dealing with the odd administrative or financial matter. A few such duties always emerged from the mail, though our friend Joy used regularly to check it and forward anything that seemed urgent.

The two weeks having elapsed, we paid a visit to the capital as we had arranged to see a West End show. This was a rarity; Joanna and I could count on the fingers of one hand the number of times we had been to the theatre together in London. But there was a special reason for wanting to attend this performance: a starring role was being played by a friend.

It was a musical of sorts, a dramatization of the epic fantasy that was once voted the most popular work of fiction in the world. I refer to *Lord of the Rings*. Shortly to end its run, it was a remarkable presentation, part singing, part dancing, part acting out the storyline, with dazzling stage effects like the 'Ents' – huge walking trees. The production needed the city's largest theatre, the Drury Lane, and had apparently cost a fortune. Our friend Andrew Jarvis, better known for his interpretation of Shakespearean roles like Richard III or King Lear, was playing Gandalf. Joanna and I, plus daughter Annabel and partner Alan, sat enthralled in the huge auditorium alongside Gillian, Andrew's wife – which prompts me to explain how we came to know her distinguished husband. The previous year Gillian, a teaching colleague, had shared an office with me at Balamand, where Andy came to visit her. I prevailed upon him to speak to my graduate class, a highly entertaining session as he got the students to participate in a couple of hilarious role-plays.

Andy had invited us to come backstage after the show so, with some others, we assembled at the back entrance. One of the 'others' was dressed in a costume resembling those worn by some of the players, with matching deportment.

'Do you think he's lost it?' I whispered to Joanna. 'Reality, I mean.'

'Very likely. Heraldry, dressing up, a new identity in a make-believe world. Someone not a thousand miles away answers to this perfectly.' She gave me a glance. 'You know who I mean. It's all very sad.'

The actors gradually began to emerge, our friend being one of the last. He invited our party in, together with some students from a drama school where he had done some teaching, and we trooped after him.

'Here are the dressing rooms,' he said as we entered a passage with doors opening onto several rooms, which we glanced into quickly. He led us to a bigger one at the end.

'This is mine,' he announced. 'I don't mind admitting, it's humbling to follow one or two former users of this room, giants of the stage like Lawrence Olivier and John Gielgud.'

Propped against the wall was a long, gnarled and weather-worn stick. 'This must be your staff,' I exclaimed, seizing it.

'It is,' he confirmed. 'And I have to say, you look good with it.'

A moment later Annabel was asking her father to pose for a photo holding this item, some of the characteristics of which – 'gnarled and weather-worn', for example – he to some extent shared.

'Great!' she said as she clicked the camera. 'White hair and white beard, wizard's wand, you really look the part!' I looked more closely at the 'wand' I was clutching – to discover it had never been cut from a tree. An important prop, it had been carefully moulded from synthetic material.

We looked at the wardrobes – more of a corridor, in fact – and the variegated garments and robes hanging there, and then moved to the stage. We marvelled at state-of-the-art electronics and hydraulics, which among other things lowered or raised sections of the stage floor. For Joanna and me it was all quite fascinating.

I should mention, finally, that besides the fact that we knew Andrew there had been another reason for wanting to see the stage version of J.R.R. Tolkien's absorbing tale. I had inherited from my father first editions of the trilogy; he was one of its earliest reviewers and these were his review copies. Indeed, he was among the first to award the work, in a learned Anglican journal, unstinting praise. For, surprising as it may seem, the epic at first had a mixed reception. My father never knew the professor personally, as he did that other famous member of the Oxford 'Inklings', C.S. Lewis, but in the realm of ideas he had a lot in common with the creator of Middle Earth. He also shared a birthday with Bilbo Baggins!

We had another musical adventure that summer, when on the first day of August we attended the opera *The Imposter King*, performed at Iford Manor in Wiltshire. The company presenting it was managed by Joanna's 'oldest' friend (and bridesmaid of yore) Judy, with husband John, and they offered us free standby seats. This was *very* different from our Drury Lane experience but in its way just as entertaining – educational, too, for semi-literates of the musical arts like ourselves.

So much for our 2008 summer holiday in UK, or so much to all intents and purposes, for three days after that opera Edmund rang to say that two-month-old William, still in Beirut with Rania and elder brother Alexander, had been diagnosed with probable meningitis. Mother and sick child, our son explained, were currently in the American Hospital, William on a drip-feed and both having further tests. In a follow-up call he asked if we could return to Lebanon earlier than expected to help the family through the crisis. He himself had been granted twelve days leave from Iran by Reuters, so we arranged to fly out to Lebanon in order to take over from him when he had to return. Two weeks later we were back in Beirut, settling into a hotel in Ayn al-Meraysi.

Our duties were largely keeping Williams' elder brother occupied. To this end we took him on trips, mostly around Beirut but once up to Balamand for the night, which he enjoyed. Meanwhile, William was doing well, with no sign of the complications that can occur though still being kept on medication.

At the end of August I arranged a lightning trip back to Sherborne, where I was due to deliver a public lecture on the topic of my book *God's Credentials*. The hundred or more in attendance received the presentation with some enthusiasm, which made me sorry I was not in a position to mount the proverbial 'author's lecture tour'. Something is better than nothing, however, and a bonus of the trip home was being treated to dinner the next day at a posh restaurant near Waterloo by my brother-in-law, Jolyon. I saw my sister too, naturally, as well as some other family members.

On arriving back in Beirut, I found little William continuing to do well, with the worries about meningitis receding. Joanna had remained in the hotel while I was away but the two of us now moved to Edmund and Rania's newly-acquired apartment in the fashionable Ashrafiah district of the capital. We arranged more outings for Alexander, including stays in Balamand, before the university term began and our long summer ended.

***

The political situation in Lebanon remained unstable following the Doha agreement of May 2008, which was essentially a compromise that satisfied no one. Elections took place in June, however, when Saad Hariri, son of assassinated Rafic Hariri and leader of an anti-Syrian bloc, gained the majority of seats in the Assembly of Representatives. The country under his premiership then saw a period of relative calm.

Elsewhere in the Arab world there were stirrings and at the end of 2010 these erupted. The commencement of what came to be called the 'Arab Spring' can be dated to 18 December, when Muhammad Bouaziz publicly ignited himself and subsequently died in Sidi Bou Saïd, Tunisia. The act provoked demonstrations and riots throughout the country, leading to the stepping down of President Zine al-Abidine less than a month later. The 'Spring' then spread to Egypt where, on 25 January 2011, there began a campaign of demonstrations and marches involving a million or more protestors, with the aim of toppling Hosni Mubarak from the presidency. This was remarkably successful, Mubarak standing down on 11 February and handing the reins of power to the military.

Elsewhere the flame of protest had already been lit: self-immolations, protests, riots, and/or violent clashes leaving behind dead and wounded, occurred in Algeria, Jordan, Mauritania, Sudan, Oman, Yemen, Saudi Arabia, Morocco, Iraq. Soon, too, Bahrain, Libya and Syria were to be added to the list.

'Syria is the big one,' Edmund had already opined when, during his holiday with the family in Beirut over Christmas, we were discussing how far revolution could fan out from Tunisia. 'Bashar al-Assad, like his father before him, is holding together a patchwork of very disparate groups. You could say he was sitting on a time bomb.'

What then of Syria, our next door neighbour, for long involved in Lebanon and its politics? Joanna and I, as already intimated, liked the country and felt affection for its people, quite a number of whom we knew as students at our university. These feelings had, interestingly, been endorsed and strengthened by my Australian cousin, who with his wife and youngest son had, only a few months earlier, come to stay with us at Balamand following a holiday in our territorial neighbour.

'Syria – a small country near Iraq and Israel, a totalitarian rogue state, member of the axis of evil along with North Korea and Iran. That summarises what many of us know about Syria. I wanted to know more and spent a month travelling this ancient Biblical land.' So David Blair began the article 'Finding the hidden side of Syria', published later on the internet blog Crikey. I will cite two further statements from that article. The first calls in question the popular view he summarises: 'Talking to many Syrians and especially members of Syria's Christian minority, I came to understand a vastly more complex situation, and the positive role of the present president as he balances and resists enormous forces.' Thus, implicitly, did he confirm our son's fears about a Syrian revolution. The second is very simple: 'The Syrians are the nicest people in the world.' Thus did my cousin confirm our own warm regard for the people of the country.

The above witnesses to the breadth of my cousin's interests, though his professional pursuits took him in a very different direction. David's academic specialism was astrophysics, in which science he had carved something of a name. I accordingly arranged for him, before he left, to deliver a lecture at Balamand on the question that consumed most of his time and energy. In presenting 'Whispers from the Dawn of Time: the search for Einstein's waves', he was able to explain to interested staff and students something of the contribution he and his team at the University of Western Australia were making towards a major project: the attempt to detect, for the first time, the 'gravitational waves' predicted by Albert Einstein.

Back now, however, to the issue of 'revolution', which did indeed, in early 2011, fan out like wildfire from Tunisia to engulf much of the

Middle East and beyond – accompanied by violence nowhere more extreme than in the country sitting alongside Lebanon's northern and eastern borders. It would be out of place here to attempt even a brief account of the course of the Syrian uprising, quickly to become a civil war, from its origin in anti-Assad graffiti scribbled on a school wall in Dara'a by students in mid-March, 2011, to the unspeakable destruction, massive human loss and grim political impasse confronting the observer some two years later. It would also be unnecessary: the world as a whole is only too aware, from incessant news-flashes, of the desperate situation that developed. My chief concern here is Lebanon. So how did the nation of our residence, at the geographical centre of this Arab-world eruption, fare from the moment of its birth?

There was fresh unrest in the country early in 2011, though this was not obviously a consequence of what was happening beyond its borders. On 12 January 2011, all ten opposition ministers resigned from the cabinet of Saad Hariri's unity government and clashes occurred between Hariri supporters and the police. Ostensibly a protest against government impotence, closer analysis suggests that the ministerial resignations were because Hizbullah operatives were about to be indicted by the Special Tribunal for Lebanon for responsibility in the assassination of Rafic Hariri – as, indeed, a few days later they were. On the resignation of a further minister, the government fell, Saad Hariri remaining as caretaker Prime Minister.

The interim period saw protests in Lebanon that more clearly reflected the influence of external events. At the end of February there were protests against the sectarian political system, ten thousand marching to the centre of Beirut to call for a secular state. Following this, supporters of the 'March 14 Alliance', which had grown out of the 'cedar revolution' of 14 March 2005, turned out in their hundreds of thousands, calling among other things for the disarming of Hizbullah. No joy for them here, however, for in June a new government took office, Najib Mikati having cobbled together a Hizbullah-led coalition. By now there were serious repercussions in Lebanon from the regional unrest, most notably the rapidly worsening situation in Syria. Violent clashes occurred in Tripoli between those who did or did not support the Syrian opposition and the friction simmered until finally, in early summer, it dramatically escalated, leaving scores of dead or wounded.

There was now much talk on the international media of the violence in Syria sparking a return in Lebanon to civil conflict, Syrian refugees by now pouring across the border. Joanna and I, naturally enough, followed events in Lebanon and the wider region with more than academic interest. We did not feel vulnerable ensconced in our university set on its coastal hill some way out of Tripoli, but whenever we were told (or could hear for ourselves) that there was trouble in the city, we kept away.

This involved a small sacrifice on my part because I had developed a fondness for Tripoli, where we would often shop, and would find excuses to drive down and stroll round its bustling, colourful *souqs*. Our car mechanic, Albert, had his workshop in the port area of al-Mina and quite often I would have to pay him a visit for repairs. While he was fixing the car, I would wander off, frequently ending up in a café doing some writing. I had earlier been asked by Dr Salem to edit the English text of a 'coffee-table' volume being brought out by the university on Tripoli, a task I was delighted to accept. *Tripoli: city of all eras*, superbly illustrated, is a fine tribute to Lebanon's multi-layered northern capital.

It was not, of course, just Tripoli that Joanna and I kept a weather eye on. As a wider family we were at the heart of the regional turmoil, with special reason to follow the situation in Egypt.

Our son Edmund had been appointed Reuters bureau chief in Cairo in 2009, with responsibility for Egypt, Sudan and Eastern Libya. Towards the end of January 2011, as already mentioned, demonstrations in the capital began and from then on he would sometimes have to bed down in the office because of danger on the streets or simply to keep abreast of a very fluid situation. Rania and our grandsons were at first confined to their home, apart from quick trips to Alexander's school, but were soon compelled to retreat to rooms on the top floor of a hotel. It soon became clear that there was a better option – refuge in Beirut. Accordingly, in mid-February, Joanna and I were at Rafic Hariri airport to meet mother and boys. The slight irony in this had not escaped us. 'How often has the Lebanese capital been considered a safe haven?' we asked ourselves.

They settled into their Ashrafiah flat for this enforced holiday and for much of it we were able to help them out since we were enjoying the university mid-year break. We had intended, as was our custom, to spend the holiday in England but cancelled our flights when we saw what was happening to the south of us. Just short of a month later, when things had to some extent quietened down in Cairo, Rania and the boys returned, impelled in particular by the need to get Alexander back to school.

Yet the removal of Mubarak on 11 February 2011 was only the beginning for Egypt. Throughout the year unrest continued as it became clear to many that the departure of the President was not enough. Parties and factions jostled for position as they looked ahead to the plebiscite. These came in the form of parliamentary elections towards the end of the year and into the next, accompanied by a measure of violence, and in June 2012 the presidential election. By a narrow margin, Muhammad Mursi, candidate of the Freedom and Justice Party set up by the Muslim Brotherhood, became the country's first democratically-elected leader. Towards the end of the year he announced a number of sweeping and unchallengeable new presidential powers. A wave of protests followed, looking remarkably like the beginnings of a second revolution. We began to wonder if our daughter-in-law and grandsons would again be seeking refuge in Lebanon.

The year 2012 became 2013 and we watched and waited. Little on the national or international scene, most especially in the 'Arab Spring', encouraged optimism. True, the Libyan forces of resistance, with help from NATO, had in October 2011 got rid of their dictator – half-clown, half-monster – Muammar Muhammad al-Ghaddafi; the following month the Yemeni people had finally pushed Ali Saleh off his perch of over thirty-three years; perhaps these were gains, though neither event did much to reduce our scepticism. Protests in Bahrain, following the government crackdown on insistent demonstrations by the Shi'a community, had by contrast failed to remove the king, helped as he was by a royal from across the water. The latter and his family, meanwhile, despite a degree of unrest among the Saudi people, remained unscathed.

Our 'Lebanese' family stayed in the Egyptian capital though the volatile situation scarcely warranted it. Changes were in the air for them, however, Edmund taking up another Reuters appointment in Nairobi at the end of February 2013. Rania, meanwhile, agreed to stay in Cairo with the boys until June so they could see out the school year.

Slowly (very slowly, this time round) the cold and storms of winter gave way to relative warmth and the blooming of flowers – a perennially cheering experience. Our professional responsibilities were as consuming as ever, especially for me, involved in preparation of literary material for the university's twenty-fifth anniversary. We nevertheless remained fully conscious of what was happening in Lebanon and just across the border, noting some disturbing developments.

There was Israel's second intervention into the Syrian crisis in May, an aerial assault on a research centre in the Damascus area, designed to eliminate the possibility of lethal weapons falling into the hands of Hizbullah. For comment on this event the BBC turned to Sir Basil Eastwood, former ambassador to Syria and friend of ours from Sudan days. He expressed no surprise at the attack, remarking that Israel had consistently threatened such action and would continue to pursue her own interests.

More significantly, there was Hizbullah's full-scale intervention into the civil conflict towards the end of May, enabling the forces of the Assad regime to wrest control of the border town of al-Qusair from the free Syrian army. The initiative, prompting further sectarian clashes down the road from us in Tripoli, was defended by Hassan Nasrallah in a video-recorded speech (he seldom appeared in public), in which he argued that Assad's Syria represented a crucial front against Israel. He then, as always, promised his followers ultimate 'victory'.

Lebanese President Michel Sleiman expressed disapproval of Hizbullah's action, reiterating the call for neutrality in relation to the Syrian conflict. Lebanese and international commentators were more pointed, arguing that Hizbullah had by taking up arms in this way given up all pretence and declared – what many had long been saying – that its fundamental loyalty was not to Lebanon but to the Iran-Syria axis.

The country Joanna and I served was now openly, perhaps irrevocably, split down the middle. Yet not just Lebanon; the region as a whole was going the same way. For even as Hizbullah from its Lebanese base was entering the fray in support of Assad, Shi'a fighters from Iran and Iraq were joining them. These latter, it was reported, considered themselves to be conducting a holy war or *jihād* against the largely Sunni anti-Assad fighters, who in turn were being encouraged by Sunni clerics in Egypt to see their struggle as a *jihād* against vicious anti-Islamic – even Satanic – forces. By mid-June, when it had become clear to all that the conflict had become regional, hopes of a political settlement had all but disappeared.

'Where will all this end?' the world was asking. The jury, as I write, is still out on that.

XVI

Signing Off

The account of my odyssey at this point comes to an end because time has caught up with me. Joanna and I are still in Lebanon as the year 2013 progresses so the odyssey itself has not ended, but I can only speculate about any further period to be spent in the Middle East.

Should I look back as I sign off, making a remark or two about what has transpired? Or should I look forward, guessing or at least expressing hope about what is yet to be? The latter is distinctly preferable, but it raises a second question. Should the guessing be personal, about me and mine, or should it be about the region that has largely been the focus of my narrative? Again, the latter is preferable.

So what of the future of this region in which we have lived so long? My thoughts on the question, few enough, will be woven around four events, which for me have something to say – at least indirectly – about that future. The events are three deaths, and a birth.

The Sunday before Christmas, 2009, Joanna and I attended the National Evangelical Church in Beirut with our 'Lebanese' family, Edmund, Rania and the boys, who were over from Cairo for the festivities, and of course Rania's mother. We attended church together because that Sunday had special family significance: one of Rania's maternal uncles was to be specifically remembered during the service because he had died, a young man, exactly fifty years before. The one surviving member of the original six brothers, Anis Sayegh, also attended with his Jordanian wife, Hilda. We were very happy to renew our acquaintance with Anis, whom we had warmed to greatly when chatting with him at Edmund and Rania's wedding in 2002. He was his usual smiling self but looking, we felt, a trifle frail. After the service we wished him and his wife 'bon voyage' as they departed to fly off to Amman. Late on Christmas Day the news came through: Rania's uncle had suffered a sudden deterioration in health and at nine in the evening had passed away.

Why do I single out this man – or rather his death – for special mention?

Anis Sayegh was a respected figure in the Arab world as historian, editor, political analyst and consultant. In all that concerned Palestine, its history and current affairs, he became an acknowledged authority. Born himself in Palestine in 1931, he championed the Palestinian cause. This and his scholarship – he obtained a doctorate in politics and history from Cambridge – prompted the Palestinian Liberation Organisation (PLO) in 1966 to appoint him Head of their new research centre in Beirut. The result was several attempts on his life by the Israelis, one of which – a letter bomb in 1972 – left him with mutilated fingers and impaired hearing and vision. Despite such provocation, he personally continued to pursue the way of persuasion rather than violence. He refused to employ armed bodyguards and, to underline his position, politely declined the gift of a firearm offered him on one occasion by the PLO leader, Yasser Arafat.

I make one comment and ask one question. Had more people of influence – on both sides of the Arab-Israeli conflict – adopted Anis Sayegh's stance, the situation in the region might be radically different today. Is it now too late for entrenched positions to change?

I referred above to reports coming through of a 'massive explosion in the Ashrafiah district of Beirut' as, on 19 October 2012, I sat in a restaurant writing about Lebanon's 'unsettled history'. The details soon emerged: a blast from a car bomb in a narrow street had killed Lebanon's top security official Wissam al-Hasan, Head of the Information Branch of the Internal Security Forces, together with four others. Brigadier General al-Hasan had played a central role in cooperating with the Special Tribunal for Lebanon.

The explosion broke the period of relative calm that followed the spate of assassinations occurring from 2004 to 2008. The March 14 opposition and political analysts duly accused the Assad regime of masterminding the outrage, a professor at the American University of Beirut commenting, 'The Syrian regime is trying to send a clear message to the international community saying, "Supporting the rebels [in Syria] will threaten security and stability in Lebanon."'

The vast majority of the Lebanese people today are utterly weary of war, I believe, so attempts to destabilise the country and reignite its civil conflict might seem futile. Yet I am not awash with optimism. It takes just one or two students set on the disruption of a class to achieve just that; it needs relatively few elements with a negative and destructive agenda to cause mayhem in a country, especially when such elements enjoy external support.

On 5 December 2012, the Patriarch of Antioch and All the East for the Greek Orthodox Church, His Beatitude Ignatius IV, died in a Lebanese hospital in his ninety-first year.

The University of Balamand was the Patriarch's creation, as we have seen. He saw the need in North Lebanon for a new centre of higher study, realised how the monastery at Balamand could be instrumental in fulfilling this need, gained support from interested parties and benefactors, and finally witnessed the dream become reality. Like the man he appointed in 1993 to the university presidency, Ignatius was a character of great imagination and vision coupled with energy and determination. The two men became close friends, the former in due course writing and publishing a well-crafted biography of the latter.

In a farewell tribute to the Patriarch, Dr Elie Salem wrote these words: 'Over his long life, Ignatius defied obstacles and crossed frontiers to live in the present and the future, to live by the power of reason and faith. The past, he argued, is replete with corpses. We can learn from looking back but we should never return to the past in order to remain there. He perceived life as a process of moving forward. It is true that Christ was born two thousand years ago, but Christ is yet with us and leads us on. The past, of course, had its pillars – pillars of society, pillars of the Church. There are saints among our forefathers. And we have our pillars today, we have our saints. These all, past and present, we shall never forget – and yet, insists Ignatius, "We look to the future." We live the joy of the Incarnation, of the Resurrection, and in this power we shall never cease to achieve.'

'We look to the future,' said this Orthodox Patriarch. We do so because into that future we all ineluctably travel. 'In the midst of life, we are in death,' we sometimes hear the parson intone at funerals. 'In the midst of death, we are in life,' the departed saint would rather have us say. Observers of today's Middle East – indeed, of today's world – might ponder the thought that every seed has to be buried before it will germinate.

***

Three deaths, and a birth.

Beatrix Mary Blair Williams, our third grandchild, was born on 21 May 2012 to our daughter Annabel and her partner Alan. The room in which she first saw the light of day looked out onto Westminster and the Houses of Parliament – an interesting fact, though not obviously auspicious. Every birth brings hope, however, and this one, being a bit special, brought a special measure of hope. It is well that it did, for the times into which little Beatrix was born seemed to demand something special. She was baptized on 4 August 2013 in our local church in Sherborne, with me doing the honours, to mark another kind of birth – the 'new birth' into the kingdom of Jesus Christ.

That same Jesus spoke of a 'new birth' of our troubled world, to be effected one day by divine fiat. This, perhaps, is our single realistic hope.